A CRISIS OF TRUTH

A Crisis of Truth

*The Attack on Faith, Morality,
and Mission in the Catholic Church*

Ralph Martin

SERVANT BOOKS
Ann Arbor, Michigan

Contents

Introduction

I ENCOUNTERED MANY CHALLENGES in the course of writing this book. I had to deal with some delicate theological questions, in a way that was both understandable to the average reader and theologically accurate. I had to provide enough documentation for the points I make concerning the reality and pervasiveness of the "crisis of truth" without badly encumbering the text or breaking the flow of the argument. Many people advised me to be specific and provide "names and places" in order not to be too general; others warned me not to focus on personalities or to draw attention to individuals who may not be fixed in their positions. My discussion of the crisis of truth in the Catholic Church necessarily involves dealing with some specifically Catholic beliefs and practices, while acknowledging that many of the problems, and hopefully the solutions that are discussed, are also relevant to the situation of many of the major Protestant Churches. I tried to do this in a way that is thoroughly Catholic yet ecumenically sensitive. I had to express the truth as I see it "without compromise," while at the same time anticipating the possibility of misunderstanding by making enough qualifications so that readers do not hear me saying something I do not intend to say or draw implications from what I say that I do not intend them to draw. I had to address the central issues comprehensively enough, while keeping the book at a manageable length. To do so, I progressively reduced the size of the book so that it is now two hundred pages shorter than the first draft.

I have attempted to solve these challenges in various ways. I hope that, overall, the average reader will find the book of genuine interest and comprehensibility even if a few chapters or parts of chapters may require closer than average attention. I also hope that readers with theological training will find the book to be responsible and accurate theologically, even if it is directed to a more popular readership. I have handled the conflicting advice concerning "names and places" by mentioning in the text those names that are generally already a matter of public knowledge and record, while relegating lesser-known individuals to the notes and supporting documentation. In this way, I hope that those readers who are not inclined to read the footnotes will still get enough documentation while reading the main text to make the argument of the book credible. At various times while writing the book

I have wondered whether its focus should be more broadly ecumenical but I have concentrated on the crisis of truth in the Catholic Church for a variety of reasons. First, I think that the crisis of truth within the Catholic Church is particularly critical now. Secondly, I think that I am in a better situation to speak to Catholics with the kind of frankness this topic requires because I am a Catholic myself, than I would be if I addressed at this time the situation in other Christian churches. Finally—and this is the most decisive reason—I think this is what the Lord wants me to do. I have, though, in the book periodically made reference and given examples of the crisis of truth in various Protestant circles to show the interplay and similar dynamics at work in both situations. I remain profoundly committed to the work of Christian unity and rejoice that my family and I are members of an ecumenical community, The Word of God, in Ann Arbor, Michigan. Some have felt that this book has a "prophetic thrust" which should not be diminished by a preoccupation with anticipating all the possible misunderstandings; others have felt that the effort to rule out misinterpretations was important. I hope in the final text that both concerns are met.

I do not intend this book to be the final or definitive word on this important area. I would be very happy if it would serve to help all of us be more aware of the seriousness of the situation that we now face in the life of the Church so that we could turn to the Lord and seek together his guidance on how to respond. This book is merely one contribution toward facing and responding to a situation where many contributions are needed.

My own understanding of the situation, as well as my understanding of how to present it, has grown and evolved over the years. This is due, in part to the many opportunities I have had, both in the United States and during my four years from 1976-80, living and working in Europe, to share concepts of this book in private conversations with many bishops, theologians, and others holding positions of leadership in the Church. Some have even taken the time to read early drafts of the book and offer valuable input. It is also due to the valuable feedback that I have received in response to both the cassette album and the video presentation entitled "A Crisis of Truth," which treat much of the material in this book.

During this time I have sought and received advice and counsel from many people. I would especially like to thank those too numerous to name who have taken the time to listen to the cassette album, view the video presentation, attend a conference where I gave these teachings, or read a draft manuscript of this book and offered their advice.

I must also thank Fr. Peter Hocken and The Mother of God Community in Maryland, as well as Fr. Patrick Egan in London, England, for their helpful suggestions. I also thank Bill Beatty and his collaborators in The People of Praise community in South Bend, Indiana, who worked so hard in the production and distribution of the videotape presentation of this material.

Special thanks must go to Fr. Michael Scanlan, President of the University of Steubenville, and his colleagues, particularly Fr. Daniel Sinisi, chairman of the theology department, who have helped me in a special way during this time. Special thanks also to members of my own community here in Ann Arbor, and in particular to Steve Clark and Bruce Yocum for their valuable comments on the manuscript, to Jim Manney for his editorial help and suggestions, Louise Bourassa for her editorial assistance during my time in Belgium, and to Nancy Pflug for her heroic secretarial help and work on the footnotes. Special thanks also to my Bishop, Kenneth Povish of Lansing, Michigan, without whose support, encouragement, and advice it would have been difficult to proceed, as well as to Fr. Robert Lunsford who, on behalf of Bishop Povish, offered his theological and pastoral resources freely.

Finally, special thanks to all those who have generously supported this work in a variety of different ways over the past several years.

Obviously, in spite of all the advice and counsel I have sought and received, my advisors cannot be held responsible for the final shape of this book. While acknowledging their help, I want to make it clear that my readers should not assume that they are in complete agreement with every point in the final manuscript. For that, I alone take full responsibility as, of course, is customary.

May God use this work for his glory, for our good, and that of all his Church.

Part One

Where Are We?

CHAPTER ONE

A Crisis of Truth

THE INFORMED OBSERVATIONS of those in the highest positions of responsibility in the Church, the experience of many ordinary Catholics,
and the results of numerous scientific surveys all indicate that the
Catholic Church is confronted today by what deserves to be called a
crisis of truth.

Paul VI saw that a confusion concerning basic Christian truth was of
such depth and pervasiveness that the very foundations of the Church
were threatened:

> Men committed to the Church are greatly influenced by the climate
> of the world; so much so that a danger bordering almost on vertigi-
> nous confusion and bewilderment can shake the Church's very foun-
> dations and lead men to embrace most bizarre ways of thinking, as
> though the Church should disavow herself and take up the very
> latest and untried way of life.[1]

John Paul I shared the views of his predecessor. A few weeks before
he entered the conclave which was to elect him pope, Cardinal Luciani
wrote an article in which he expressed concern about the widespread
confusion of truth being propagated in the name of "aggiornamento."
He cited the decline of preaching as an example. The homily may have
indeed been restored to its proper place in the liturgy, he said, but now
the word that is promoted there is often distorted. Today's preaching
"never speaks of the following tragedies of original sin, purgatory,
hell, the last judgment," the Cardinal said. He went on: "Rare are the
preachers who speak to the young about continence and self-control.

Often the preachers let it be believed, explicitly or implicitly, that such points of Catholic doctrine, taught until recently, are false, superficial, or depasse." Cardinal Luciani cited the example of homilies given in one large church in Italy. One week, a theologian denied the humanity of Christ; a week later, a second theologian denied the divinity of Christ; and a few weeks after that, another preacher cast doubt on the historical existence of Jesus.[2]

Cardinal William Baum, former head of the American Bishops' Doctrinal Committee and now head of the Roman congregation that oversees Catholic education and seminaries, warned the American bishops about the increasingly frequent attacks on the fundamental truths concerning the nature and person of Christ:

> The mystery of the Incarnation is being challenged in a profound new way by many theologians and if you have not yet felt the effects of this in your own local dioceses, you will in time. These effects already are being felt in our seminaries and universities, and undoubtedly will affect preaching and teaching in the local churches.[3]

Cardinal Baum went on to say that many of these present-day attacks are similar to ancient fourth and fifth century heresies which were condemned by the councils of Nicea, Constantinople, Ephesus, and Chalcedon.

John Paul II has repeatedly expressed his concern for the destruction of faith and morality going on in the Church today, even at the hands of some of her own priests. He has called for "priests endowed with a sound theological sense, listening attentively to Holy Scripture, Tradition, and the Magisterium. We need priests who, teaching faith and morality, will construct and not destroy."[4]

This sense of alarm is not confined to those officially charged with guarding the truth of Catholic Christianity. Many ordinary Catholics are confused and worried. Virtually every day I receive letters, often heartbreaking, which witness to the corruption of basic truth in much of Western Catholicism.

A group of concerned Catholic parents in one European country sent a letter to their bishops which I am able to partially cite here. In it they express grave reservations about the condition of the Church in their country:

> Many in our country who are Catholics in name no longer ask themselves when seeking the truth: What does Holy Scripture say? What does the church teach us? but: What is my opinion? What do I think is best for me? What do other people accept? What do our theologians say? . . . The consequences are confusion and uncertainty

by many believers. . . . The situation of religious classes in school is tragic. Many priests and deacons no longer talk of revelation, but simply of human experiences and the human sciences. . . . To young children with their hearts open to receive Christ and his word is given only confusion and disbelief.

Alarming statistical evidence backs up the impressions of parents like these. For example, a poll in the Netherlands revealed that only forty-seven percent of Dutch Catholics still believe that Christ is the Son of God. In 1966, seventy percent believed in Christ's divinity. Even fewer Dutch Catholics believe in a personal God or life after death.[5] Unfortunately, the Netherlands is not unique. The undermining of Christian truth and its sources in scripture and tradition has contributed to a similar decline in belief in most of the Western countries.[6]

In another European country, a young student at perhaps the most esteemed Catholic university in Europe wrote a letter to the rector, sharing his experiences of Christianity there. The student shared this letter with me:

> After a year and a half of being in _____, I'd like to share with you some of my thoughts, that might interest you. Every day we students are being stormed at by professors and other students with propaganda for Marxism, homosexuality, strife, fighting, claiming power, etc. Every day we hear, even in the courses, cynicism and the tearing down of deepest Christian values. To give you an example: up till now I have never heard a professor contribute to the Christian aspect of our life during the lessons; many though have regularly broken it down. Is it normal that in a "Catholic" university, students as well as professors fight for and live according to all but Christian ideals? Is it normal that work-groups to promote, for example, homosexuality can just go their way as members of a Catholic university without being bothered by anybody? Is it normal that in between these voices and ideas coming out of our university, practically no Christian voice is to be heard? . . . Those are questions that I ask you, not as a blame, nor as a demand, but as a means of exposing to you a wound that exists in my heart, in that of many others, and overall in that of God.

This crisis of truth is certainly not the only crisis that the Church is facing today, nor the only aspect of Christian life that needs to be emphasized today. But unless it is faced and resolved, the Church will not be able to meet the other crises which it faces. A firm and clear grasp on the authority and truth of God's Word is fundamental to the Church's existence.

I believe this observation is borne out by what scripture reveals to us of the fundamental satanic strategy employed in the Fall of mankind, a strategy which is continuously employed with great success in our current situation.

Jesus identified the intentions of Satan toward the human race as its destruction, and his strategy as deception. In talking to people who were rejecting him, Jesus said: "The father you spring from is the devil and willingly you carry out his wishes. He brought death to man from the beginning and has never based himself on truth. The truth is not in him. Lying speech is his native tongue. He is a liar and the Father of lies" (Jn 8:44).

The initial revelation of Satan as the one who seeks the destruction of humanity through falsehood is contained in the third chapter of Genesis. This chapter is well worth reflecting on as we begin our exploration of how God's Word is being undermined among his people today.

The serpent, later revealed as Satan, is described as the most cunning of all the animals that God had made. The serpent approaches the woman and asks a question: "Did God really tell you not to eat from any of the trees of the garden?" The woman, apparently recognizing that the serpent is not representing God's Word accurately, replies: "We may eat of the fruit of the trees in the Garden; it's only about the fruit of the tree in the middle of the garden that God said, "You shall not eat it, or even touch it, lest you die.' " Some scholars think that the woman herself in response to the serpent may have added the "or even touch it," which is not contained in the earlier Genesis account of God's command (Gn 2:17); others, though, think perhaps it is just a fuller recalling of the previous version.

The serpent, who began by questioning and distorting God's Word, now proceeds to outrightly deny it. "You certainly will not die. No, God knows well that the moment you eat of it, your eyes will be opened and you will be like gods who know what is good and what is bad."

In the process of denying the truthfulness of God and His Word, the serpent tries to get the woman to doubt God's intentions toward her; he seeks to get her to suspect that God's Word is restrictive and narrow, that it keeps her from some experience, power, or fulfillment that is rightfully hers.

The serpent then appeals to what the first epistle of John later referred to as "carnal allurements, enticements for the eye, the life of empty show" (1 Jn 2:16). In the end, both the woman and the man prefer the word of the serpent to the Word of God, and they suffer the consequences. Instead of the abundant life that the serpent promised, they receive death. They find themselves under the sway of him whom they trusted and believed in preference to God.

I believe that this same satanic strategy employed in the Fall of the human race is being repeated in our midst day after day in the lives of countless human beings, many within the Church. They are first led to question and doubt God's Word, and then eventually to deny it. The dehumanization of man, both within and outside the Church, follows inevitably.

Increasingly a question mark is being placed over God's Word, its reliability questioned, its authority denied, its clarity obscured. Increasingly a relativistic and skeptical attitude to truth is arising even within the hearts of many Catholics, even among those who hold positions of responsibility.

Pilate's skeptical and relativistic approach to truth made him vulnerable to the various pressures that were working for Jesus' crucifixion and to undo the plan and purpose of God. As growing numbers of even those dedicated to the Church shrug their shoulders with Pilate and say, "What is truth?" it becomes that much easier for spiritual and temporal forces to undo the work of God in the world and crucify Jesus in his Body, the Church. The satanic intentions and strategy did not cease with the Fall of the first human beings, nor with the crucifixion of Jesus. They continued on into the life of the early Church, and on into the life of the Church today. As St. Paul wrote, "My fear is that, just as the serpent seduced Eve by his cunning, your thoughts may be corrupted and you may fall away from your sincere and complete devotion to Christ" (2 Cor 11:3).

Paul VI identified this satanic element in the corruption of truth the Church is experiencing today:

Satan's smoke has made its way into the temple of God through some crack. . . . one no longer trusts the Church; one trusts the first profane prophet that comes along . . . doubt has entered our consciences and it entered through windows which should have been open to the Light. It was believed that after the second Vatican Council there would be a day of sunshine in the history of the Church. There came instead a day of clouds, storm and darkness, of search and uncertainty. This came about through an adverse power; his name is the Devil. . . . We believe that some preternatural thing has come into the world precisely to disturb, to suffocate the fruits of the Ecumenical Council.[7]

There is a time for everything under the sun. I believe that we are in a time now when God's people need to become clear again about the authority, clarity, and accessibility of God's Word. God's Word is the foundation of the life and mission of the Church. It is time, I believe, for the Word of God, which is sharper than any two-edged sword, to again be proclaimed in clarity and power, and to accomplish its task in our day.

John Paul II stated this priority in a recent speech: "Today, our first concern must be with truth. Both for our own interior needs and for our ministry. We cannot sow error or leave people in the shadow of doubt."[8]

With the above as a framework let us now turn to an analysis of some of the ways in which God's Word is being undermined today.

CHAPTER TWO

Undermining God's Word

IN THIS CHAPTER, I would like to examine five main ways in which I see God's Word being undermined today. The first of these is simply the direct denial of the authority of God's Word as it comes to us in scripture, through tradition, and the teaching of the Church.

Direct Denial

Often the denial of specific Christian truths is rooted in a previous denial that scripture and Christian tradition are truly authoritative in our contemporary situation. The scriptures, authentic Christian tradition, and, for Catholics, the teaching authority of the Church then become just one opinion among many that Christians should consult as they decide how to think and act. People with this mentality do not deny all authority. Rather they replace the authority of scripture, Christian tradition, and Church teaching with the authority of "experts," opinion polls, or of one's own subjective opinions and preferences.

A faculty member of a major American Protestant seminary provided an extraordinary example of this mentality in a convocation address delivered to an audience composed of seminarians, faculty, and staff. This statement starkly reveals an attitude now commonly held, although often in an implicit way, among many Catholics:

What does ancient Christian tradition, with its archaic language and individualistic ethos, have to do with the necessarily social and secular expression of Christianity today? What is the point any more of teaching or studying the classical disciplines when the bases for our action are given with sufficient clarity by contemporary ethics and the adjunct studies of sociology and psychology? I suspect that many of us here, if our back were against the wall, would honestly have to answer, "Very little indeed." We may have some aesthetic interest in tradition, but we are no longer in any danger of confusing aesthetic with normative judgments. There is thus probably a widespread, intuitive acceptance of two affirmations: (1) the New Testament and the creeds are no longer in any way authoritative or canonical for us; (2) the Christian today can find sufficient guidelines for his faith and action in contemporary statements and solutions.

We are thus in no secure place. We have found no single authoritative standard from the past of what to say or how to live. Neither have we a secure self-understanding erected on the basis of our immediate experience. We in fact find ourselves in the abyss of a continual uncertainty, but we are kept from falling into chaos by the very tension between past and present. Our specific spot over the abyss is the result of our own individual dialogue. We have no assurance that where we happen to be is the best or final place to stand.[1]

It is important to note that this seminary professor is describing an implicit attitude. The faculty and seminarians he is addressing do not explicitly and consciously reject God's Word. Rather, he is saying that, when pressed to define their actual position, he and his colleagues would find that they have in fact abandoned their commitment to the authority of God's Word as the supreme authority in their lives.

It is uncommon to find statements as blunt as the above in Catholic circles, although they are not unknown. However, one does commonly encounter both "professional" and ordinary Catholics who regularly speak and act in a way that indicates that God's Word as it comes to us in scripture, tradition, and the teaching of the Church no longer holds supreme authority in their lives.

For example, Hans Küng would like to make the academic community, principally the theologians, the authoritative interpreters of scripture and tradition, in effect replacing the pope and bishops.[2] Rosemary Reuther, a prominent Catholic theologian, not only applauds Küng's effort, but advises what is required to accomplish it:

This is really what Küng is calling for: that the academy replace the hierarchy as the teaching Magisterium of the Church. This cannot be accomplished by the academy itself. It entails the equivalent of the French Revolution in the Church, the deposing of a monarchial for a democratic constitution of the Church.[3]

Another American Catholic theologian, David Tracy, a man who is often referred to as one of the most brilliant of American Catholic theologians, advocates that Christian theologians make their primary commitment and have their primary loyalty to the norms and principles of the academic community. He says this commitment must encompass not just their professional work as theologians, but also their personal lives and beliefs as well.[4]

This shift of loyalties and commitments is affecting the life of religious communities. The leading official in the Maryland Province of a congregation of Catholic nuns resigned her office because she was no longer able to support in conscience the "renewal" plan being worked out in her congregation. She said the plan elevated the sisters' personal experience over God's Word as the supreme authority for the community:

"The Renewal for Mission Plan" shifts the center of life from faith in God's action to concentration on ourselves, the members of the congregation. The "lived experience of the Sisters" is the authoritative source of knowledge governing actions and decisions, replacing rather than complementing the authoritative sources of revelation in the Church. In fact, lived experience is made the criterion for assessing revelation, the basis for selection and interpretation of Scripture passages and teachings of the Church; social analysis is made the point of departure for theology.[5]

Such implicit or explicit rejection of the authority of God's Word is not simply a theoretical, abstract doctrinal question restricted to speculative theology. My concern here is not primarily to draw attention to abuses of the academic freedom which theologians need in order to work creatively. Rather, I am concerned about the spread of such attitudes and teaching throughout the Church far beyond the academic community, often, it seems, with the explicit purpose of leading God's people away from His Word, and sometimes to the active encouragement of immorality.

For example, the editor of a Catholic magazine devoted to the renewal of parish life (a magazine which is sold in the magazine racks of many parish churches) just a few years ago wrote an article in his magazine which advocated the practice of bisexuality. He rejected the authority of God's Word and installed in its place the authority of subjective desires:

Persons—young and old, Hollywood beauty and spiritual beauty— have all become sex "objects" for me.

So why not male and female? . . . Surely each of us is, at least a little bit, bisexual—capable, in the proper circumstances, of lovingly and rewardingly expressing our sexuality with a person of either sex. . . . If

I'm really honest with myself, I can see and feel—via a kind of extrapolation, interior and visceral and not just mental, from teenage fantasy to real live bodies to the female person as *female* to the female person as *person*—that it's really the *person* as *person* that I desire sexually, or could, or ought to, in my mind, heart, and loins. So why not the male person?

The law of God, you say? Come on, let's grow up theologically too. We say we don't hold an anthropomorphic God, a kind of great puppeteer, old, male (and hetero-sexual, may one suppose?), so let's really not hold one. No, God works the wonders of his providence, of his love and his laws, right down inside the concrete, living, *individual* natures he creates and sustains.[6]

Behind the offensively humorous tone of this encouragement to immorality lies a disregard—even contempt—for the sources of Christian truth. The words of St. Augustine bear repeating here:

It is necessary that we become meek through piety so that we do not contradict Divine Scripture, either when it is understood and is seen to attack some of our vices, or when it is not understood, and we feel that we are wiser than it is and better able to give precepts. But we should rather think and believe that which is written to be better and more true than anything which we could think of by ourself, even when it is obscure.[7]

Another magazine that provides abundant examples of the undermining of God's Word is *U.S. Catholic*. For years now, *U.S. Catholic* has regularly run articles undermining the authority of God's Word as it comes to us in scripture, tradition, and the teaching of the Church. Published by the Claretian Fathers in Chicago, it is distributed throughout the United States in parish magazine racks by Paulist Press.[8]

Increasingly in the Church today, God's Word is rejected when it conflicts with personal preferences, the opinion of the secular academic community, or contemporary "causes" and movements. This has led some to boldly proclaim that we simply omit from scripture those passages that teach something unpalatable to the contemporary mind. This remedy is applied with particular passion to the scriptural teaching on the structure and order of family and church, and the question of men's and women's roles. An article in one theological journal put it bluntly: "Then we can say with a clear conviction and without fear or guilt that if Jesus was not a feminist, he was not of God."[9]

"Theological" pronouncements like the above have led many clergy to a rather remarkable approach to "explaining" God's Word in this area. As one clergyman put it when commenting on 1 Corinthians 11:2-16:

Because at bottom he [Paul] knew he was wrong, he became angry, argued from propriety, nature and proof texts which did not prove. We are saying that he was not ignorant of the gospel here. Rather, he knew it and could not face it.[10]

Such attitudes toward scripture are not restricted to theological journals, nor to the clergymen who are exposed to this type of thinking, but are increasingly becoming characteristic of the "ordinary Christian."

A few years ago I wrote a book on family life in which I essentially reaffirmed the teaching of scripture and authentic Christian tradition about the life of the Christian family.[11] My book was reviewed by a nationally syndicated Catholic columnist in a popular American Catholic family magazine. This woman's column appears in many diocesan newspapers, and she was a keynote speaker at the American Bishops' conference for their "decade of the family" program.

The reviewer did not like my book. For our purposes, the merits of the particular book are not relevant, but the reasons why she criticized the book are an interesting commentary on where many see the locus of authority in the Catholic Church today.

She criticized the book because "it puts itself on a collision course with today's culture, changing womanhood, and most respected mental health schools." The reviewer expresses surprise that a former president of the American Bishops' conference endorsed the book, since "it so contradicts the precepts of the Pastoral Ministry Plan for Families passed by the American bishops in May of 1978." The reviewer went on to say that she worked on a commission that helped the bishops formulate their plan.[12] She said that some of the major scriptural foundations of family life as presented in the book are "archaic issues as far as parents are concerned." The reason? "We listened to their needs—825,000 of them—and tried to present a ministry of and by the people which takes into account today's family struggling in today's culture."[13]

What is particularly troubling about this review is that it did not deal at all with the book's contention that family life had to be based on God's Word. This is simply dismissed as irrelevant because scripture is on a collision course with certain elements of contemporary society. The new sources of truth are "today's culture," "changing womanhood," and the results of an opinion poll. No attempt is even made to justify replacing the old sources of truth with the new.

The root question this kind of attitude raises can be posed in a number of different ways. Do we approach scripture with the intention of trying to get it to support certain currently popular social and political trends such as radical feminism and Marxism? Or do we look to scripture and the teaching of the. Church with a view toward forming our approach to life by them, and evaluating contemporary trends in their light? To phrase the question more succinctly, if contemporary trends and authentically interpreted scripture conflict, where does our allegiance lie? Who has to yield? The teaching of the Church and scripture, or "today's culture," "changing womanhood," and the opinions of 825,000 average American Catholics?

Another example of this attitude is a letter that appeared in a Catholic diocesan newspaper:

> I'm sorry, dear editor, but I don't believe that the excerpt from Paul to the Ephesians is the word of the Lord; and if believing is living what we believe, neither does anyone else, be they husband or wife! Paul's words are fossils, to be kept in libraries for scholars to read and remark to each other about how primitive people were in "Bible times," how uncivilized.
>
> Furthermore, if these readings are so difficult to understand, and their occurrence in our liturgy is the cause of people losing faith, then those people in Rome are saying: "It is better to insist that Paul's words are the word of the Lord and lose souls than it would be to strike Paul's archaic language from the liturgy and use something meaningful in its place."
>
> . . . The books of the Bible were put together as one book by men. Let wiser men take them apart.[14]

There is certainly the need to raise, in a responsible manner, questions of culture, of literary form, of the author's intention, in the interpretation of scripture, but the facile rejection of scripture that disagrees with contemporary ideologies, evident here, is frightening. What a contrast there is between the increasingly hostile attitude toward scripture on the part of many and the attitude of the early Fathers of the Church. When confronted with such arrogant approaches to God's Word as we have encountered above, they responded bluntly:

> They have not feared to lay hands upon the sacred Scriptures, saying that they have corrected them. Nor is it likely that they themselves are ignorant of how very bold their offense is. For either they do not believe that the sacred Scriptures were spoken by the Holy Spirit, in which case they are unbelievers, or if they regard themselves as being wiser than the Holy Spirit, what else can they be but demoniacs?[15]

What a contrast between so many contemporary attitudes toward God's Word and the teaching of the Second Vatican Council on the inspired, inerrant nature of God's Word.

Those divinely revealed realities which are contained and presented in sacred Scripture have been committed to writing under the inspiration of the Holy Spirit. Holy Mother Church, relying on the belief of the apostles, holds that the books of both the Old and New Testament in their entirety, with all their parts, are sacred and canonical because, having been written under the inspiration of the Holy Spirit (cf. Jn 20:31; 2 Tm 3:16; 2 Pt 1:19-21; 3:15-16), they have God as their author and have been handed on as such to the Church herself. In composing the sacred books, God chose men and while employed by Him they made use of their powers and abilities, so that with Him acting in them and through them, they, as true authors, consigned to writing everything and only those things which He wanted.

Therefore, since everything asserted by the inspired authors or sacred writers must be held to be asserted by the Holy Spirit, it follows that the books of Scripture must be acknowledged as teaching firmly, faithfully, and without error that truth which God wanted put into the sacred writings for the sake of our salvation. Therefore "All Scripture is inspired by God and useful for teaching, for reproving, for correcting, for instruction in justice; that the man of God may be perfect, equipped for every good work" (2 Tm 3:16-17).[16]

Ambiguity and Vagueness

While the direct denial of the authority of God's Word and of specific Christian truth is widespread today, another common problem is the surrounding of the truth and the authority of God's Word with question marks and uncertainty, so that those who hear or read such preaching or teaching arc left in vagueness and confusion. Uncertainty is inherent in the "scientific" study of scripture as it is commonly practiced today, and rightly so. Since scientific statements are always susceptible to correction by further scientific findings, one can scarcely ever conclude that something is certain, on that basis alone. This spirit of uncertainty, tentativeness, and ambiguity has become a very common characteristic of contemporary Catholic life. Since clarity and certainty are a necessary foundation for fervent Christian life and evangelization, the seriousness of this development cannot be underestimated.

John Paul II frequently speaks of this undermining element often seen in Catholic scripture scholarship and theology today. He deplores the over-extension of "scientific" approaches to scripture that undermine the certainty and clarity of God's Word as it has been authentically interpreted in the Councils of the Church, lived in its prayer life and liturgy, witnessed to by the Fathers, doctors, and saints, and authoritatively interpreted for our time by the pope and bishops.

In passing one refers here to the relationships between the "human sciences" and Revelation. Some people expand the field proper to these sciences to such an extent that they empty the mystery of Christ of its content as Saint Paul very much lamented, and in their exaggeration of the importance of human wisdom they despise the foolishness of the Cross.[17]

The pope has begun to deal with some of the more prominent practitioners of theological and doctrinal denial and ambiguity. He has issued warnings in his speeches and has also moved directly against some prominent individuals through disciplinary actions administered through the Congregation for the Doctrine of the Faith. These are important cases precisely because they involve prominent individuals whose writings and ideas well illustrate the lethal extent of uncertainty about basic Christian truth.

For example, a French Dominican theologian, Fr. Jacques Pohier, was publicly corrected, with the pope's approval, for holding views not compatible with Catholic doctrine. In doing so, the Vatican wished to call attention "to the seriousness of the errors here denounced and to the impossibility of considering them as opinions left to the free discussion of theologians." The Vatican found that one of the priest's books negated the following truths: Christ's intention to give a redeeming and sacrificial value to his passion; the corporeal resurrection of Christ and his permanence as a real subject after the end of his historical existence; the survival, the resurrection, the eternal life with God as a vocation of man; the presence in the Holy Scriptures of a true teaching, having objective sense, which faith can recognize and which the teaching of the Church, assisted by the Holy Spirit, can authentically determine.[18] The Vatican noted danger even in Pohier's various "affirmations":

> One finds other statements, so ambiguous and of such a nature as to generate uncertainty in the minds of the faithful about the following important articles of the Christian faith. . . . as far as regards the divinity of Christ, the author expresses himself in such an unusual manner, that it cannot be determined whether he still professes this truth in its traditional Catholic meaning.[19]

Recently, the Vatican drew attention to questionable statements, ambiguity, and uncertainty in the work of Edward Schillebeeckx, the well-known European theologian, and, following discussions with him, despite initial press reports to the contrary, asked him to publish some extensive clarifications to dispel confusion and uncertainty he had engendered in his readers.[20] Roman theologians were not alone in their concern. Some of the English-language reviewers of his recent work, *Jesus: An Experiment in Christology*, were not sure what Schillebeeckx is saying: Does he contend that Jesus rose from the dead, or that he merely lived on in the understanding of the disciples? Does he affirm Jesus' divinity or not? An American Jesuit theologian, writing in a journal normally sympathetic to such theology, had this to say about Schillebeeckx's recent work:

> Despite my genuine praise for this book, I contend Schillebeeckx has seriously neglected the New Testament tradition which calls Jesus "God." Schillebeeckx gives us a creaturely Jesus by reducing "hypostatic union" to mean "being in, of, and by God.". . . An interest in the reality of Jesus' appearances and the empty tomb, moreover, cannot be dismissed as "pseudo-empiricism," "supernatural hocus-pocus," or a "naive and crude realism." . . . despite his "pastoral" motivation in writing this book, it is so theologically controversial (and flawed, in my view) and pastorally misleading, it is better left to professional theologians.[21]

This quote from a review obviously does not function as an adequate treatment of the merits of Schillebeeckx's book or of his personal orthodoxy. Such a discussion is beyond the scope of this book. However, this quote does illustrate a serious theological problem with grave pastoral consequences. When even theological peers sympathetic to Schillebeeckx's work cannot find unambiguous affirmations of basic Christian truth, what will be the result as views like his are popularized in the numerous summer workshops and theological renewal seminars, and are then passed on to ordinary Catholics through preaching and the press?

Just after Schillebeeckx was called to Rome for a discussion of his views, the Vatican—once again with the direct and personal approval of the Pope—declared that Hans Küng, a Swiss theologian teaching in Germany, could no longer be considered a Catholic theologian. This final step was preceded by Küng's repeated refusal over the years to meet with Vatican theologians, and by his final refusal to retract those aspects of his teaching contrary to faith.

It is notable that these recent attempts to restore clarity and certainty to the faith have involved some of the most influential theologians of the conciliar and post-conciliar years. Men like Schillebeeckx and Küng have had their works published and translated all over the world. They have lectured widely, given interviews, and appeared on television, and their books are used in Catholic seminaries and universities to train the future leaders of the Church. They have blazed a trail that many others have followed. Thus the attacks on Christian truths and ambiguities to be found in their works is only the tip of the iceberg. Their spirit and attitude, if not their actual conclusions, are reflected widely and deeply throughout many Catholic theological and scripture faculties today and among millions of ordinary Catholics.

Behind this widespread hesitancy to make unequivocal affirmations of Christian truth often lies an actual hostility to the idea that Christian truth can be known certainly and proclaimed authoritatively. John Paul II's attempts to restore clarity and authority have often evoked hostile responses which reveal themselves to be opposed in principle to the possibility that we can know Christian truth with any certainty.

Even journalists writing in the secular press are able to spot this attitude. On the occasion of John Paul II's visit to the United States, a syndicated secular columnist wrote perceptively about the hostility expressed by certain Catholics to the pope's clear and certain proclamation of basic truth:

> Scholar-journalist Garry Wills, writing in New York Magazine, uses words such as "disturbing," "old-fashioned," "theocratic," "right-wing," "rigid," "self-defeating," and "anachronistic" to convey his sense that this pope is unfit to lead the Church of What's Happening Now. He quotes an Italian politician who complains that John Paul, unlike Paul VI, has "no doubts at all" about his role in the world, a state of certitude he finds downright "scary."
>
> The politician is also a "Marxist." Now Marxists aren't noted for self-doubt about their role in the world, but that is only one of the ironies that eludes Wills. An article like this one illustrates the plight of religion in America. If there is any orthodoxy today, it is liberal secularism—which can't countenance claims of religious truth. As a result, many people try to hold on to the forms of religion while avoiding a real show-down with unbelief. . . .
>
> That is what is so exciting, I think, about John Paul II: He is felt to be a reminder that religious "preference" has to be subordinate to religious truth.[22]

In my own speaking and writing about the gospel, I have encountered many Catholics who seem to have become addicted to an atmosphere of religious ambiguity. After a simple presentation I gave about Christian truth concerning the final judgment, a teaching which I had reviewed with a well-known scripture scholar who found it "balanced," I received a letter which illustrates this attitude. The writers said:

> We feel that this manner of oversimplifying is unproductive because it does not generate movement toward a reflective theology. Though you may personally reflect on God's love, mercy, judgment, and

condemnation, you should not present it in such a way as to close off dialogue on these issues.

Despite the merits or lack of them of this particular talk, the tragedy of this kind of response is that it may reflect an inability to receive God's Word as *God's* Word, revealing a hostility to the very notion of clearly revealed and binding truth. There's a powerful current today that tends to reduce Christian belief to the level of personal opinion: religious doctrines are not to be held to have a universal component of truth but simply to provide grist for the unending "reflection" of theology. This view drains God's Word of its purpose. God's Word is not primarily intended to "generate movement toward a reflective theology" or to open up "dialogue," but rather to call for adherence, obedience, and change of life. The preaching of Jesus, the apostles, the Fathers and Doctors of the Church, and the authoritative teaching magisterium today are all intended to call men and women to conversion. They are not simply one of many words, or opinions that provoke dialogue. Jesus preached with authority. "The people were spellbound by his teaching because he taught with authority, and not like the scribes" (Mk 1:22). His successors—those preachers and teachers who carry out their mission in union and harmony with the authority of Jesus, the apostles, and the teaching Church—share in Jesus' authority. It is indeed through this grass-roots teaching and preaching that the Church is to be built up. Yet, if the trumpet gives an uncertain sound, who will come for battle?

In some ways today the hostility toward certainty, clarity, and authority in connection with God's Word is linked to an idolatry of "the search" or "the journey." Searching or journeying toward truth and meaning has been so elevated into a value, or assumed as our proper stance, that the very notion of finding truth that is clear, authoritative, and binding is consciously or unconsciously rejected or avoided.

During my undergraduate years as a student at the University of Notre Dame, and as a graduate student at Princeton, this love for the "search" was pervasive. For a period of time I rejected the teaching of Christ and the Church, and "searched" for truth. After a time, I came to realize that I often avoided those trains of thought or contact with certain people that would challenge or threaten my love of the "search." The prospect of finding or discovering the truth threatened me. If I found the truth, I would have to submit to it. I saw that I had come to love the "search for truth" more than the truth itself. I had to repent of such idolatry in order to truly serve him who calls himself, quite simply and definitively, the Truth.[23]

Indeed, an attitude which lies behind much of the attack on truth in the Church today is a growing doubt that human beings can know *anything* with clarity and certainty. Perpetual uncertainty is an intellectual posture quite congenial to contemporary, secular culture. All truth is suspect. All statements about reality, not just religious statements, are brought under a thoroughgoing skepticism. Thus, in many circles in the Church, the "search for truth" is a permanent attitude which actually prevents "finding" it. Great antagonism greets the suggestion that the search for some truths is over—that God has revealed his will about some important things certainly and clearly, in ways that human beings can understand and act upon. Christians who believe that God has spoken this way are often incorrectly labeled "fundamentalists" by those who doubt that the truth can be known.

Cardinal William Baum, quoting the official teaching of the Church, shows how this skeptical attitude toward truth is incompatible with the Church's beliefs:

> The Incarnation of the Truth means that "the faithful must shun the opinion . . . that dogmatic formulas . . . cannot signify truth in a determinate way, but can only offer changeable approximations to it." It means that the truth cannot be considered "like a goal that is constantly being sought by means of such approximations."[24]

Citing the teaching of both Vatican Councils, Cardinal Baum pointed out that truths concerning God and basic morality are in principle accessible to human reason (Rom 1:20). Because of Revelation, they "can be known easily, with a firm certainty and without any admixture of error." Because of the importance of this statement, I would like to quote the exact text promulgated by the Constitution on Divine Revelation, from Vatican II:

> This sacred Synod affirms, "God, the Beginning and End of all things, can be known with certainty from created reality by the light of human reason" (cf. Rom 1:20); but the Synod teaches that it is through His revelation "that those divine realities which are by their nature accessible to human reason can be known by all men with ease, with solid certitude, and with no trace of error, even in the present state of the human race."[25]

In *Catechesi Tradendae*, a forceful document about instruction in the faith, Pope John Paul II warns against the dangers of deceitful or beguiling language. He then notes that certain philosophical approaches are undermining theology and pastoral practice because they have at their center a hostility toward certainty and clarity:

> A more subtle challenge occasionally comes from the very way of conceiving faith. Certain contemporary philosophical schools which

seem to be exercising a strong influence on some theological currents and, through them, on pastoral practice, like to emphasize that the fundamental human attitude is that of seeking the infinite, a seeking that never attains its object. In theology, this view of things will state very categorically that faith is not certainty but questioning, not clarity but a leap in the dark.[26]

The pope says that while we must not claim certainty for things that are not certain, we must also resist the inclination to question everything and to ignore the absolute certainty that Christ has provided us in the important matters relating to our salvation and how to live our life:

> The letter to the Hebrews says that "faith is the assurance of things hoped for, the conviction of things not seen" (Heb 11:1). Although we are not in full possession, we do have an assurance and a conviction. When educating children, adolescents, and young people, let us not give them too negative an idea of faith—as if it were absolute non-knowing, a kind of blindness, a world of darkness— but let us show them that the humble yet courageous seeking of the believer, far from having its starting point in nothingness, in plain self-deception, in fallible opinions or in uncertainty, is based on the word of God who cannot deceive or be deceived, and is unceasingly built on the immovable rock of this word.
>
> The most valuable gift that the Church can offer to the bewildered and restless world of our time is to form within it Christians who are confirmed in what is essential and who are humbly joyful in their faith.[27]

The notion of "pilgrim people" expressed in the Council documents has been so twisted and distorted that it has come to signify a people who is unsure of its own identity, its mission, its destination, and its route. This interpretation is in precise opposition to the intention of the Council and the biblical meaning of "people of God." God's people are supposed to be characterized by their assurance of who they are, who has called them, what their way of life is, what their mission is, and what their final destiny is to be. They are, after all, followers of him who is the Way, the Truth, and the Life.

Silence

Another way in which God's Word is being distorted and undermined in the Church today is simply through silence. For some years, the general environment of the Catholic Church has been marked by a tendency to discuss, teach, preach, and celebrate only parts of God's

Word, usually those parts which are most congenial to the general secularized environment of Western culture. This produces tremendous distortions in the lives of people exposed to such one-sided input. We have heard much about the "affirming" aspects of God's love, much less about his justice and judgment. We have been taught how Christianity helps us develop a positive self-image and to "feel good" about ourselves; we have not been taught nearly as much about the reality of sin and the need for repentance. After years of hearing about how every human being is a "beautiful person," the notion that we need to preach the gospel to those who do not know Christ is met with skepticism. Years of encouragement to seek "self-fulfillment" and to "do your own thing" have made many Catholics hostile to the call to renounce all to follow him and to die to ourselves in order to live to him. In short, many preachers and teachers have largely fallen silent about the demanding and unpleasant aspects of the gospel, such as the call to obedience and submission to God and His Word when it is both convenient and inconvenient. Many Catholics now have a pronounced tendency to pick and choose from among God's Words those that they find pleasant and "affirming." This caricature of God's Word is producing a tremendous distortion and softening of Christian character.

This silence about the "hard" parts of the gospel fits the general climate of ambiguity and vagueness in the Church and society today. Since so many are plagued by doubt and unbelief, there is a strong tendency to preach or teach only those parts of God's Word that modern man finds congenial. And modern man wants to avoid many hard parts of his Word that go against the grain of fallen, rebellious mankind—the truths that sin, Satan, and death are real; the need for redemption, for faith, repentance, baptism; the reality of the Lord's return in glory and the judgment of the living and the dead, the resurrection of the body, and eternal blessedness or punishment, heaven or hell.

Silence about such truths over a period of years can erode the faith and confidence of God's people as effectively as outright false teaching. It can sap our will to live lives of godliness and holiness when faithfulness to God's Word is inconvenient, when it is uncomfortable, when it is scorned by the world.

Inauthentic Reinterpretation

When I was critical of Christianity and the Church during part of my university years, I admired the "honesty" and "fidelity to human experience" of certain French existentialist philosophers and writers. In particular I admired Albert Camus when he declared, "I cannot believe in a God who allows innocent children to suffer." I approved his strong commitment to his experience of justice and injustice, and his refusal to accept a God that did not conform to his strongly experienced and strongly held ideas about justice and injustice.

As I came to encounter the living God in a renewed way just before I graduated from the university, I came to see this position as foolish and arrogant. For I discovered that it is folly and arrogance to judge God in light of human experience, norms, and convictions. Rather we should judge human experience, norms, and convictions in light of God and His Word, which can neither deceive or be deceived.

Unfortunately, many people in the Church today, even those holding positions of responsibility, place man's norms above God's. They approach God very much as Camus approached God, insisting that he conform to our experience, values, or ideological commitments if he is to be truly acknowledged as God. Many people today insist that God support their firmly held convictions, respect certain deeply felt values, and validate certain "profoundly experienced" intuitions. A crucial part of the crisis of truth is the failure of Christians to submit those convictions, values, experiences, and intuitions to God and His Word, and to value and judge them in light of His Word.

Camus' folly was to insist that God's justice had to fit into the narrow, restricted, time-and-space-bound frame of reference of the "natural" man. God's Word explicitly tells us that the plan and wisdom of God cannot be perceived by the natural man, but only by the man who has repented, believed, and partaken of God's Spirit (1 Cor 2:10-11). Indeed the suffering of innocent children cannot be reconciled with the ideas of "natural man." It can only be understood in light of what God has revealed about himself and his character, and about sin and Satan, reward and punishment, the resurrection of the dead, and final justice at the judgment of all mankind.

Many who study and interpret scripture and Church teaching today make the same mistake Camus made. They have made prior commitments to ideologies, causes, and movements. They interpret God's Word to conform to these prior commitments. These previous commitments then motivate an attempt to "reinterpret" scripture so it does not contradict the commitments already made. This results in a twisting and distortion of scripture.

In this connection it is worthwhile to note the influence of Rudolf Bultmann on contemporary scripture scholarship. Bultmann began the study of scripture already having made a commitment to a scientific view of his time that held that supernatural events, like miracles, cannot happen because they apparently break the laws of nature. Bultmann and his followers thus treated the scriptural accounts of miracles as merely metaphorical or symbolic. He demythologized and reinterpreted much of God's Word to fit the anti-supernaturalist biases of the science of his day. There continue to be scholars today who approach God's Word in the same way, judging it on the basis of some previously held ideological commitment. As one scholar described the benefit of this type of approach:

> The value of liberal theology was that it reassured Christians that they did not need to sacrifice their intellects to assent to conceptions that are simply silly in our century.[28]

Or as another scholar described it, the problem with much of scripture is that it contains "concepts which are often outmoded and meaningless to 20th century man" and speaks in "metaphors and analogies [which] are archaic and distasteful to modern sensibilities."[29]

Unfortunately, there has been little agreement about which conceptions are really "silly," "outmoded," and "distasteful to modern sensibilities." Since the personal views and opinions of scholars vary widely, this approach to interpreting scripture has tended to shred it into a myriad of subjective judgments and preferences. It has become clear that this approach is often not "objective" science at all, but is rather the reading back of prior subjective commitments into God's Word. This approach has wreaked so much havoc in certain circles of scholarship and Church life that both Protestant and Catholic scholars have begun to raise serious questions about it because of its predominantly negative results.[30]

The effort to control the grossly subjective and ideological presuppositions of this approach to scripture in the Catholic Church has not been totally successful. Even such prominent Catholic scholars as Raymond Brown can declare that Jesus and Paul were simply wrong in their belief in demons.[31] Obviously, such opinions, disseminated widely in the Catholic press, affect the beliefs and actions of many Catholics.

Behind this approach to God's Word is an attempt to reinterpret scripture so as to support what the writer or speaker has already accepted as an absolute value. Thus those committed to certain political movements will insist that "authentic Christianity" would support them. The pressure to reinterpret is especially pronounced in relation to sexuality. Those who "can't believe in a God who would insist that a gay person remain chaste," or that "God would not expect teenagers in our culture to abstain from sex," will find an interpretation of scripture that suits their views on sexual behavior.

This twisting of scripture to suit a particular purpose sometimes becomes so strained that its practitioners finally admit that their views indeed cannot be justified by scripture, tradition, or Church teaching. They end up rejecting the authority of God's Word or even Christianity itself.

This has happened in certain sectors of the feminist movement. One prominent nun, acknowledging the awkwardness of reinterpreting scripture to fit feminist values, finally declared:

> The Scriptures are unredeemably sexist. Even though here and there women may appear in a favorable light, the overwhelming stance of the writers toward women is that they are inferior to men, weak, needing protection, and foolish. Wickedness in a woman is worse than in a man. To say that this portrayal reflects the cultural condition of the age in which the books were written in no way solves the problem. In my view, that explanation ignores the claim made by both synagogue and church: that the books purport to contain God's Word. If the Word of God can be so corrupted by the mores of the culture in which it is received and on a matter of such centrality, it is in need of correction.[32]

Some Catholic feminists have become so committed to an alien ideology that they have gone "beyond God the Father."[33] Some have become explicitly involved in devotion to pagan goddesses.[34]

Such open rejections of God's Word are easier for most Christians to deal with than the subtle attempts to reinterpret God's Word to support previously accepted values. One article in a prominent Christian magazine addressed the situation of readers who found themselves no longer able to assent to traditional Christian concepts as expressed in the Creed and liturgy. The author urged such people not to leave the Church, but to reinterpret Christian beliefs and stay.[35] Many people have taken this advice. We now face a situation in the Church in which growing numbers of people hold on to the forms and language and rituals of Christianity but profoundly corrupt their meaning and purpose. God's Word is twisted and distorted, sometimes so perversely that sin and infidelity are encouraged.

Of course, there is a genuine need for theological creativity. One of the roles of theology is to attempt to relate the unchanging Word of God to the various cultural shifts characteristic of human history. We can see from the tradition of the Church that the richness of understanding and expression of God's Word has benefited from such theological attempts and cultural interaction over the centuries. Yet for such contemporary restatement or enriched understanding of unchanging truth to be authentic and legitimate, it must remain faithful to the original meaning and intent of the Word of God, and adequately retransmit this in contemporary terms. This often does not happen today. Some have abused the legitimate responsibility of theology to relate with contemporary culture. Instead, they reinterpret God's Word so that it is not only emptied of its meaning, but even perversely used to justify the very thing it identifies as sin and infidelity.

"Vain and Futile Speculation"

As we have already said, there is a legitimate and important place for responsible theological speculation and a need for the appropriate measure and kind of academic freedom in which such speculation can take place in a sound manner. But today there are a considerable number of people who have suspended various aspects of Christian faith and commitment because of what can only be called an addiction to the "latest thinking." There is an appropriate and wholesome speculation, possible in theology and yet there is also what scripture refers to as "vain and futile speculation" (Rom 1:21). It is important that certainty and clarity not be attributed to what is not certain and clear. At the same time, it is important that what has been clearly and certainly revealed by God—the fundamental truths concerning our salvation and the way of life of Christians, and which has been definitely and authoritatively interpreted for us in the various Councils, Creeds, and authentic teachings of the Magisterium—not be obscured or approached as if these teachings were only speculation. Inappropriately speculating on God's Revelation instead of receiving it with thanksgiving, faith, and worship and acting on it, is only to provoke a deeper spiritual blindness, which lends itself to moral disorder (Rom 1:21ff).

Many Christians today have held back their full assent to God's Word, including its summons to a life of commitment and holiness and generous service and mission, out of a fear that the next scholarly article may make their belief and commitment appear naive and foolish. A desire not to appear unsophisticated has led many to reserve wholehearted commitment, in the fear of what implications the "latest theory" may have for their life and belief.

I personally have met a number of Catholic and Protestant missionaries in several countries who have abandoned efforts to directly preach the gospel in the hope of leading people to an explicit acknowledgement of Jesus as Savior and Lord, because they have been exposed to theological speculation which states that all mankind is already implicitly or "anonymously" Christian. We will deal with the issue of Christian mission in detail in Chapter Four. Here it is sufficient to note that a not inconsiderable part of the missionary workers of the Church are ignoring the direct command of Christ to preach the gospel to every creature, in favor of theological speculation which in some of its forms empties God's Word of its power and content.

There are also many who, having been exposed to speculation in the field of moral theology, have abandoned lives of holiness and righteousness to engage in pre-marital, extramarital, and homosexual activity, and who have killed the life of the child within their wombs.

A heavy responsibility rests upon those who teach:

Not many of you should become teachers, my brothers; you should realize that those of us who do so will be called to the stricter account. (Jas 3:1)

But a heavy responsibility also rests upon those who hear: "people will not tolerate sound doctrine, but, following their own desires, will surround themselves with teachers who tickle their ears" (2 Tm 4:3).

One reason why many people today are insecure in their faith, unsure of what to believe, reserved and ambiguous in their commitment and action, "addicted to the latest theories" is an excessive regard for and dependance on the results of academic studies. These studies sometimes overextend their actual sphere of competence. John Paul II described the problem this way:

We live in a culture which subjects everything to critical analysis and, in so doing, often absolutizes partial criteria, which by their very nature are unsuited to the perception of that world of realities and values which escapes the control of the senses.[36]

The various sciences that pertain to the study of God's Word and its application to contemporary life have a very real, but limited and subordinate contribution to make to the understanding of God's Word. We value the contribution that various archaeological, linguistic, historical, cultural, and literary studies can make to help us understand the original meaning and intention of the Word of God in its original languages and contexts. We also value whatever light psychology and sociology can cast on God's Word and its application to human life. For the work of many, many dedicated scholars we should be grateful. But these various sciences, even in their soundest and most responsible contributions, can never bring certainty in their interpretations; as Catholics we believe that certainty and confidence in belief rests with the direct action of the Holy Spirit and the authentic interpretation of the Church, initially in the Church's witness and testimony to what constituted the actual books of inspired scripture, then through the ages in the important conciliar, creedal, liturgical, and theological witnesses to God's Word. The various sciences are always subject to revision, modification, even contradiction in the "next article." This is proper; it is the nature of human science. Thus, if we primarily look to these sciences for certainty and clarity, we will never have it. Our commitment will always be muted and reserved or subjectively based. The role of the sciences is properly subordinate to the teaching authority of the Church, and the spiritual and moral factors which God's Word speaks of as necessary for its true understanding, factors which we will consider in more detail in the following chapter.

Cardinal Baum warns that an excessively critical approach to scripture with the intention of purifying it of cultural influences of the time misunderstands the profoundly incarnate nature of Christian Revelation. In some ways everything about God's Word is culturally conditioned, preeminently Jesus himself. It is precisely into and through a culture that God has prepared that he chose to manifest himself. It is impossible in many instances to separate God's Word from the form in which he chose to bring it to us!

What God has done is to intervene in our history. The word became flesh, one of us. The Gospel is therefore "incarnational." There is no "truth" which can be so detached from concrete deeds and words that these are considered entirely accidental, that is, arbitrary. Some particular deeds, and these alone, are redemptive in God's plan; some words, and not others, express the truth. Therefore the formulation of the truth, the proclamation and interpretation of the deeds, cannot be thought to depend entirely on cultural, historical factors.[37]

Sometimes today a tentativeness in belief and commitment is rooted in a misunderstanding of the way in which the Church freely acknowledges a legitimate place for what has been called "development of doctrine." But an authentic development of doctrine—a richer appreciation of a truth's dimensions and implications—must always proceed in such a way as to never deny what has previously been held, but only to develop and enrich doctrine in a way which is consistent with previous formulations and interpretations. Whether in the teaching of St. Vincent of Lerins or of Cardinal Newman or of John Paul II, there can be no such thing as a "development of doctrine" which actually contradicts what has previously been officially held and taught in the area of faith and morals.[38]

The pope has recently attempted to deny as explicitly as possible the possibility that the Church can ever change her understanding of God's Word in the area of marriage and human sexuality, an area where immense pressure to change is arising from secular influences even within the Church. The pope said, "the Church will never dilute or change her teaching on marriage and the family."[39]

Individual bishops in their local dioceses are also taking action to clarify the confusion about what can change and cannot change in our understanding of God's Word. As Archbishop Bernardin expressed it to those responsible for religious education in the Archdiocese of Cincinnati:

We must never expect that theological speculation will substantially change the "deposit of faith" which the Apostles received and which, for example, Paul passed on to Timothy. Despite all the speculation in theology today, such basic doctrines as the divinity and humanity of Christ, the Real Presence of Christ in the Holy Eucharist, the sacramental forgiveness of sins in the Sacrament of Penance, and the charism of infallibility by which the Church preserves pure and undefiled her deposit of faith can never be substantially changed.[40]

If human sciences, even when employed responsibly and competently can only play a supporting role in helping us understand God's Word, what are the primary components of such an understanding? To this we now turn.

CHAPTER THREE

Knowing God's Word

THOSE OF US who are Catholics are not fundamentalists in our approach
to the scripture. We realize the Bible is a collection of books written
over many hundreds of years in many different styles and literary
forms. We realize that understanding the Semitic mind and Semitic
culture, as well as the original languages in which the scriptures were
written, is important and that it takes work, study, and all the help of
the applicable sciences to acquire this knowledge. And we are grateful
for the work of the many dedicated scholars who have undertaken
these studies. However, science alone cannot bring us to an adequate
understanding of God's Word. For that, an action of God himself is
necessary. For God to act, certain moral and spiritual conditions need
to be met.

As Walter Burghardt, editor of *Theological Studies*, said in a convocation address given at the Jesuit School of Theology in Berkeley, California:

> What I do deny is that the world needs desperately the kind of
> theologians many of us have become. To do theology, it is not
> enough to know *about* God; I must know God. . . . From my own
> checkered past, I urge on you in the years to come a burning,
> humbling question: For all you know about God, do you really know
> God? Can you say that, like Ignatius Loyola, you have truly encoun-
> tered God, the living and true God? Can you say that you know
> God Himself, not simply human words that describe Him? If you
> cannot, I do not say you will be an unhappy theologian, unproduc-
> tive. . . . But . . . you will not be the theologian our world desperately
> needs.[1]

The scripture and the teaching of the Church make it clear that spiritual and moral factors—not technical knowledge—are the primary criteria for understanding God's word. As Jesus himself said to scripture scholars of his day:

Search the Scriptures
in which you think you have eternal life—
they also testify on my behalf.
Yet you are unwilling to come to me
to possess that life. (Jn 5:39, 40)

Learning is useful, but in the context of a right posture before God. We will examine some of the more important of these elements in detail because many Christians today are rapidly losing sight of them.

Fear of the Lord

An attitude of deep reverence and respect before God is a prerequisite for truly understanding His Word. The knowledge that it is God who is speaking creates an appropriate "fear." This inspires a deep respect toward God and His Word. "The fear of the Lord is the beginning of knowledge" (Prv 1:7).

It is possible to know many technical facts about God's Word and yet not to know His Word at all. Scholars can know many things about the archaeological, linguistic, and literary nature of scripture, and yet completely miss its meaning and relevance because they fail to appreciate the vast significance of the fact that scripture is indeed *God's Word*.

An attitude of reverence and respect for God's Word has been characteristic of the great expositors and interpreters of scripture throughout the ages. Today, however, a "scientific" arrogance has sometimes supplanted it. Compare, for example, the attitude of St. Augustine and St. Justin Martyr with some of the attitudes encountered in the previous chapter. St. Augustine, one of the greatest interpreters of scripture in the early Church, was reverent before the difficulties of his work:

If we are perplexed by an apparent contradiction in Scripture, it is not allowable to say, "The author of this book is mistaken"; but either the manuscript is faulty, or the translation is wrong, or you have not understood. . . . But in consequence of the distinctive peculiarity of the sacred writings, we are bound to receive as true whatever the canon shows to have been said by even one prophet, or apostle, or evangelist; otherwise, not a single page will be left for the guidance of human fallibility, if contempt for the wholesome authority of the canonical books either puts an end to that authority or involves it in hopeless confusion.[2]

St. Justin Martyr, another early expositor of scripture, had the same attitude:

I am entirely convinced that no Scripture contradicts another. I shall admit rather that I do not understand what is recorded, and shall strive to persuade those who imagine that the Scriptures are contradictory, to be rather of the same opinion as myself.[3]

Scripture says that "fear of the Lord" functions as a bulwark against sin. It is a necessary safeguard against the profound tendency of human beings to exalt themselves and their own knowledge and opinions above the Word of God—intellectual sin that causes human beings to become spiritually blind. Strands of pride and self-sufficiency are deeply intertwined in certain widely held attitudes toward scripture today. These need to be dissipated by a renewed fear of the Lord, the indispensable prerequisite for a true knowledge of God and a true wisdom. As Cardinal Newman put it:

Fear of God is the beginning of wisdom; until you see God as a consuming fire, and approach him with reverence and holy awe, because you are sinners, you will not be able to say that you are even in sight of the narrow door. . . . Fear and love must go together; continue to fear, continue to love until the last day of your lives.[4]

The Role of the Holy Spirit

Scripture makes it clear that the Holy Spirit, in union with the Father and the Son, knows and reveals the things of God. The scriptures were written under the inspiration of the Spirit; they must be read under the same inspiration to be properly understood. A living union with God—a genuine life in the Spirit—is a necessary precondition for an adequate understanding of the Word of God. Flesh and blood alone, working simply from its own skills and resources, can never understand and grasp the significance of God's Word. Only the working of the Holy Spirit can bring true understanding.

Jesus himself referred directly to the spiritual source of divine revelation. When Peter confessed faith in him, Jesus replied, "No mere man has revealed this to you, but my heavenly Father" (Mt 16:17). Before he returned to his Father, Jesus said that he would continue to be with his disciples through the Holy Spirit. This operation of the Holy Spirit in

their lives was the main way they would be able to continue to understand His Word. It is the same for us.

> The Paraclete, the Holy Spirit
> whom the Father will send in my name,
> will instruct you in everything,
> and remind you of all that I told you. (Jn 14:26)

> When he comes, however,
> being the Spirit of truth
> he will guide you to all truth.
> He will not speak on his own,
> but will speak only what he hears,
> and will announce to you the things to come. (Jn 16:13)

This was also the clear teaching of the apostles:

> No one knows what lies at the depths of God but the Spirit of God.
> The Spirit we have received is not the world's spirit, but God's
> Spirit, helping us to recognize the gifts he has given us. We speak of
> these, not in words of human wisdom but in words taught by the
> Spirit, thus interpreting spiritual things in spiritual terms. The natu-
> ral man does not accept what is taught by the Spirit of God. For him,
> this is absurdity. He cannot come to know such teaching because it
> must be appraised in a spiritual way. (1 Cor 2:11b-14)

The teaching could not be clearer: we cannot understand the things
of God without the help of the Holy Spirit and without the perspective
of the "spiritual man" who lives by that Spirit.

The knowledge and wisdom of the world is not just incapable of
truly perceiving or understanding God and His Word. Scripture even
acknowledges a certain opposition between prevailing human philoso-
phies and the truth and wisdom of God:

> The message of the cross is complete absurdity to those who are
> headed for ruin, but to us who are experiencing salvation it is the
> power of God. Scripture says,

> "I will destroy the wisdom of the wise,
> and thwart the cleverness of the clever."

> Where is the wise man to be found? Where the scribe? Where is
> the master of worldly argument? Has not God turned the wisdom
> of this world into folly? Since in God's wisdom the world did not
> come to know him through "wisdom," it pleased God to save those

who believe through the absurdity of the preaching of the gospel.
(1 Cor 1:18-22)

See to it that no one deceives you through any empty seductive
philosophy that follows mere human traditions, a philosophy based
on cosmic powers rather than on Christ. (Col 2:8)

As John Paul II put it:

The "Word of God" is always effective, because in the first place it
puts human reason in a crisis: merely rational and temporal philoso-
phies, purely humanistic and historicist interpretations, are thrown
into confusion by the "Word of God," which replies with supreme
certainty and clarity to the questions posed to man's heart, enlight-
ens him about his true destiny, which is supernatural and eternal,
and points out to him the moral conduct to practice as the authentic
way of serenity and hope.

Certainly, the "Word of God" is disturbing, because the Lord says:
"My thoughts are not your thoughts, neither are your ways my
ways" (Is 55:8); it causes a crisis, because it is demanding, it is as
sharp as a two-edged sword and it is based not on persuasive
speeches of human wisdom, but on the manifestation of the Spirit
and his power (cf. 1 Cor 2:4-5).[5]

Our age is particularly characterized by the kind of scientific and
philosophical mentality that can block true understanding of God and
his Word. John Paul II speaks pointedly of the foolishness of the
"wise":

Not the "wise" and the "intelligent": they've formed a vision of their
own of God and of the world and are not ready to change it. They
think they know everything about God, that they possess the solution, that they have nothing to learn: for this reason they reject the
"good news," which seems so strange and in conflict with the principles
of their "Weltanschauung." It is a message that proposes certain
paradoxical changes, which their "common sense" cannot accept.[6]

The pope applies this to faith in basic Christian truths like the resurrection:

One thing is clear, beloved brothers: faith in the Risen Christ is not
the result of technical knowledge or the fruit of scientific qualifications (cf. 1 Cor 1:26). What is asked of us is to announce the death of
Jesus and to proclaim his resurrection (cf. Liturgy). Jesus is alive.
"God raised him up, having loosed the bonds of death" (Acts 2:24).[7]

"A true theological commitment," the pope says, "can neither begin nor conclude except on one's knees, at least in the secrecy of one's interior cell, where it is possible 'to worship the Father in spirit and truth (cf. Jn 4:23).' "[8]

Humility

Humility—a recognition of our limits, finiteness, creatureliness, our complete dependence on God—is indispensable for attaining to Christian truth. "God resists the proud but bestows his favor on the lowly" (Jas 4:6).

Spiritual pride, intellectual "self-sufficiency," and "autonomy" produce a deadly spiritual blindness. God reveals himself to the humble, not to the proud. And the pride that produces spiritual blindness often includes an intellectual pride.

At that moment Jesus rejoiced in the Holy Spirit and said: "I offer you praise, O Father, Lord of heaven and earth, because what you have hidden from the learned and the clever you have revealed to the merest children.

"Yes, Father, you have graciously willed it so. Everything has been given over to me by my Father. No one knows the Son except the Father and no one knows the Father except the Son—and anyone to whom the Son wishes to reveal him." (Lk 10:21-22)

John Paul II movingly comments on this passage:

. . . in the solemn words one feels almost a quiver of exultation. Jesus sees far ahead; he sees in the course of the centuries the innumerable host of men and women of all ages and from all walks of life, who will adhere joyfully to his message. . . . They have one characteristic in common: they are little, that is, simple, humble. . . . Christ does not ask man to renounce his own reason. And how could he, if it was he himself who gave it to him; what he asks of him is not to yield to the old prompting of the tempter, who continues to conjure up before him the deceptive perspective of being able to "be like God" (cf. Gn 3:5). Only he who accepts his intellectual and moral limits and recognizes that he is in need of salvation, can open up to faith, and in faith, meet Christ, his Redeemer.[9]

In the Church today, sometimes the "learned and clever" are destroying the genuine, God-revealed faith of the "merest children." Some of these "merest children" are literally children, those who have had their faith undermined or blocked by deficient catechetical programs. Many are ordinary Catholics whose faith has been subverted by warped confessional advice or inadequate adult education programs, often leaving them bitter, cynical, and leading lives of rebellious sin. Some are Catholics in the Third World whose "conscientization" is systematically exchanging their genuine faith in Christ for a pitiful hope in a secular revolution.

Unless we who are sometimes regarded as "learned and the wise" cultivate humility, we will almost surely succumb to intellectual error and moral decay. Scripture makes it clear that the proud man who trusts in his own ability and training is susceptible to being misled by the "spirit of the age"; he will fail to distinguish what is from God from what is not. A person's moral and spiritual condition is a prime determinant of what truth he will be able to comprehend and grasp. Wrong attitudes of the heart will lead eventually to wrong belief, and often to wrong behavior. Purity of heart, love, reverence, humility—these are all prerequisites for knowing God and His Word.

John Paul II stressed the need for humility in a particularly striking passage in an address to the assembled faculties and student bodies of the Pontifical Roman universities and colleges:

> So weak is our intelligence, so limited our experience, so short our lives, that what we can succeed in saying about God seems more like the babbling of a child than a dignified discourse, exhaustive and conclusive. . . . This is the fundamental conviction with which the theologian must approach his work: he must always remember that, whatever he may be able to say about God, it is always a question of the words of a man, and therefore of a tiny finite being, who has ventured upon exploration of the unfathomable mystery of the infinite God.[10]

In his address, the pope recalled a story about St. Thomas Aquinas. It is said that the great theologian had had an overwhelming mystical experience near the end of his life. Shortly afterward, his secretary exhorted him to continue writing the *Summa Theologica*. St. Thomas is said to have turned away his friend's urgings by recalling his mystical experience. "Brother," he said, "I cannot go on. Everything that I have written seems to me straw."

Obedience and Faith

Obedience and faith go along with humility. In fact, Jesus says that a willingness to obey God's Word is a condition for recognizing and understanding it:

My doctrine is not my own;
it comes from him who sent me.
Any man who chooses to do his will
will know about this doctrine—
namely, whether it comes from God
or is simply spoken on my own. (Jn 7:16-17)

This is perhaps what "men of good will" means: men disposed to
seek God and his truth and obey it. Accepting and carrying out
Christ's Word simply on the basis of his authority unfolds the meaning
of the Word: "If you live according to my teaching, you are truly
my disciples; then you will know the truth, and the truth will set
you free" (Jn 8:31-32).

By contrast, the attitude too common in the Church today is just the
opposite: "I don't understand, so I won't obey." Too many Christians
have this attitude even about authoritative teaching, which is clearly
expressed and solemnly communicated. The consequence of this refusal
to obey is an even deeper spiritual blindness.

Understanding God's Word depends on faith. Believing and trusting
the Word of God, even when we do not fully understand it, is a key to
future understanding and experience. This, in fact, is a characteristic of
God's dealings with man. Throughout history, he has required human
beings to believe in and obey His Word simply because it is His Word,
not because they understand completely the "reasoning" behind it.

John Paul II has been pointing out how central is this connection
between believing and understanding in the tradition of the Church:

Man, St. Thomas points out, while he is *in statu viae*, can reach a
certain understanding of the supernatural mysteries, thanks to the
use of his reason, but only to the extent to which the latter rests on
the unshakable foundation of faith, which is participation in the very
knowledge of God and of the blessed who behold him face to
face. . . . It is the view of the whole theological tradition and it is in
particular the position of the great Augustine: "By believing you
become capable of understanding; if you do not believe, you will
never succeed in understanding. . . . May faith, therefore, purify
you, so that you may be granted the privilege of reaching full
understanding."

The conclusion which the Bishop of Hippo reached was to become
classic: "Understanding is the fruit of faith. So do not try to understand
in order to believe, but believe in order to understand." This is a
warning on which anyone who "does theology" must reflect.[11]

The attitude of "I don't understand, so I don't believe" is especially evident in sexual morality, but it affects and infects the whole range of Christian truth, as we will see in subsequent chapters.

The Teaching of the Apostles

Because of their special relationship with Jesus, and because of the special help of the Holy Spirit he promised and gave to them, the apostles were able to authoritatively interpret their master's intent and the reliable meaning of his words and actions. The role of the apostles is an essential element in God's plan of salvation, in the authentic proclamation and interpretation of His Word and saving acts. This was true from the very beginning of the Church. Following Pentecost, the Jerusalem believers "devoted themselves to the apostles' instruction and the communal life, to the breaking of bread and the prayers" (Acts 2:42).

In the early Christian communities, the apostles settled disputes about the proper interpretation of the scripture and the teaching of Jesus. Under the inspiration of the Holy Spirit, they taught the proper way to understand the death and resurrection of Jesus. The apostles formed the life of the early communities and established their "traditions" and pastoral approaches to adequately reflect the mind of the Lord.

The Christian Churches today currently differ about the authority of this apostolic tradition and the practices of the apostolic churches in guiding the proper interpretation of scripture. Christians also differ about what degree scripture has been authentically interpreted by the Fathers of the Church, the decisions of the general councils, and the formulations of the creeds. Yet there is much room for agreement as well. Many Protestants agree that authentic Christian tradition expressed in early liturgy, the consensus of the Fathers, and the formulations of the creeds and councils has significant weight as a guard against arbitrary subjectiveness in the interpretation of scripture.

Those of us who are Catholics place great weight on the authority of tradition. Our understanding of God's Word is guided not just by a solid firsthand knowledge of scripture and the direction of the Holy Spirit, but also by the authentic tradition of the Church, which we see as being an expression of God's faithful love. (Yet even for Catholics, scripture holds a unique place in relationship to tradition and the magisterium. Only scripture is positively inspired, and the central function of both tradition and magisterium is to insure its proper interpretation and application.) For Catholics, this tradition is expressed in the writings of the Fathers, the formulations of creeds and documents and decisions of councils, and the lived faith of Christians throughout the centuries. This tradition is expressed today in the liturgy, and it is defended and interpreted by the official teaching authority of the Church in harmony with scripture.

This is why the effort to undermine God's Word in scripture has been accompanied, in the Catholic Church, by a concerted attempt to discredit the apostolic tradition of the Church as well. The elements of tradition—the Fathers, the councils, the creeds, the teaching of the bishops as a whole, the teaching of the popes, the witness of the liturgy, the lives of the saints—all combine to make a remarkably consistent testimony to the correct understanding of scripture and its teaching. It is not surprising that the same arrogance and skepticism that many have lately turned on scripture is also being turned on tradition.

It is certainly true that historical studies can cast a helpful light on certain aspects of tradition, just as historical and literary analysis can help us understand scripture. It is possible to distinguish among different layers of Church tradition of varying value and authority. Literary analysis can clarify the precise meaning of certain statements in tradition. However, this method of analysis when misused or overextended can produce the same excesses in the study of tradition as it has in the study of scripture. The abuses follow a familiar course. A "critical" approach, legitimate in itself, too often becomes an irresponsible and misguided effort to separate the "real" tradition from "general" or "culturally determined" tradition, with the criteria of judgment being what is most "meaningful" to modern man. Distasteful aspects of authentic tradition are sometimes rejected, and the modern critic can end up accepting only whatever is congenial to him. This approach often places the modern scholar in judgment over tradition; it robs tradition of its power to protect the truth.

But there is something even more fundamentally awry with conducting some modern analyses of tradition in a critical spirit. Attempts to "purify" scripture or tradition, efforts to make them more "meaningful," are often attempts to do away with the Incarnation and its consequences, what St. Paul called the "scandal" of Christian truth. The fallen human mind in its natural state truly cannot abide the whole notion of Incarnation. Confronted with the truth that Jesus is fully God and fully man, the fallen mind tries to do away with either Christ's humanity or his divinity in order to make his person and mission more "meaningful," more "tasteful."

Scripture and the Church both share in the incarnate mystery of Jesus, and both invoke the same skeptical reaction from fallen minds which cannot abide it. Scripture is both the words of men and the Word of God. Our approach to its study must therefore proceed with a reverence and humility similar to that with which we approach the mystery of Jesus himself. We should be realistic about our tendency to rebel against the incarnate mystery and to break it apart so it can be made more palatable to the human mind.

The same is true for the Church. Since, for a Catholic, the Church is both the Church of the Holy Spirit and the Church of the apostles, it too shares in the mystery of Incarnation. Again, the fallen human mind is strongly compelled to try to destroy the incarnate nature of the Church by making it either a solely spiritual body or a solely institutional one. But the two are profoundly linked and united—similar to the incarnate mystery of Jesus himself, and of the scripture.

God chose to save the world through the modality of Incarnation. The incarnate nature of Jesus is reflected in scripture and the Church— the ways he chooses to continue to communicate his Incarnation to each new generation. An attack on one becomes, in its ultimate outworking, an attack on all three.

Respect for Tradition

Any Christian who wants to understand God's Word must approach scripture in humility, with an attitude of obedience and faith, in fear of the Lord who is speaking, with respect for the teaching of the apostles, and with primary reliance on the action of the Holy Spirit to reveal the truth to him. In the Catholic Church, however, similar attitudes should also mark the Catholic's approach to the teaching authority (Magisterium) of the Church when it teaches in the areas of faith and morality. Catholics believe that God's Word is made accessible through authentic apostolic tradition, creedal affirmations, conciliar decisions, and the official teaching of the Church in areas of faith and morality. If Catholics are to be faithful to these beliefs, they should approach the teaching authority of the Church with respect and humility.

For Catholics, this means coming to grips in practical terms with our relationship to the legitimate teaching authority of the Church. This, of course, does not mean we should uncritically accept whatever bishops or even popes say. In the past, and again today, bishops have departed from the true faith, becoming captive to corrupting cultural ideas, philosophical and theological currents, and political pressures. Later we will examine distressing instances in today's Church where it appears that even bishops have been engulfed by the crisis of truth. It is important to be able to realistically face up to these situations in the interests of truth and, for Catholics, for the sake of authentic Catholicism.

Nevertheless, for those of us who are Catholics, a commitment to Christian truth means a commitment to its authentic expression, elaboration, and defense in Christian history—tradition—and to the official teaching authority of the Church today in the area of faith and morals. This means accepting the official teaching given by the pope and those bishops teaching in union with him in the area of faith and morals as a reliable guide to the correct understanding of God's Word.

Such teaching is infallible, and is to be received with the submission of faith, when given by the pope *ex cathedra* or by an ecumenical council when it solemnly defines. But even when it is not a matter of the pope and council solemnly defining, the bishops of the world, when they are in concurrence in matters of faith and morals, can proclaim Christ's teaching infallibly. (See Vatican II, Constitution on the Church, 15.) Even the ordinary teaching of the bishops, and especially the pope, on matters of faith and morals is to be received by Catholics wholeheartedly. As the Second Vatican Council stated this responsibility:

> Bishops, teaching in communion with the Roman Pontiff, are to be respected by all as witnesses to divine and Catholic truth. In matters of faith and morals, the bishops speak in the name of Christ and the faithful are to accept their teaching and adhere to it with a religious assent of soul. This religious submission of will and of mind must be shown in a special way to the authentic teaching authority of the Roman Pontiff, even when he is not speaking ex cathedra. That is, it must be shown in such a way that his supreme magisterium is acknowledged with reverence, the judgments made by him are sincerely adhered to, according to his manifest mind and will. His mind and will in the matter may be known chiefly either from the character of the documents, from his frequent repetition of the same doctrine, or from his manner of speaking.[12]

The fact that the pope's teaching is almost always simply a reaffirmation for our time of scriptural truth, or applications of the implications of scriptural truth held by the Church throughout the ages, does not diminish its importance for Catholics, especially in the current climate of uncertainty and confusion. As the Constitution on Divine Revelation from the Second Vatican Council states:

> The task of authentically interpreting the word of God, whether written or handed on, has been entrusted exclusively to the living teaching office of the Church, whose authority is exercised in the name of Jesus Christ. This teaching office is not above the word of God, but serves it, teaching only what has been handed on, listening to it devoutly, guarding it scrupulously, and explaining it faithfully by divine commission and with the help of the Holy Spirit; it draws from this one deposit of faith everything which it presents for belief as divinely revealed.
>
> It is clear, therefore, that sacred tradition, sacred Scripture, and

the teaching authority of the Church, in accord with God's most wise design, are so linked and joined together that one cannot stand without the others, and that all together and each in its own way under the action of the one Holy Spirit contribute effectively to the salvation of souls.[13]

This is the issue at stake in the attacks on infallibility by Hans Küng and other theologians. They are not simply challenging the teaching authority of the pope and bishops. They are undermining the entire teaching authority of the Church and the creedal and conciliar decisions that guard and protect scriptural truth. A spokesman for the German Catholic bishops explained this connection when the German bishops corrected Hans Küng:

The dogma of infallibility in the church can seem at first sight to be marginal in the totality of the faith. In reality, in it are concentrated fundamental problems, such as, for example, the knowledge of truth and interpretation of revelation, its verbal form and its tradition, the certainty of the faith and the grounds of the power of authority in the church. In this area that serves true knowledge of divine revelation, the appearance of errors brings damage to the faith itself.[14]

John Paul II's call for understanding of and commitment to authentic Church teaching in the area of faith and morals is an effort to safeguard the way the Holy Spirit defends and explicates the faith and keeps it free from the whims of subjective or academic opinion from age to age. Humility, the pope has said, is the right attitude the theologian should have toward the Church. He is humble before the Church because "he knows that the 'Word' has been entrusted to her, to proclaim it to the world, applying it to every age, and thus making it really relevant. As a man of the Church, the theologian loves the Church's past, meditates on her history, venerates and explores Tradition." The attitude of scripture scholars should be the same. "God entrusted holy scripture to his Church and not to the private judgment of specialists," the pope has said. The exegete's faithfulness to the Church's teaching authority is a question "of faithfulness to the spiritual function given by Christ to his Church."[15] Or as Cardinal Baum has put it:

The magisterium of the Church does not depend entirely on the result of scholarship in order to know with certainty what Catholics must believe and how they must live. This certainty is a gift of the Lord; it is a communication of his authority, the authority that evoked the admiration of the people confused by the debates between experts: "Jesus left the crowds spellbound at his teaching. The reason was that he taught with authority and not like the scribes." (cf. Mt 7:28-29)[16]

The Responsibility of Teaching Christian Truth

Scripture says that those who teach Christian truth have a particularly grave responsibility, and they will be held accountable for their work: "Not many of you should become teachers, my brothers; you should realize that those of us who do so will be called to the stricter account." Teachers of Christian truth must also bear in mind the solemn words of Jesus: "It would be better if anyone who leads astray one of these simple believers were to be plunged in the sea with a great millstone fastened around his neck" (Mk 9:42).

In light of these warnings, we might well ask how much of the teaching in religion classes, adult education programs, catechetical situations, Catholic schools and universities, seminaries, and summer workshops for theological "updating" has met the scriptural criteria for the knowledge of Christian truth. How much of it has been a faithful transmission of Christian truth, and how much has been personal opinion, speculative theories, or "worldly" wisdom masquerading as God's Word? How often has this teaching been rooted in bitterness, pride, resentment, rebellion, and delight in destroying "simple faith?"

Scripture instructs us to examine the character of the men and women who teach Christian truth. Their characters should be marked by loyalty and fidelity to the teaching they have received, to the "deposit of faith." As Paul wrote to Timothy, "The things which you have heard from me through many witnesses you must hand on to trustworthy men who will be able to teach others" (2 Tm 2:2).

It is possible and useful to examine the situation of the Church today sociologically. But it is even more important to use the spiritual and moral criteria provided in scripture to understand the current situation.

In that perspective, things look different.

Many missionaries have become confused and stopped evangelizing. Many men and women have not heard the gospel because a theory of "anonymous Christianity" has convinced missionaries and ordinary Catholics that nonbelievers are probably already Christian without knowing it. Many have stopped obeying the explicit command of Christ to preach the gospel to every creature.

Many thousands of people have been led to commit grave sin because of erroneous scriptural exegesis popularized in the Catholic press and purveyed by Catholic publishers run by Catholic religious orders. Marriages have been destroyed, babies conceived out of wedlock, abortions performed, people come into bondage to homosexual disorders, and religious and priestly vows abandoned because moral theologians have exercised "freedom" to not only question Church and scriptural teaching, but to publicly reject it. Children have not been born because the advice of the confessional encouraged selfishness rather than generosity. Falsehood has been believed and taught by religious educators who have found ideas from moral theologians which provide rationalizations for their own desires. Many thousands of Christians have been dissuaded from generously giving themselves to lives of holiness and obedience because the Word of God has been shrouded with ambiguity and uncertainty.

No moral or spiritual neutrality is possible in theology and scripture study. There is no such thing as "just doing theology" or "simply being an exegete." Every word spoken and published by any of us, theologians and exegetes included, has a moral and spiritual dimension and will be judged by God accordingly. We will have to answer for every word that has come out of our mouth or our pen. Scripture says:

> I assure you, on judgment day people will be held accountable for every unguarded word they speak. By your words you will be acquitted, and by your words you will be condemned." (Mt 12:36-37)

Those of us with a responsibility for Christian teaching today need to heed the words of Jesus: "Woe to you lawyers! You have taken away the key of knowledge. You yourselves have not gained access, yet you have stopped those who wished to enter!" (Lk 11:52).

How much do the words of John Paul II also need to be heeded:

> In catechesis it is Christ, the Incarnate Word and Son of God, who is taught—everything else is taught with reference to him—and it is Christ alone who teaches—anyone else teaches to the extent that he is Christ's spokesman, enabling Christ to teach with his lips. Whatever be the level of his responsibility in the Church, every catechist must constantly endeavour to transmit by his teaching and behaviour the teaching and life of Jesus. He will not seek to keep directed towards himself and his personal opinions and attitudes the attention and the consent of the mind and heart of the person he is catechizing. Above all, he will not try to inculcate his personal opinions and options as if they expressed Christ's teaching and the lessons of his life. Every catechist should be able to apply to himself the mysterious words of Jesus: "My teaching is not mine, but his who sent me."[17]

The Fall and the Redemption of the Mind of Man

As we survey the condition of the Church, we must be aware that man's mind is as thoroughly fallen as his body. The human mind had much to do with bringing about the Fall, and our minds suffer greatly from its effects. The mind and body of man in their natural state are wounded, fallen, inclined to rebellion and perversity. The mind is not simply a neutral element residing in a fallen body; the lusts of the mind are no less real than the lusts of the body.

It follows that the mind needs redemption as much as the body. The mind needs to be renewed, to be converted and transformed under the power of the Spirit and the Word of Truth in order to reflect the mind of Christ. As Paul says:

Do not conform yourselves to this age but be transformed by the renewal of your mind, so that you may judge what is God's will, what is good, pleasing and perfect. (Rom 12:2)

The mind's natural state is to be vulnerable, conformed to and dominated by the thinking of this age—a way of thinking which is influenced by Satan and by the lusts of fallen man. Christians must pass over from the way of thinking of the world to the way of thinking of the age to come. They must learn to think like Christ himself. Christians must aim to "bring every thought into captivity to make it obedient to Christ" (2 Cor 10:5b). Only to the extent that this happens will our words be words of truth, words of life.

Let us turn now to a consideration of how the attack on the authority of God's Word in scripture and tradition extends in its logical outworking to an attack on the person of Jesus himself and the unique claims that he makes about his own person and role in God's plan of salvation for the human race.

CHAPTER FOUR

Silencing the Gospel

THE TRADITIONAL CHRISTIAN CLAIM, based on a multitude of scripture texts, is that God established Jesus as *the* one who alone is able to effect reconciliation between God and man. Jesus' claim to be *the* door through which men enter the kingdom of God is both unique and absolute. It forms the basis for the Church's whole missionary endeavor.

Jesus' unique claims—and the whole basis for Christian mission—are now being undermined in the attack on the authority of God's Word. The true identity of Jesus, as uniquely both fully God and fully man, is being undermined and obscured by denial, ambiguous formulations, inadequate "reinterpretations," and simple silence. This undermines man's understanding of Jesus' unique salvific role and, along with it, the whole foundation of Christian mission. When Jesus' identity as "true God" and the reality of his bodily resurrection are denied and obscured, Jesus is inevitably compared to other "great" religious leaders like Buddha and Mohammed, men who were not "truly God" nor truly raised from the dead, but who left a lasting impression on their followers.

We now turn to a consideration of how the attack on God's Word in scripture and tradition as it is authentically interpreted by the teaching authority of the Church very quickly leads to an attack on the identity of Jesus himself as the unique Son of God. This attack particularly shows itself today in a blurring of the differences between Christianity and the non-Christian world religions, with a subsequent blurring of the unique role of Jesus in God's plan for the world, which effectively silences the effective preaching of the gospel.

Is Christianity Unique?

Many Christians today are uncertain about the relationship of Christianity to what are commonly called "the great world religions"—namely, Judaism, Islam, Buddhism, and Hinduism. Because of the special link between Judaism and Christianity, a distinction must be made between Judaism and the other world religions. This chapter will primarily focus on the relationship between Christianity and non-Judaic world religions. However, it must be said that the link between Christianity and Judaism in no way implies that Catholics have no responsibility to work in a respectful way to bring Jewish people to Christian faith. While Judaism is in a special way related to Christianity, the missionary mandate of the Church fully extends to the Jews, as well as to adherents of other world religions.

Catholics have the vague impression that the Second Vatican Council somehow changed the Church's position regarding the world religions. It is thought that Christians are now supposed to appreciate the "religious insight" of non-Christians and stop trying to bring them to Christ. One's religious identity is viewed as something determined by personal preference or cultural accident, and that this should not bother anyone. "After all," goes the refrain, "aren't all religions basically the same, and all valid ways to God?" This attitude, of course, is accompanied by a strong tendency to underplay, "reinterpret," or ignore the unique and absolute claims of Christ, and to put him on the same level as "other great religious leaders."

The result is an intellectual and practical "syncretism," a mixing together or putting on the same level things that do not necessarily belong together. Even when the unique and absolute claims of Christ are not clearly rejected on an intellectual level, syncretism often fosters an emotional hostility to such claims. This creates an atmosphere that saps the strength of Christianity as effectively as explicit apostasy. If belief about the unique and absolute claims of Christ is unclear, then faith is corrupted, worship becomes enfeebled and distorted, and evangelism ceases.

I first encountered confused notions about the uniqueness of Christianity in the late sixties and early seventies among Catholic high school and university students and some of their teachers. Today, syncretism has spread far beyond students. It also affects their parents and families and has begun to pervade Catholic life as a whole. The principal of a Catholic school told me how difficult it is to find teachers who have a firm grasp on the absoluteness of Christ's claims. Even worse, he said, was the fact that more and more Christian parents are encouraging their children to study different approaches to God and to choose the beliefs that best suit them. The principal was deeply concerned. "In these circumstances," he said, "it's impossible to pass on the faith. The next generation of children may still call themselves Catholic or Christian, but they will mean something quite different by it than what Christ and the Church mean."[1]

Relativistic and indifferentist approaches to Christianity are even being openly promoted in the Catholic press. In one article that appeared in a British Catholic newspaper, an ex-seminarian called for an approach in Catholic schools that would "let pupils discover the truth by being given a panoramic view of the alternatives and choosing for themselves the most convincing religion."[2] In response one reader rightly called this proposal a foolish approach to religious education:

> Any such "panorama" can only be superficial and probably also confusing. To suggest that it could form a basis for conscientious choice would seem naive in the extreme. It would be more likely to result in the baffled youngster's opting for no religion at all or for the nebulously humanistic amalgam of the lot![3]

Unfortunately, many millions of Catholic youth have found themselves possessors of just such an amalgam of "nebulously humanistic" views rather than a clear structure of Christian truth and life. In one European city, the Catholic Church sponsored a "Praise and Prayer" festival where Christian, Jewish, and Muslim young people were invited to come together to celebrate the "good news." As is so often the case, the "good news" was never defined. A vague "celebration of creation" and an "opening to the city" was invoked as the focus of the celebration.[4]

Missionary work is also suffering from widespread confusion about the nature of the redemption wrought by God in Christ. Many missionaries, priests, nuns, and laypeople no longer understand what they are supposed to be doing as missionaries. Some have "reinterpreted" their mission to mean virtually the opposite of what missionary work has always meant.

One nun in Africa summed up her changed approach for me. She no longer viewed her work among Moslems as an opportunity to lead them to see and receive Christ as their Savior and Lord, but rather "to make them better Moslems." This is not the confused opinion of one individual. The largest Catholic missionary society in the United States devoted an issue of its popular mission magazine to a consideration of relationships between Muslims and Christians. The editors declared:

> Maryknoll missionaries work side-by-side with Muslims in the Philippines, Bangladesh, Tanzania, Yemen, the Sudan and other nations.

In fact, Maryknoll's apostolate in Bangladesh, where there are few Christians, is designed specifically as a service to Muslims, without the ulterior motive of conversion.[5]

A Maryknoll missionary in Yemen expresses the new focus of his missionary commitment like this: "Respecting one another's religious vocation, as God makes it known to us, some Muslims and I now work together for our common conversion to the values of the kingdom of God."[6]

These "values of the kingdom of God" often turn out to be focused exclusively on improving this world:

Their challenge today is to better understand this common religious heritage and to draw closer together, not only as individuals but as communities of believers who face many similar problems in the modern world and who seek the same unifying goals—world peace and justice.[7]

The missionary magazine of the Columbans, another major missionary order, published major articles in its December, 1980, issue which were devoted to extolling Hinduism.[8] In this "Christmas" issue, the focus was more squarely on the "incarnation of Krishna" than on the incarnation of Christ. One article described how one of the order's missionaries sought spiritual enlightenment at the feet of a Hindu holy man. Nowhere in the articles was any attempt made to point out any inadequacies in Hinduism as a religion. The articles conveyed the impression that there very well might not be any inadequacies, and that Hinduism might be a totally adequate way to God also. This magazine, the publication of an order devoted to missionary work, never mentioned the need to work to bring Hindus to a saving knowledge of Christ, nor of any efforts their order was making to do so.

I think I can fairly say, from my extensive travel and firsthand observation, that missionary work today is affected by great uncertainty about whether Christians are still supposed to work to bring others to a knowledge of Christ. Missionary work which is directed toward conversion is rarely accompanied by a sense of urgency, as if something really depended on it. The vitality of the Church's missionary effort has been sapped by the belief that potential converts are "Christians already, even if they don't know it," or they are "anonymous Christians," or they already have within them "the hidden Christ of Hinduism."[9]

Much spreading syncretism in the Church's missionary work takes place under the rubric of "cultural adaptation of the gospel to indigenous cultures." Of course the gospel must be transmitted in a way comprehensible to people in different cultures. Uniquely Western cultural values should not be presented as essential elements of Christian faith. Thus, attempts to create a genuinely African or Asian Christianity are very important. But these efforts at cultural adaptation must be carried out by Christians who have a firm grasp on the meaning of the gospel, particularly when other local religions are involved. Unfortunately, this has not always been the case. In some situations the legitimate need for cultural adaptation has led to an explicit or a silent denial of the message of salvation. In some places, it has resulted in religious syncretism.

For example, some Catholic priests I have met in India are so culturally adapted that their words and appearance witness for Hinduism rather than Christianity. I have attended "Indianized" liturgies where more reverence is accorded to the Hindu scriptures than to the Bible. I have visited Western monasteries where monks seek spiritual wisdom at least as seriously from the visiting Hindu swami as from Christian sources.

The extent to which such confusion and syncretism pervades the atmosphere of the Church today should not be underestimated. One article that typifies the problem appeared in the national Jesuit magazine of the United States. The writer, discussing how Jesus can be revealed to others without his name being spoken, casually includes Mahatma Gandhi in a list of Christian examples: "Pope John XXIII revealed Jesus in the way he waved his hands, Gandhi in the calmness with which he dealt with his adversaries. . . . Helder Camara in his smile."[10] Whether Christ is significantly revealed in handwaving or smiles is another interesting discussion. But to include Gandhi in this list gives the impression that whether one is explicitly Christian or not is not of great importance.

The Catholic news media often promotes syncretistic approaches to other religions and spiritualities. One national Catholic newspaper in the United States ran a photo of an Apache Indian puberty ritual on its front page. The accompanying story made positive references to this benign intermingling of the Apache pre-Christian religion and the Christian religion.

Adam Lupe, a Catholic, and also a practitioner of the Indian religion, appeared glad to see the white visitors, including the nuns. He had no problem with the synthesis of the two religions. "These are our ways, Jesus and the Virgin Mary gave them to us."

Lupe was educated in a Catholic boarding school. "When I was a little boy they brainwashed me, they told me this was superstition and the medicine men were no good." But he said both religions deal strongly with symbols, meditation, prayer and ritual and nothing in one excludes the other.[11]

Other examples abound. A noted scripture scholar in an interview published in a popular Catholic magazine was asked to respond to this question: "What about the scriptures of other religions, like the Hindu religion? Are they valid?" His response was: "I don't have any problem with that. . . . I have no problem accepting in any sense at all the fact that we can speak of those scriptures as being divinely inspired."[12]

A large-circulation Catholic family magazine has highly recommended that ordinary Catholics read and use a book called *Invitation to a Great Experiment: Exploring the Possibility that God May Be Known*. The author of the book takes a syncretistic approach. In his introduction, he describes his firm commitment to what he calls "spiritual mongrelism":

Although now a professing Christian, I am still a mongrel, in that I find truth, get help, and take delight in other religions, past and present, in nonreligious spiritual movements, and in religiously unlabeled spiritually-oriented men. I do look everywhere for my light, and I do not find the process confusing but, on the contrary, illuminating and edifying. I believe that it is possible and necessary for many of us today in seeking the face of God to look not only high but low and not only at home but abroad. This outlook is rooted in deep conviction. I am stuck with it, and, if you read further, so are you.[13]

The atmosphere of the book is heavy with religious relativism, indifferentism, and syncretism. The author puts the scriptures of the "great religions" on the same level of truth and reliability. He completely sidesteps the absolute and unique claims of Jesus; for him, Christianity is just one of various ways to spiritual enlightenment.

The material in this book is, unfortunately, not especially unusual in contemporary Catholic religious writing. What is unusual is that a popular mass-circulation Catholic magazine, run by a religious order dedicated to the preaching of the cross of Christ, and edited in a diocese under a Catholic bishop, should give cover-story treatment to a book so thoroughly subversive of genuine Christian faith.[14]

Currently, a multi-volume series of classics of Western spirituality is being published by the largest Catholic publisher in the United States. The series includes works by Muslims, Jews, heterodox Christians, the Church Fathers, and orthodox Christian mystics.[15] These "Classics of Western Spirituality" are being promoted to Catholic schools and libraries, as well as to general readers. The publishing house which sponsors this syncretistic enterprise is operated and controlled by a religious order that was founded to preach the gospel and bring people to Christ and his Church.

Another large publishing house, this one with its roots in the Episcopal Church, publishes a review of religious books. In one issue a section recommending books for prayer and meditation recently lumped together such diverse works as the *I-Ching*, *Transactional Analysis*, and Carlos Castaneda's openly occult works—along with the *Philokalia* and the *Imitation of Christ*.[16]

Another source of confusion and ambiguity is the retreat and continuing education programs sponsored by some diocesan religious education departments, religious orders, and retreat houses. Recent course offerings by Catholic institutions in a large East Coast American city included such courses as "The Story of Jung," "Yoga and Meditation," and the "Feedback Meditation Workshop."

This last course offers instruction in the "Journal" approach to spirituality, a method that has become very popular in many Catholic retreat houses and spiritual renewal centers. The systematic sequence of Journal Workshops, as devised by their founder, Dr. Ira Progoff, deserves a close look. One of Dr. Progoff's works, called "The Image of An Oracle," is described in promotional literature as "twelve interviews with the four 'control' figures of medium Eileen Garret." Dr. Progoff's extended commentary outlines a new " 'third approach' to parapsychic experience."[17] Thousands of priests, nuns, and lay people, as well as official Catholic "spiritual renewal" institutions, are enthusiastically embracing this method. While the method may have useful features, its link through its founder to openly occult sources and practices is well worth noting.

Catholics have also been tragically receptive to other occult-connected meditation and spirituality programs. Prominent examples are Transcendental Meditation, featuring worship of a dead Hindu guru, and Silva Mind Control, which promises two "spirit guides."[18] Catholics in this same East Coast city can renew their spirituality in the Enneagram Workshop, described as "an ancient Sufi approach to personality study." The workshop is taught by two nuns and is sponsored by a Jesuit renewal center named after a Jesuit martyr to the faith.

The same English Catholic newspaper that carried the article suggesting the "panorama" approach to religious education reported on a meeting between Buddhist and Benedictine monks where "the Buddhists joined their Catholic brethren not just in theological dialogue, but in worship." The Catholics and Buddhists agreed that

their goal was identical; only the means were different. The Buddhists were pleased to enter into the experience of western spirituality. The Benedictines were glad to gain a deeper insight into Zen Buddhist forms of meditation which are so attractive to European youth—especially to those alienated from Christianity. They were also deeply impressed by the importance of silence in the Buddhist tradition.[19]

This particular experiment occurred in a German monastery, cited as one of several in Europe that have "spiritual encounters" of this sort.

Obviously, important and complex issues are involved in the situations we are examining, issues that need careful thought and evaluation. Cultural adaptation is a real issue. It is valid to ask whether and to what extent techniques from non-Christian religions can be useful for Christian purposes without adulterating Christian faith, life, or worship.

Yet Catholics today seldom grapple with these issues in a responsible and thoughtful manner. Rather, the practical effect of the way such issues are generally presented is to make them serve as a vehicle for adulterating Christian faith, weakening worship, and undermining evangelism and catechesis of the young. Unsound theological theories are propounded as gospel truth. Eastern religious practices are purveyed to a mass audience with little concern for their effects on clarity of doctrine and on one's actual relationship with God. Their often-hidden occult underpinnings are ignored.

The instances of syncretism I have cited so far are not isolated examples which can be attributed to ignorance or naivete. Syncretism is common. The fact that these are not isolated examples is an indication of a pervasive shift in the attitudes and beliefs of many people. The stream of theological and popular statements that put Christianity on the same level as the other world religions is indicative, I believe, of a profound and widespread loss of confidence in the truth of the claims of Christ. Many people have come to a profound uncertainty not only regarding the truth and authority of the Word of God in scripture, but of the actual person, identity, and claims of Christ himself.

The campaign for openness to other religions is carried out with such moral fervor that it becomes increasingly hard to mention—much less defend—the unique and absolute claims of Christianity. Orthodox Christians are scolded as narrow and uncharitable; they are labelled "closed" when they refuse to adopt the syncretistic thinking and practices advocated by the "open," the "knowledgeable," and the "broadminded." The new syncretists invoke the authority of "the consensus of leading theologians" and "the spirit of Vatican II." Sadly, these invocations in many cases amount to justification for destroying the Christian faith.

How did we get into this situation? And how can we get out of it?

"The Spirit of Vatican II"

Much of the confusion regarding the relationship of Christianity to the world religions has been disseminated as being in "the spirit of Vatican II." Attempts to hold to the absolute and unique claims of Christ as the foundation of all missionary effort have often been dismissed as outdated, "pre-Vatican II" ideas. Thus it is worth asking what the Council did teach about the relationship of Christianity to the world religions.

The Council clearly acknowledged the positive elements found in the world religions. This was in keeping with its overall pastoral strategy pertaining to the relations between the Church and elements outside itself. It attempted to create a climate of friendship and respect and to establish an ongoing "dialogue." The Council hoped that this atmosphere would afford a better chance to effectively present the claims of Christ and also prepare the ground for possible joint cooperation for human development.

The Council's efforts to create a positive climate in no way implied that any religion other than Christianity was an effective way to salvation. Its efforts to set up a dialogue with the world religions in no way implied that its ultimate aim was anything other than to find opportunities in which Christ could effectively be proclaimed as the unique and absolute revelation of God and the only way to the Father.

Let us look at those passages in the Council's "Declaration on the Relationship of the Church to Non-Christian Religions" which are often inaccurately cited as instruction to abandon explicit missionary activity among non-Christians:

> The Catholic Church rejects nothing which is true and holy in these religions. She looks with sincere respect upon those ways of conduct and of life, those rules and teachings which, though differing in many particulars from what she holds and sets forth, nevertheless often reflect a ray of that Truth which enlightens all men. Indeed, she proclaims and must ever proclaim Christ, "the way, the truth, and the life" (Jn. 14:6), in whom men find the fullness of religious life, and in whom God has reconciled all things to Himself (cf 2 Cor. 5:18-19).
>
> The Church therefore has this exhortation for her sons; prudently and lovingly, through dialogue and collaboration with the followers of other religions, and in witness of Christian faith and life, acknowledge, preserve, and promote the spiritual and moral goods found among these men, as well as the values in their society and culture.[20]

Like isolated scripture passages, a proper interpretation of isolated passages from Council documents requires an understanding of their context and their relationship to other documents. For example, in order to fully understand the implications the above passages might have on the missionary activity of the Church, it would be necessary to consult the document on that subject. Also, as John Paul II has recently pointed out, the Council itself must be interpreted in the light of scripture and of the whole Church tradition that has preceded it.

However, even without this necessary interpretation, the meaning of the above passage—the strongest Council statement on the positive aspects of relating to non-Christian religions—is very clear. They reaffirm the need to proclaim the gospel to all men, and they stress that a witness of Christian faith and life is a necessary element of the dialogue.

Yet even during the Council itself, and in the months immediately following, efforts were made to push the interpretation of these and other passages in a direction antithetical to the Council Fathers' intentions. For example, in the dominant English translation of the document on non-Christian religions, translation choices are made that push the interpretation in the direction of blurring the distinction between Christianity and non-Christian religions. For example, in the section just quoted above, after the positive elements of the religions are mentioned, the call to preach the gospel is preceded by the English word "indeed." The best translation of the word in the official Latin text (*vero*) would be "however" rather than "indeed."[21] This claim is borne out not only by the original Latin but also in reviewing the decision made by the French translators, who render *vero* as *toutefois*. Yet the choice of "indeed" makes it appear that the two parts of this passage are contrasted less sharply than they in fact are. The effect is to blur the distinction between Christianity and the non-Christian religions.

Another English mistranslation of the same Council document has the effect of blurring the difference between the Church and the world. One passage in the document cites 1 Peter 2:12, which literally means "maintain good conduct among the gentiles" or "behave yourselves honorably among the pagans." The English translator chose the unusual translation "maintain good fellowship among the nations." This makes it ambiguous whether Christians are to maintain good conduct among themselves, to be a good example to the nations, or perhaps to maintain fellowship among and with nations. A footnote to the English translation explains that the passage was translated this way in order to better "catch the spirit of the Council document."[22] However, the translation obscures the plain meaning of the Council document and even tends to reverse it.

Pope Paul VI wrote *Evangelii Nuntiandi* in part to counter and correct these misinterpretations of the Council:

Neither respect and esteem for these [non-Christian] religions nor the complexity of the questions raised is an invitation to the church to withold from these non-Christians the proclamation of Jesus Christ. . . . [Christianity] effectively establishes with God an authentic and living relationship which the other religions do not succeed in doing, even though they have, as it were, their arms stretched out toward heaven.[23]

Paul VI could not have stated the Church's teaching more clearly: Non-Christian religions are unable to reconcile men with God effectively. The need to proclaim the gospel of reconciliation through Christ remains as urgent as ever.

John Paul II has continued to point out the unique and absolute claims of Christ and the need to announce him to all men. In addition, he has specifically issued this call to those responsible for the dialogue with non-Christian religions. In a meeting with the members of the Plenary Assembly of the Secretariat for Non-Christians, the Vatican body responsible for Catholic dialogue with the non-Christian religions, the pope defined such exchange as a "dialogue of salvation," a part of the Church's great evangelistic mission to call all men to Christ:

A Christian finds it of the highest interest to observe truly religious people, to read and listen to the testimonies of their wisdom, and to have direct proof to their faith. . . . At the same time the Christian has the tremendous responsibility and the immense joy of speaking to these people with simplicity and openness. . .of "the mighty works of God" (Acts 2:11), of what God himself has done for the happiness and salvation of all at a particular time and in a particular man, whom he raised up to be our brother and Lord, Jesus Christ, "descended from David according to the flesh . . . Son of God in power according to the Spirit of holiness" (Rom. 1:4).

I am happy to see that the Secretariat has adopted as its own this will to enter into communication, which is characteristic of the Church as a whole, and that it has put this communication into practice through what Paul VI called "the dialogue of salvation."[24]

John Paul II further declared that the notion of dialogue is motivated by nothing other than the desire expressed by St. Paul to become "all things to all men in order to save at least some of them," and to cultivate a variety of approaches "for the sake of the gospel."[25]

On his visit to Japan he asked to meet with leaders of the non-Christian religions and while affirming respect for their values, the need for dialogue, and for joint collaboration where possible to serve the needs of mankind, he very boldly proclaimed the gospel to them:

Yes indeed, in many things you are already with us. But we Christians must also say that our faith is Jesus Christ; it is Jesus Christ that we proclaim. We shall say even more, repeating the words of Saint Paul: "I have decided to know nothing among you except Jesus Christ and him crucified" (1 Cor 2:2)—Jesus Christ who is also risen for the salvation and happiness of all mankind (cf. 1 Cor 15:30). Accordingly, we bring his name and his joyful message to all peoples and, while sincerely honoring their cultures and traditions, we respectfully invite them to listen to him and to open their hearts to him. When we enter into dialogue, it is in order to witness to Christ's love, or, in concrete terms, "to foster unity and charity among individuals, indeed among peoples, by reflecting in the first place on what we have in common and what tends to promote fellowship among us" (cf. Nostra Aetate, 1).[26]

The Theory of "Anonymous Christianity"

A wrong understanding of dialogue and "the spirit of Vatican II" is only one source of the confusion about the relationship of Christianity to non-Christian religions. Another source is widely-publicized theological theories that have given many Christians the impression that it is no longer so important to explicitly proclaim the gospel and bring nonbelievers to repentance, faith, baptism, and membership in the Church.

The best-known of these theories is the notion of "anonymous Christianity."[27] Briefly, variations of this theory hold that many people who are consciously and explicitly Buddhists, Hindus, or even atheists may in fact be Christians and members of the Body of Christ because they "accept their own humanity fully," or "embrace the mystery of their existence." Variations on this theme speak of "the hidden Christ in Hinduism," implying that even though Hindus consciously reject Christ's claims, they already know Christ, have implicit faith, and are therefore saved.

While the exploration of theological possibilities like "anonymous Christianity" is certainly a legitimate part of the theological enterprise, and theology needs a legitimate sphere of freedom to undertake such exploration, the pastoral effect of what is in fact simply speculation has been devastating. This is not the place for a full discussion of the pastoral responsibility of the theologian in tension with legitimate theological freedom. However, it is perhaps worth noting again the solemn responsibility God's Word lays on those in teaching and theological service in the Church: "Not many of you should become teachers, my brothers; you should realize that those of us who do so will be called to the stricter account" (Jas 3:1). Or as Jesus said, "It would be better for anyone who leads astray one of these little ones who believe in me, to be drowned by a millstone around his neck, in the depths of the sea" (Mt 18:6).

Our concern here is not with the question of how theological freedom should be exercised, nor even with the theory of "anonymous Christianity" in itself. (Although it must be said that while leading proponents of the theory counsel readers not to stop evangelizing, the logic of their argument is sufficiently undermining of the scriptural and Conciliar teaching that motivation to evangelize is effectively sapped.) Rather we are concerned with the pastoral effects of the widespread promulgation of these theories.[28]

In some cases, such theories lead to a syncretistic amalgamation of Christianity and Hinduism. Recently, a Catholic priest from India told me that the superior of one religious order in his country was seeking to build some basic Christian communities that would include both Christians and Hindus. He was basing this project on theological theories maintaining that Hindus are already Christains even if they do not know it, and that they do not need repentance, faith, and baptism as prerequisites to full participation in Church life.

The devastating effects of the popularized theories of anonymous Christianity are especially visible in a country like India, where Christians are a small minority in a culture dominated by another religion. In 1979, an Indian theologian gave a talk in the Philippines to a conference of thirty-seven Catholic bishops from Asia, Europe, and North America. In the course of his talk, the theologian gave a startling rationale for the virtual abandonment of Christian missionary activity in India. According to a report of the bishops' conference, the theologian suggested

> that the fact that members of the higher religions, such as Hindus and Buddhists, do not convert may be a sign that they are not meant to convert. There is nothing in the New Testament, he said, about all men becoming Christians as we ordinarily understand the term. Mankind, not the church, is the basic community or people of God, as shown in Genesis. The Church is a sign community witnessing to certain truths, but there may be other sign communities, the higher religions, for example, that have their own and equally valid role in God's total plan. If so, the church is called to sincere dialogue and mutual sharing to realize the larger truths.[29]

The writer of this report, a member of the staff of the Federation of Asian Bishops' Conference Office for Human Development, found the theologian's views convincing:

Even a visitor to India . . . can understand somewhat the difficulties a sensitive theologian finds in the identification of the people of God with the church. If the tiny group of Catholics, or Christians as a whole, is the people of God, who are the other 600 million men, women and children that crowd that nation, some of whom one meets daily in the marketplace or slums or on the bus? They are as engaging and human as Christians. God loves them as He loves the Christians. He has given them their religions in which they find meaning. They do not seek to convert to Christianity. To define their lives in terms of church and traditional theological concepts may be completely contrary to what God in His wisdom has established. Maybe in the end it will be necessary to do so, but do not love and respect for our brothers and sisters and humility in the face of God's mystery require us to seek new theological insights that will give greater dignity and equality to non-Christians and their religions and allow us to see the sweep of God's plan?[30]

This Church official, holding an influential position on the staff of the Asian Bishops Conference, concluded with the remarkable suggestion that Christians begin to view other religions as "salvific." The sensitive Christian, he said, needs

conviction that the other religions are salvific, that conversions are not necessary and that Christianity has much to learn from God and about God through Islam, Hinduism and Buddhism.[31]

Such ideas have become widespread in the Church today, not just among avant garde intellectuals, but among pastoral leaders and ordinary Catholics. They are also widespread in certain segments of Protestantism and continue to be actively propagated with devastating results to actual missionary work in the Protestant missionary enterprise. A United Church of Christ missionary, who is also president of a missionary research center in the Philippines and consultant to both the World Council of Churches and the U.S. National Council of Churches, declared in an interview that Christian-Moslem dialogue should focus on mutual understanding and social change and that efforts to bring Muslims to Christ are obsolete. "The times of converting are over," he said.[32]

Such theories—judged in themselves and by their fruits—are at complete odds with the Word of God in scripture and in the teaching of the Church. In fact, they work to directly and perniciously undermine the Church's whole missionary effort. Whether they flow from unexamined presuppositions in a modern European philosophical anthropology, a prior commitment to the "saving value" of Hinduism, or an eagerness to submerge questions of truth in favor of joint political activity, they lead Christians away from proclaiming the saving message of Christ to all nations.

Syncretistic theories and approaches not only drain the Church of its missionary vitality. They will eventually lead to the abandonment of any recognizable form of the Christian faith. Already, some "advanced" Christian thinkers have taken this final step.

One Protestant clergyman, for example, wrote an article for a leading Christian journal in which he lucidly and fearlessly spelled out the underlying and often unconscious assumptions of syncretism. "We are increasing contact with other religions of the world," he wrote, "and an insistence on the uniqueness of the historical Jesus can only be a hindrance." He continued:

> Christians should never have made a god out of Jesus. It is just too preposterous to believe that God gave his/her world-embracing love uniquely through Jesus. We Christians may use such phrases as "anonymous Christian" and "the cosmic Christ" in our attempts to universalize Christianity, but then we should empathize with such terms as "the universal Buddha" or "the plurality of avatars." The world-embracing love of God cannot be confined to any particular historical person, including Jesus. I stated earlier that in comparison to 20 years ago there is little mention now of the once-for-allness of Jesus. Still it seems as though everybody tries hard to lay claim to the man from Nazareth—the revolutionary and the pacifist, the Marxist and the capitalist, the evangelical and the liberationist. I suggest that we leave him alone for a while. Just as Jesus said to his disciples, "It is best for you that I depart. For if I do not go, the Advocate will not come to you" (Jn 16:5), so, too, must we have the courage to say that it is best for Jesus to depart for the sake of the love of God.[33]

The compromise of basic Christian truth in the Catholic Church may be at this time more a matter of confusion, naivete, and loss of confidence than an explicit desire to do away with Jesus. The effect, however, is the same. Also, it is well to note that there are some, as the above article's excerpt makes clear, who are consciously and explicitly working to undermine confidence in the unique and absolute claims of Christ.[34] Their goal is to bend all the world religions to a cooperative endeavor to serve various political, social, and economic programs.

The New Testament describes such efforts as the very work of the spirit of anti-Christ:

> Who is the liar? He who denies that Jesus is the Christ. He is the antichrist, denying the Father and the Son. Anyone who denies the

Son has no claim on the Father, but he who acknowledges the Son can claim the Father as well. (1 Jn 2:22-23)

In times past there were false prophets among God's people, and among you also there will be false teachers who will smuggle in pernicious heresies. They will go so far as to deny the Master who acquired them for his own, thereby bringing on themselves swift disaster. Their lustful ways will lure many away. Through them, the true way will be made subject to contempt. (2 Pt 2:1-2)

It must be recognized that just as in New Testament times, there are those in our midst today who call themselves Christians and are members of various Christian churches but are serving the purposes of the antichrist.

The Experience of Failure

A third source of the Church's missionary weakness—along with misinterpretation of Vatican II and the influence of certain theological theories—is the experience of failure which Christian missionaries have in their work. Missionary work is very difficult. Results have been meager in post-Christian Western Europe, in Marxist dominated Third World countries, in nominally Catholic Latin America and in Asia. Many Christian missionaries have become eager to embrace any theological idea or pastoral strategy that might make their apparent ineffectiveness seem less painful. Considering the masses of Hindus who seem unresponsive to Christian missionary efforts, it is all too easy to embrace such theories as the "hidden Christ in Hinduism." Considering the skepticism of modern European man in a post-Christian society, along with the obvious weakness of many parts of the European Church, a theory of "anonymous Christianity" becomes attractive. Islam's seeming imperviousness to the gospel helps to explain why truncated concepts of "dialogue" become popular. Losing confidence in the truth and power of God's Word helps to account for the dominant theme in modern missionary circles of the need for the missionary to be "converted" by those they serve and "learn from" those to whom they have been sent. While growth in commitment and knowledge is of course to be encouraged, the picture often given today is predominantly of the missionary being a recipient and not also the bearer of a precious treasure and irreplaceable message.[35]

Even some members of the hierarchy seem to be affected by the experience of failure. Sometimes theologians and bishops from Third World countries betray exhaustion and dashed hopes in some of their statements. A bishop from one Asian country expressed this mentality candidly:

We do not seek to convert the Muslims or the Hindus. We have tried and largely failed and there is almost no hope in the foreseeable future of conversions among the mainline Buddhists, Muslims, or Hindus. And, as I said, their religions are of God. Conversion will come later, perhaps, maybe centuries from now in God's own good time.[36]

Or as a bishop from Bangladesh strikingly put it:

Evangelization is broader than making Christians by baptizing people, etc. After all, faith is a gift of God and not my work. . . . Islam and Hinduism are salvific, for how could the good God abandon them? What, then, is the role of the church? If you have something you think is good and valuable to you, you want to share it with others. I believe Christianity is a fuller revelation and can gladden the lives of all my brothers, so I share it. It's not so much that I think the Muslims need it. You don't offer a cigarette to a friend because he needs it but because you enjoy it and want him to share your joy.[37]

The experience of failure—the tension between the claims of the gospel and the seeming lack of response to it—can tear a man or woman apart if it goes on too long. A missionary in this situation has two options: either to change the gospel so as to make it more acceptable, or to seek God for ways of presenting it more effectively, for strength to persevere in the effort, no matter what the results. Tragically, many missionaries have chosen to change the gospel or to abandon their efforts to preach it, assuaging their conscience with misinterpretations of the Council or erroneous theological theories. The Christian solution to the problem lies in the other direction: a turning toward God for wisdom, strength, support, and power, in the conviction that to labor for him is never in vain, even when results are not apparent.

In this connection it is worth noting the extraordinary success of pentecostal and charismatic movements in places where many of the mainline churches have given up. Even in places where the mainline churches are considered to be strong, such as Africa, the various pentecostal and charismatic independent churches are drawing the loyalty of many Protestants and Catholics with their fervor and freedom of worship, warmth of fellowship, and ministries of healing and deliverance where the power of God is tangibly manifest. It is also worth noting that in Japan, where traditional, Westernized Christianity has not made any significant advances in hundreds of years, the most vital of the new Japanese religions, which incorporates ministries of healing and deliverance, has grown rapidly.

John Paul II has adverted to the overwhelming pressure of seeing the masses of human beings who do not yet know Christ, and to the magnitude of the task before us. He proposes a solution: not a change in the gospel, but a change in us and in our grasp of gospel truths.

> The spiritual needs of the present-day world are immense! If we look at the boundless forests of buildings in modern metropolises, invaded by numberless multitudes, we cannot but be frightened. How can we reach these persons and bring them to Christ?
>
> We are helped by the certainty of being only instruments of grace: it is God Himself who acts in the individual soul, with his love and mercy.
>
> Our real and constant goal must be that of personal sanctification, to be suitable and effective instruments of grace.
>
> The truest and most sincere wish I can form for you is just this: "Make yourselves saints and do so quickly!"[38]

And again, on the occasion of World Mission Sunday:

> The only and indispensable strategy for missionary work is precisely deep, personal, convinced, ardent love of Jesus Christ! . . . Love is intrepid and courageous: Jesus is still unknown to three-quarters of mankind! The Church therefore needs so many, willing missionaries, men and women, to proclaim the Gospel! . . . Life is noble and great only to the extent that it is given! Be fearless. . . . Love of Christ urges us to bear witness, to announce, proclaim the Good News, to everyone and in spite of everything!
>
> Precisely in these times you must be witnesses and missionaries of truth: do not be afraid! Love of Christ must drive you to be strong and resolute, because "if God is for us, who is against us?" (Rom. 8:31). No one, in fact, can "separate us from the love of Christ" (Rom. 8:35).[39]

CHAPTER FIVE

Is Jesus the Only Way?

CHRISTIANS HAVE DRIFTED into religious indifferentism and syncretism for many reasons, but the central issue remains one of truth. The real question is this: Is Jesus the only way to the Father? Is Jesus, as the scriptures and the Church proclaim, the only way men can be saved?

To answer this question, we must first understand the nature of mankind's need for reconciliation with God. Scripture tells us that God's view of man's situation is different from the "natural" man's. Furthermore, it tells us that God's views are the accurate ones. Thus it follows that the appropriate attitude for us to take before God is one of silence and of listening, so that we might hear His Word and learn the truth about our situation and about his provisions for it. If we are quiet before God and receive His Word, he will tell us about the nature of our situation, our need for salvation, and the way we can receive that salvation.

God's Word tells us that the human race in its "natural" condition is in a state of fundamental rebellion against him and his ways. The evil consequences of this state of sin are vast in scope. Because of this sin and rebellion, all men and women are now living a "fallen" existence, subject to disease and, ultimately, death and our race continues to commit abominations against God himself and against our fellow humans. Scripture further tells us that a host of evil powers, led by an evil genius, Satan, has gained access to the human race and exerts a hold on it.

Human history is therefore a history in which evil abounds: greed and fear, anger and hostility; it is the story of murder on a mass scale, of unfaithfulness, theft, treachery, fornication, homosexuality, adultery, oppression, war, brutality. The veneer of civilization and of human solutions to problems fails to mask the underlying tragedy and horror of our fallen existence.

The facts of our condition force us to ask fundamental questions: What would it take to overcome the evil that allowed civilized Germany to murder six million Jews? What kind of humanity has been created in the modern, progressive Soviet Union and China through the starvation and execution of tens of millions of their citizens? What could be offered to the Creator as reparation for the hundreds of millions of infants murdered in the womb or strangled on the birth-bed throughout the history of the human race? And what of the grievous exploitation of the poor by the wealthy and powerful so commonly seen throughout history? What could ever make up for a demonic nuclear exchange?

Even if some men and women during the ages have led moral lives, what of the rest of us? What of the praise, gratitude and worship due to God, which even many moral men and women withhold? What of the disease that strikes even moral men and women, and the death that takes us all?

The Elements of Salvation

As we reflect on God's Word, it becomes clear that the salvation we need includes a number of specific elements.

1. It must include pardon for the enormity of the sins of the human race, for its original, fundamental, and continued rebellion. This can come only from the one primarily offended—God himself. "We know that everything the law says is addressed to those who are under its authority. This means that every mouth is silenced and the whole world stands convicted before God" (Rom 3:19). "All men have sinned and are deprived of the glory of God" (Rom 3:23).

2. Repentance, with subsequent forgiveness, must always be accompanied by restitution. The wrong that is done must be made up for. The just demands of God's Word in Genesis—"the moment you eat from it you are surely doomed to die" (Gn 2:17)—must be fully satisfied. These words are echoed in Romans 1:32: "They know God's just decree that all who do such things deserve death." An eternal and just decree of God declares that rebellion against God is justly punished by physical and spiritual death. The just demands of this decree must be satisfied. The consequences of our personal and collective sin must somehow be fully expiated if we are to be reconciled to God.

3. The power that Satan and his infernal legions exercise over the human race must be broken. Man on his own is not equal to the task of overcoming he whom Jesus referred to as "the prince of this world" (Jn 16:11) and whom the apostle John described as having the "whole

world" under his control (1 Jn 5:6).

4. Justice must be established—justice that somehow reaches backward in time, beyond death, to correct millenia of oppression and injustice. Justice must deal with the fact that the wicked have often flourished at the expense of the righteous, with the fact that those who were first in the eyes of the world often deserved to be last. Salvation and reconciliation require that all of man's longings for justice be satisfied.

5. Death and disease must be conquered. Somehow the seed of death now inherent in our nature must be plucked. "What a wretched man I am! Who can free me from this body under the power of death?" (Rom 7:24). Our nature, now mortal and corruptible, cries out to somehow be made immortal and incorruptible.

6. And the effects of sin on the physical creation itself must be removed. "Cursed be the ground because of you! In toil shall you eat its yield all the days of your life" (Gn 3:17). "Creation was made subject to futility, not of its own accord but by him who once subjected it. . . . Yes, we know that all creation groans and is in agony even until now" (Rom 8:20, 22).

7. Men and women must undergo a fundamental change in their natures so that they can live in a way pleasing to God with both the desire and power to do so.

It is Christianity's unique claim that in Jesus Christ, and only in Jesus Christ, all that is required for man's salvation is provided. All the requirements are met. God's Word tells us that through the incarnation, death, and resurrection of Jesus, salvation for the human race is accomplished.

1. Sin is forgiven:

> Just as a single offense brought condemnation to all men, a single righteous act brought all men acquittal and life. Just as through one man's disobedience all became sinners, so through one man's obedience all shall become just." (Rom 5:18-19)

2. Atonement is made:

> There is no condemnation now for those who are in Christ Jesus. The law of the spirit, the spirit of life in Christ Jesus, has freed you from the law of sin and death. The law was powerless because of its weakening by the flesh. Then God sent his Son in the likeness of sinful flesh as a sin offering, thereby condemning sin in the flesh, so that the just demands of the law might be fulfilled in us who live, not according to the flesh, but according to the Spirit." (Rom 8:1-4)

3. The power of Satan is overcome:

> Now, since the children are men of blood and flesh, Jesus likewise had a full share in ours, that by his death he might rob the devil, the prince of death, of his power, and free those who through fear of death had been slaves their whole life long. (Heb 2:14, 15)

> The man who sins belongs to the devil, because the devil is a sinner from the beginning. It was to destroy the devil's works that the Son of God revealed himself. (1 Jn 3:8))

4. Justice is reestablished:

> Since everything is to be destroyed in this way what sort of men must you not be! How holy in your conduct and devotion, looking for the coming of the day of God and trying to hasten it! Because of it, the heavens will be destroyed in flames and the elements will melt away in a blaze. What we await are new heavens and a new earth where, according to his promise, the justice of God will reside.
> (2 Pt 3:11-13)

5. Death and disease are conquered:

> O death, where is your victory? O death, where is your sting?
> (1 Cor 15:55)

6. The curse on the physical creation is lifted:

> Indeed, the whole created world eagerly awaits the revelation of the sons of God. Creation was made subject to futility, not of its own accord but by him who once subjected it; yet not without hope, because the world itself will be freed from its slavery to corruption and share in the glorious freedom of the children of God. Yes, we know that all creation groans and is in agony even until now. Not only that, but we ourselves, although we have the Spirit as first fruits, groan inwardly while we await the redemption of our bodies.
> (Rom 8:19-23)

7. Men and women are born again by the Spirit of God and made partakers in the divine nature:

> By virtue of them he has bestowed on us the great and precious things he promised, so that through these you who have fled a world corrupted by lust might become sharers of the divine nature.
> (2 Pt 1:4)

Between Jesus' first and his second comings, some of these results of the redemption will be experienced only in an initial way. But all will be fully realized with his second coming. Already Jesus' resurrection and our experience of Pentecost validate his claims to be the one sent by God; they confirm the truth of his message and mission, as well as make it possible.

This is why the traditional Christian and scriptural belief in the physical resurrection of Jesus is so important. As Paul said in 1 Corinthians, "if Christ was not raised, your faith is worthless. You are still in your sins" (15:17). The resurrection is the sign that Jesus really was who he claimed to be. It is God the Father's public vindication of Jesus as the one truly sent by him to effect reconciliation between God and man. The resurrection is the sign that the sacrifice of Christ on the cross has been received by God the Father as a sacrifice that is truly able to "take away the sins of the world."

Jesus as the Son of God was fully God, and as the Son of Man was fully man. If he had been just a great religious leader or a holy man, his death would not have had the atoning value sufficient to cancel the debt of the human race. Yet his resurrection is God the Father's sign that Jesus was who he said he was, and that his death did have the atoning value sufficient to cancel the sin of centuries, to break the hold of Satan, to put an end to disease and death, to lift the curse from the human race and the creation itself, to re-create men and women, and to establish justice at the end of time. Thus the resurrected body of Jesus is a pledge of our own resurrection and an assurance of our reconciliation with God through the atoning death of his Son. It is also the assurance that salvation has been accomplished. Jesus alone meets all the conditions. His life, death, and resurrection alone have the power to atone for the Auschwitzes and abortion clinics of all the ages.

Other Ways to God

When we are told that there may be another way to reconciliation with God, we should ask some questions in return. Does this "other way" effectively deal with the actual requirements of our fallen condition? Does it make atonement for sin, win pardon, overcome death and Satan, establish justice, re-create the human race? Paul VI pointed out that the non-Christian religions are reaching out to God with arms extended toward heaven. However, as man's efforts to reach out to God, they cannot effectively reconcile men with God or win pardon for our offenses. As Jesus put it: "You will surely die in your sins unless you come to believe that I AM" (Jn 8:24). God himself must act. No matter how great the human effort, no matter how spiritual and fervent the attempt, only the sacrifice of Jesus on the cross has been deemed acceptable by God the Father as the basis for reconciliation with him and forgiveness of sins.

In addition to asking whether this "other way" to God is truly effective, we also need to ask on whose authority this "other way" has been established, and who has sent its messengers. If Jesus is God's appointed Messiah and prophet, should we not justly call all others who claim this role in his place false messiahs and false prophets? We may justly admire the things we share in common with Islam, for example—a similar moral code, a belief in afterlife and eternal judgment, a reverence for Mary. But we must also point out that the Prophet Mohammed distorted Christ's words and tried to supplant him as the final and definitive revelation of God. We must also keep clearly in mind that Islam is hostile to the gospel and Christianity and that Mohammed's way contributes to keeping about 700 million human beings from coming to Christ. Finally, what spirit inspired Mohammed? The Holy Spirit could not be the dominant influence in a religion that rejects Christ as Savior and Lord. Then what spirit was the dominant spirit?

It is sometimes claimed that the non-Christian world religions are providentially guided to prepare for the fuller revelation of God in Christianity. This was certainly the case with Judaism, but the Jews as a whole rejected the full revelation of God in Christ and held on to what God intended as preparation.

It is difficult to regard Islam as preparation for Christianity. It appeared six centuries after Christ as an explicit attempt to supplant Christianity and to deny the unique identity and function of Jesus in God's plan. As a matter of practical fact, Islam has not prepared its adherants to become Christians, but instead has consciously attempted to make conversion to Christianity as difficult as possible.

Buddhism and Hinduism preceeded Christianity, but, despite what well-meaning theoreticians may say, they have not served as "doorways" to Christianity. Instead, their systems of thought and worship make conversion to Christ, or even comprehension of his claims, exceedingly difficult.

While the non-Christian world religions certainly contain "glimpses of truth" and manifest impressive examples of dedication and devotion, the teaching of Christianity is that they are not salvific as religious systems. Individuals within them may be saved if they have not heard the gospel—and if they sincerely seek God and live according to the light received. These individual non-Christians will be saved by God's mercy and because Christ reconciled man to God. However, on the practical level of religious practice and worship, the non-Christian world religions function in the lives of their adherents for the most part in opposition to the claims of Christ. They seek to keep their adherents from encountering him or responding to him, to their great eternal peril.

The religious experience of many devout non-Christians, particularly adherents of Eastern religions, can often be more sinister. I once discussed the question of practical, day-to-day religious experience with a Christian teacher and scholar who had been raised in a devout Hindu family before his conversion to Christianity as a young man. I wanted to know what the average devout Hindu experienced of God in the course of day-to-day worship. He replied that in his view much of the worship of the average Hindu was a primitive effort to propitiate demonic forces. A regular part of the Hindu's life consists of offering sacrifices to obtain favors, exact vengeance, and to escape retribution. My friend pointed out that non-Hindus who study Hinduism usually ignore the primitive and demonic quality of this "grass roots" experience of the religion. They usually focus on Hindu literature and philosophical systems which were, he thought, a mixture of genuine insights into God and his nature and predominantly human attempts to understand God. In actual practice, he stated, worship of false gods and sacrifice to demonic powers are not uncommon.

A reminder from John's Gospel is relevant here: "Truly I assure you: Whoever does not enter the sheepfold through the gate but climbs in some other way is a thief and a marauder. . . . I am the gate" (Jn 10:1,6). Or as John Paul II put it recently, echoing these words of Jesus:

> Note it well. Does not Jesus say in the Gospel that he is "the way, the Truth, and the life" (Jn 14:6)? . . . he defines himself as the Way, that is the highway, the route that is at once obligatory and sage for those who wish to go to the Father and thus reach salvation. It is certainly an image similar to the one that presents Jesus as Light (Jn 8:12) or as the Door (Jn 10:7). These images are based on a substantially identical teaching: it is necessary to walk following the way marked out by Jesus, illuminated by Jesus; or more simply it is necessary to follow Jesus.[1]

The Urgent Need to Evangelize

Catholics who stress the praiseworthy elements of non-Christian world religions while ignoring or denying their inadequacies go far beyond what Vatican II intended. The Council Fathers said that while the Church looks with "sincere respect" on other religions, "she proclaims and must ever proclaim Christ, "the way, the truth, and the life,' in whom men find the fullness of religious life, and in whom God has reconciled all things to himself."[2] "All must be converted to Him as He is made known by the Church's preaching. All must be incorporated into Him by baptism, and into the Church which is His body."[3]

The New Testament clearly teaches that all nations and cultures, all human beings, indeed, all of creation, is to submit to Christ, to come under his rule, become part of his body, and be presented by him to the Father.[4] Scripture insists that in Jesus one finds the full, definitive, and final revelation of God. It presents Jesus as the last chance for the human race, as God's final offer.

> In times past, God spoke in fragmentary and varied ways to our fathers through the prophets; in this, the final age, he has spoken to us through his Son, whom he has made heir of all things and through whom he first created the universe. This Son is the reflection of the Father's glory, the exact representation of the Father's being, and he sustains all things by his powerful word. When he had cleansed us from our sins, he took his seat at the right hand of the Majesty in heaven, as far superior to the angels as the name he has inherited is superior to theirs. (Heb 1:1-4)

John Paul II is proclaiming and reaffirming this Word of God in scripture today. In an address to a group of bishops from India, where there exist powerful pressures to accommodate Christianity to the Hinduism, Buddhism and Islam of India and its neighboring countries, he reaffirmed the need to proclaim Jesus as the only savior of the human race:

> One of the greatest services then that we can give to our people is to proclaim to them, day in and day out, "the unsearchable riches of Christ" (Eph 3:8), pointing out that Christianity is a unique and original message of salvation to be found in the name of Jesus Christ and in his name alone.[5]

To another group of Indian bishops he spoke similar words:

> The message that we proclaim is proclaimed in his name—in the name of Jesus, the Saviour of the world. Ours is a proclamation of salvation in him—salvation in his name. This truth is the explicit object of apostolic teaching, being proclaimed by the Apostle Peter under the inspiration of the Holy Spirit. And today the Successor of Peter wishes to proclaim it anew, to you and with you and for you, and for your people: "There is salvation in no one else, for there is no other name under heaven given by which we must be saved" (Acts 4:12). It is in the name of Jesus that all our ministry is performed. Repentance and the forgiveness of sins are preached in his name to all nations (cf. Lk 24:47). We ourselves have been washed and sanctified and justified in the name of our Lord Jesus Christ (cf. 1 Cor 6:11). Through faith we have "life in his name" (Jn 20:31).[6]

Or again, on the occasion of a World Mission Sunday, the pope proclaimed:

> St. Paul wrote to his disciple Timothy: "God desires all men to be saved and to come to the knowledge of the truth" (1 Tim 2:4). The truth that saves is only Jesus Christ, the Redeemer, the Mediator between God and men, the one and definitive Revealer of man's supernatural destiny. . . . In fact, if unity in faith is lacking, who and what is proclaimed?[7]

The Fate of Non-Christians

As we consider Christ's imperative command to preach the gospel to every creature, a troubling question arises: what will be the fate of those who never hear the gospel, despite our best efforts?

The scriptural teaching on this question is largely contained in the first two chapters of the Epistle to the Romans. This teaching is well summed up and explicated in the foundational document of the Second Vatican Council—The Constitution of the Church:

> Those also can attain to everlasting salvation who through no fault of their own do not know the gospel of Christ and of His Church, yet sincerely seek God and, moved by grace, strive by their deeds to do His will as it is known to them through the dictates of conscience. Nor does divine Providence deny the help necessary for salvation to those who, without blame on their part, have not yet arrived at an explicit knowledge of God, but who strive to live a good life, thanks to His grace. Whatever goodness or truth is found among them is looked upon by the Church as a preparation for the gospel. She regards such qualities as given by Him who enlightens all men so that they may finally have life.
>
> But rather often men, deceived by the Evil One, have become caught up in futile reasoning and have exchanged the truth of God for a lie, serving the creature rather than the Creator (cf. Rom. 1:21, 25). Or some there are who, living and dying in a world without God, are subject to utter hopelessness. Consequently, to promote the glory of God and procure the salvation of all such men, and mindful of the command of the Lord, "Preach the gospel to every creature" (Mk. 16:16), the Church painstakingly fosters her missionary work.[8]

Thus it is possible for people who have never heard the gospel to be saved, but only under certain conditions: that their ignorance of the gospel be through no fault of their own; that they sincerely seek God;

and that they try to correspond to his will as they know it, helped by his grace. Yet the Council—and scripture—realistically points out that these conditions may in fact not commonly be met. As a matter of plain fact, vast portions of the human race seem to be in bondage to sin, deceived by Satan, and in desperate need of the liberation that the gospel brings. Therefore, while it is possible for people who have never heard the gospel to be saved by God's grace, even so by virtue of the death and resurrection of Christ, it is by no means to be presumed. It is to everyone's great advantage to hear the gospel, and imperative for those who know it to preach it.

At issue is our obedience to an explicit and solemn command of Christ, repeated by the apostles, and affirmed by the authentic tradition of the Church through the centuries. To seize on theological hypotheses that deflect from this obedience jeopardizes our own salvation. After pointing out that God, in his mercy, gives a possibility of salvation to those who have not heard the gospel, Paul VI asked: "Can we gain salvation if through negligence or fear or shame . . . or as a result of false ideas we fail to preach the gospel?"[9]

A mentality that does not aim at explicit conversion—that views Christian missionary work as primarily or exclusively helping people to improve their lot as human beings or helping them to become better believers in non-Christian religions—is a travesty of the gospel. This mentality grossly distorts Vatican II and betrays a blindness to the heart of the good news of salvation.

The absolute claims of Christ are nothing to be ashamed of. They are not unreasonable or unfair, as some Christians today seem to think. Christ's claims are merciful. Through them, the overwhelming mercy of God provides a savior able to fulfill all that is required for the salvation of the human race. They represent the merciful truth and we should greet them with joy.

To complain that God did not provide us with another savior, or with a dozen saviors, or with a choice of saviors is to miss the point of our actual situation. To rebel at the claim that Jesus is the sole means by which the human race can be saved is to risk losing the last chance for a new beginning. The human race rejected the first chance for a blessed existence. That we should pit our sense of what is fitting and fair against God's sense of what is fitting and fair is a sign of the rebellion that requires repentance, of the sickness that requires healing. The Word became flesh and dwelt among us precisely for this purpose— to atone for our rebellion, to make repentance possible, and to heal our fallen condition.

Because the gift of God in Christ Jesus is so great, and the redemption offered so exquisitely and powerfully appropriate, the consequences of accepting or rejecting it are great. "Then he told them: 'Go into the whole world and proclaim the good news to all creation. The man who believes in it and accepts baptism will be saved; the man who refuses to believe in it will be condemned' " (Mk 16:15-16).

Scripture and the tradition of the Church do not tell us everything we might like to know about how God will deal with human beings. His ways are not our ways. Our curiosity about everything does not need to be satisfied. But we do know two things with absolute certainty: there is salvation in no one else but Jesus; and it is our responsibility to proclaim this good news clearly and confidently to every creature.

CHAPTER SIX

Christianity and
Social Concern

IT HAS ALWAYS BEEN a challenge for the Church to properly discern and guide its interaction with the various social, political, and economic patterns of society. Historically, Christians have not always had the solid biblical perspective, acute spiritual discernment, and practical wisdom necessary to conduct the Church's relations with society successfully. The Church has often become compromised in its relations with the state and the contemporary culture. Perspective, discernment, and wisdom are as urgently needed today as in the past. In many places they are conspicuously lacking or purposely ignored.

In many countries of the world, Church leadership is trying to disentangle itself from some kind of alignment with political and economic forces. In some cases, these are right-wing forces, some of them brutal and oppressive. In the process, however, some Church personnel seem to be contracting new alliances with left-wing forces, many of them as brutal and oppressive as tyrannies on the right. To exchange complicity in the oppression of the right for complicity in the oppression of the left is not a wise exchange.

For centuries, the Church in Western Europe and Russia was implicated to some degree in the injustices of a sometimes oppressive "ancien regime." When movements to change these inequities came, the Church was very slow to support them. Fifty years after the *Communist Manifesto*, in the closing years of the nineteenth century, Pope Leo XIII wrote his encyclical *Rerum Novarum*, in an attempt to deal with some of these social problems from a Christian perspective.

A similar situation obtained in the Third World. The Western powers which colonized these countries introduced Christianity, along with an often exploitive and oppressive colonial system. In many of these countries, the Church quite naturally became aligned with the colonial powers and with the elite of the country which cooperated with and benefited from the colonial system. When the colonial system disintegrated, the Church's alignment with the collaborating economic and political elites gave it a credibility problem. It was sometimes hard to view the Church as an organism in its own right, hard to disassociate it from the economic and political injustices of the colonial powers which had introduced and established it.

The Church was in an especially difficult position in those Third World countries that were predominantly nominally Catholic. Here, the Church had presided over—and oftentimes left uncorrected—a social situation in which rich Christians often prospered at the expense of poor ones. This left a vacuum of leadership which anti-Christian forces were quick to fill. They were also quick to point out and exploit the Church's failures. Marxism in many ways has served as a goad and a stimulus for the Church to distinguish its unique role and mission from the prevailing political, economic, and social systems in which it must live. One of the positive contributions of the liberation theologies which openly acknowledge their debt to Marxism has indeed been to help the Church become aware of the ease with which Christianity can become identified with the status quo in all its strengths and weaknesses.

The Church has learned necessary lessons from this historical experience. It tries to avoid a wrong identification with the status quo, understanding that such identification often implies assent to serious institutionalized injustice. It has become more concerned to exercise leadership in efforts to correct injustice. These efforts are often good in their own right. They also reflect the Church's awareness of the danger in allowing the initiative for social change to pass into non-Christian hands. It developed an impressive body of social teaching that tried to chart out a "third way" between the deficiencies of either classic capitalism or communism, a social teaching which is still too little known and applied.[1] However, hasty and ill-considered attempts to implement these lessons often put the Church in the same position under a different guise. If, in the past, the Church was often a tool of the repressive right, today it runs the risk in many countries of becoming a tool of a repressive and anti-Christian left.[2]

I would like to consider two aspects of this danger: in this chapter the explicit Marxist infiltration of the Church in many countries, and in the next chapter the ascendancy of an anti-Christian secular humanism. Both these developments are seriously damaging the Church.

Marxist Infiltration of the Church

The Marxist attitude toward the Church is no secret. Marx himself, and other Communist theorists, have written clearly about the Church, and their ideas and tactics have been put into practice in Marxist states in Eastern Europe, Africa, the Caribbean, and Asia. Briefly, Marxists view the Church as an enemy and an obstacle to revolution. The Church pledges loyalty to an authority higher than the Marxist state, and the Church's analyses of the importance, quality, and method of social and economic change differ from Marxist ideas. When Marxists do not hold power, their strategy includes an attempt to discredit the Church's authority. They try to sow disunity in the Church, to subvert and infiltrate it, and to enlist it as much as possible in Marxist causes, always looking ahead to the day when the Church will be directly under Marxist control.

Marxist revolutionaries struggling for power typically offer Christians freedom of worship. In practice, this freedom of worship is extremely narrowly defined. When they gain power, Marxist governments always try to strictly control and limit the Church. They impose the forced atheistic education of the young, and try to secure control over ecclesiastical appointments. Christians are discriminated against, harrassed, persecuted, and sometimes tortured and killed. The Marxist goal is to ensure the eventual disappearance of the Church as a truly vital and independent force. In the ideal Marxist society, the Church will no longer exist because man's "superstitious needs and fears" will no longer exist.

One clear tactic in both Marxist theory and practice is to cultivate sympathizers within the Church. Marxists try to identify and enlist people who may not accept the whole Marxist program, but who are disposed to support Marxist causes that promote the revolution. In most countries, this tactic is aimed at the Church's full-time professionals: bishops, priests, nuns, brothers, seminarians, and full-time lay leaders. This tactic is designed to ultimately subvert the Church and bring it under Marxist control.

The first step in this process is to identify those Church personnel within a region or country who combine sympathy for the poor with positions of influence—a cynical but effective approach. These candidates for "conversion" are then bombarded by appeals to their humanitarian and Christian sensibilities. They are asked to get involved in Marxist-sponsored direct action programs for the poor. Here, Marxist analyses of the root causes of oppression are presented and illustrated by carefully prepared "testimonies" from the Marxist-indoctrinated poor themselves. Church personnel are then urged to act on their new convictions by supporting Marxist-controlled political and social fronts and "conscientization" programs. Finally, trusted Church leaders who have been sufficiently won over to the Marxist view of their particular country's social situation are asked to funnel Church resources toward the cause—gifts of money, use of buildings and printing presses, public support of party fronts and causes. People with access to Church publications, speech writers for bishops, officials responsible for cate-chetical instruction, school curricula, and adult education programs will be assisted in using these organs to publish ostensibly Christian articles, catechetical material, and documents that will help the Marxist cause.

Some Church leaders may be invited to candidate membership in the Marxist party without being required to explicitly repudiate their per-sonal "faith" (as long as their faith does not interfere with their will-ingness to follow the party line in practice). Other leaders are thought to be more valuable as sympathizers outside the party. This usually gives them a wider influence within the Church, influence they can be counted upon to use at certain critical junctures to turn Church policy in a direction favorable to the party.

Bishops and other Church leaders who cannot be won over openly or covertly to the Marxist cause will find themselves under pressure to remain silent. Key Church personnel will criticize uncooperative bish-ops as "reactionary" and "not favoring the poor." The goal is to silence and discredit such Church leaders. The passivity of neutral and uncer-tain Church leaders is an asset to the Marxist program.

Examples of the success of these subversive tactics abound in Third World countries today. A well-known archbishop from a Third World country, traveling on one of his frequent trips to the developed coun-tries, was asked in an interview if he were "Red." He replied, "I don't have any problem with Marx, but I have some with the Marxists because they make of Marx an absolute."[3]

All Christians should have a problem with Marx. He and his follow-ers are atheists, hostile to Christianity, and totally secular and material-istic in their analyses of reality. Could it be that Church leaders like this archbishop are ignorant of Marx? Or do they make such statements unaware of their consequences, carried away by a taste for poetry or the well-turned phrase? Or, in an interest to see their cause prevail, do they ignore important truths inimical to their desires?

What I have just described is not simply a nebulous idea: it is a well worked-out strategy that has been applied successfully in many coun-tries. The state control of the Russian Orthodox Church is painfully evident today; it is clearly subservient to Soviet policy. Even in those areas of Eastern Europe where the Catholic Church still shows some strength, it suffers from continuing Marxist efforts to infiltrate and subvert it. Christian and Catholic fronts, composed of priests in many cases, will often attempt to divide the Church in a particular country by cooperating with the state. The Vatican finds that it must be very careful whom it appoints as bishops, because a small but significant number of priests in these Eastern European countries are Marxist sympathizers or agents. Some party members have even been assigned to enter seminaries and become priests. In China, a systematic campaign of discrediting Church leaders and sowing division in the Christian Churches paved the way for their takeover by Communists.[4] In Vietnam or Nicaragua today it is not clear whether catechists and Church authorities will be firm enough to resist attempts to make Christian education an instrument of Marxist indoctrination.

In 1980, an American bishop talked with several of his fellow bishops from Marxist-ruled countries at the Synod of Bishops in Rome. I quote at some length from his report of these conversations:

One bishop spoke to me about the atmosphere of fear, subtle coercion and constant surveillance he undergoes. His reports to diocesan groups are being monitored constantly by government agents planted within the Church. He said that if I should visit him in his country, we would have to plan very carefully where we should visit together.

Another bishop, a quiet and reflective man, revealed that some of the priests even within his own home who share meals with him (we were having a meal together at the time he was telling this story to me, and he gestured with his right hand and then his left) owe their first allegiance to the government. They report everything happening within the diocese to the government, especially areas of difficulty which the government might exploit.

Under virtual house arrest, he is unable to talk anywhere without permission. He was allowed to leave his country to visit Italy because the government wished to use the occasion for propaganda purposes.

Seminarians have been arrested. As a result, many are preparing for ordination in a kind of underground church. He keeps a small piece of luggage always packed because he expects to be arrested at any time. His mail is being constantly monitored, so he advised me not to write directly. . . .

Lay people at the Synod spoke of the power of their governments over their children and young people. Some countries aggressively attempt to win the minds and hearts of children and young people from their Christian faith through schools, youth activities and clubs. Employment and economic discrimination are practiced against Catholics and other believers.

In some Asian countries lay people are preparing themselves for a time when priests will not be allowed to minister to them any longer. Small households of faith, composed of a few families, are being encouraged under the leadership of catechists and others, when priests may no longer be allowed to exercise their priesthood. This fear especially pervades some Churches in Asian countries bordering on Communist areas.[5]

Catholics in Marxist states are often openly persecuted and harrassed, but they have the advantage of perceiving the government as an enemy of the Church bent on its destruction. When the enemy is clearly seen as the enemy, the Church can fight back more easily. The Catholic Church in Poland, of course, is the outstanding example of a Church that has in some ways grown stronger under persecution.

By contrast, the Church in many non-communist Third World countries and in Western Europe faces more insidious infiltration by Marxists because the process of subversion is hidden from view. Church authorities often deal with it less effectively than bishops under openly Marxist regimes.

For example, many French priests have become open proponents of the Marxist vision, adopting not only its aims but even its methods and its terminology of class struggle. A group of eighty-seven French priests, both diocesan and from religious orders, have appealed to all their fellow clerics to become involved in the "class struggle" on the side of the "oppressed." This group of priests has formed a "collective" (a standard Marxist vehicle) in response to the advice of friends, lay people, and "non-Christian revolutionaries, anxious for the conversion of the Church." This will serve as an action group to enlist more and more priests in the class struggle.[6]

Christians who try to enlist Church resources in the Marxist plan of revolution have often completely lost their grasp of the distinctiveness of the Christian mission and its incompatibility with Marxist goals and methods. Fr. Bernard Marchal, a French Catholic priest who is also the secretary of the local section of the Communist Party, expressed it this way:

> I fail to see why it would be absurd and contradictory to be both a Christian and a Communist. I will go further: I see no contradiction between being a Marxist and being a man who questions his faith and the ministry he has received from the hands of a bishop. I even dare ask myself and others this question: if Marxist analysis led me to atheism, would this evolution not in fact express the very freedom of the movement of which I am a part, and would this freedom not be the freedom of the Gospel?[7]

The remarkable suggestion that atheism be viewed as an expression of "the freedom of the gospel" could only come from someone who utterly misunderstands what the gospel is, or who understands it but is working to undermine it. Similar efforts to bend Christian language to the support of certain political ideologies are widespread in areas where liberation movements are at work.

The point is not that liberation movements as a whole are either good or bad; they are almost always a mixture. The Church in individual countries and individual Christians must judge them and all political movements in the light of Christian criteria, criteria which are being enunciated clearly for our time by John Paul II.[8] Sadly, the Church does not always do this.

The situation is especially difficult for the Church in Third World countries where the colonial heritage and depth of economic problems provide a fertile field for Marxist efforts.

In Mexico a well-known Mexican Methodist pastor, director of the Coordinating Center for Ecumenical Projects (an organization supported by the World Council of Churches), announced that he would seek a seat in Mexico's Chamber of Deputies as a candidate of the Communist Party. He declared that "even if it [the Church] should become atheist, the Church cannot fulfill what the Gospel requires in our day without Marxism." The pastor, repeating Marxist dogma, said he regarded God as a human creation and declared that he has not defected from the faith but has "found the faith in leftist political practice."[9]

This use of Christian terms like "gospel" and "faith" to indicate something quite different from their orthodox Christian meaning is an important element in the Marxist subversion of Christianity. When we hear people mouthing reassuring Christian words, we need to know what they are really talking about. What is the content of the "gospel" they profess? Who or what is the object of their "faith?"

This Methodist-Communist pastor apparently worked within the Church for years as an agent of Marxist infiltration. He tried to divert it from its full mission into an exclusive focus on aiding the "oppressed classes." One of the leading figures of Mexican Methodism had this to say:

> For many years he tried to sail two currents and play two hands of cards. Now he has torn off the mask of what he pretended to be, and has revealed his true face. Backed by the World Council of Churches and the Methodist Board of Missions, and supported by "imperialist dollars," he acted as an instrument of Marxist infiltration.[10]

The more serious problem for the Church is not Marxists who leave the Church but those who remain, those who still try to serve two masters or—even worse—only the wrong one. This is an acute problem in Latin America. Some priests and nuns who maintain the outward form of Christianity, using its language and celebrating its rituals, are now primarily committed to a secular and materialist revolution. They use the influence of their outwardly Christian presence to enlist the support of the people. In Nicaragua, a country where a leftist junta came to power through a revolution that took many lives, a member of the ruling revolutionary junta publicly acknowledged the important role of Catholic priests and nuns. He said they gave people confidence to support the revolution:

> Catholic religious men and women have been very important to the success of the revolution. . . . I think these priests who decided to commit themselves to the revolution in Nicaragua played an important role. They were able to use their credibility among the Nicaraguan people. The Catholic church remains a real power within Nicaragua.[11]

The Church in this particular country in years past was previously allied with a right-wing regime. A new archbishop moved it to a more moderate position. Radical priests and nuns then actively took part in the armed struggle and encouraged the people to do so. The Church's earlier complicity with a right-wing regime was hardly commendable, but it is now in danger of domination by a left-wing government. Already some of its policies, institutions, and personnel are in danger of being subverted to governmental ends. For example, some catechetical materials printed since the revolution are written to present the revolution as the fulfillment of Christian truth. The cover illustration on one of these books shows a picture of a guerrilla fighter, rifle in hand, emerging from a drawing of the crucified Christ. Some have even gone so far as to present the revolution as a fulfillment of the "second coming" of Christ, or as ushering in "the kingdom of God."

The killing of Church personnel in situations of political turmoil is often used for the purpose of advancing revolution. The dead priests and nuns are often proclaimed "martyrs," and their deaths are used to identify Christian commitment with a particular political cause. When Archbishop Oscar Romero of El Salvador was murdered, his death was immediately used by many as an opportunity to rally Christians to the support of a particular "liberation movement." Support for this movement was often presented as the only way to be a real Christian. Fr. Miguel D'Escoto, a Maryknoll priest who had major responsibility for Maryknoll's publications until he became the foreign minister in Nicaragua's revolutionary government, had this to say about Archbishop Romero's death:

May Archbishop Romero's spilt blood help us to see with clarity that to be a Christian is to be a revolutionary. And to be a revolutionary is to make the revolution. And to make the revolution is to struggle against the inevitable consequences of the reactionary egoism which motivated the violent assasination of our great friend Oscar Arnulfo Romero.[12]

This particular liberation movement may or may not do a better job at governing justly and effectively, but it is a mistake to identify being a Christian with a particular political preference or membership or support of a particular political party.

A Catholic bishop from another Latin American country, a man known as a moderate, recently expressed to me in a private conversation his increasing uneasiness about the results of the "conscientization" programs used by many priests and nuns on that continent. These programs attempt to raise the consciousness of poor people about their "oppressed" situation. The bishop thought that, in practice, these programs seemed to be replacing whatever genuine faith, hope, and love the poor had with hatred and class struggle. He thought that even some of his fellow Latin American bishops have come to see the gospel almost exclusively in secular, revolutionary terms. There is a particularly serious problem, he said, with nuns who tend to accept blindly whatever they are taught by certain Marxist-oriented priests who are systematically enlisting them in the cause. Furthermore, he claimed, some members of religious orders are working unhindered as Marxist agents within the Church. Their bishops cannot control them and their own religious superiors fear them.

Although often presented as simply a "value-free" contribution to educational methodology, "conscientization" is often in practice and theory a tool for political indoctrination. The materials are often written from a Marxist perspective and are intended to foment class struggle and hatred. The materials prepared and circulated by the World Council of Churches under the inspiration of sometime staff member Paulo Freire, perhaps the most well-known proponent of conscientization, are often blatantly ideological in content.[13]

Ironically, some of the leading voices of the Third World are in fact doing nothing but repeating echoes of a Western ideology, Marxism, which did not develop in the Third World, which in many ways is incompatible with deeply held family and religious values indigenous to the Third World, and which continues to find its world center in the Soviet Union—a foreign imperial and colonial power. It is interesting to note that European and American missionaries have played a prominent role in Third World countries by being the "voice of the voiceless." Many of the indigenous Third World Church personnel have had their "voices" formed at European universities. For example, Camilo Torres, the Colombian priest who was killed while fighting with a guerrilla band, did a significant part of his studies at Louvain, in Belgium. One of Torres' fellow students at Louvain was Gustavo Gutiérrez, a Peruvian who is perhaps the most prominent of the liberation theologians who openly acknowledge their dependence on Marx, and who tend to see the kingdom of God on earth coming in the vehicle of a Marxist revolution.[14]

There are signs that this imposition of a first world ideology is in fact resented by many who are its supposed beneficiaries. A report in a Hondurian newspaper is interesting in this connection. It begins:

"Residents in Disagreement with Priests Because They Only Speak About Marxism to Them"

Very disgusted because the priests are only talking to them about Marxism, the residents of three towns, Macuelizo, Azacualpa, and San Marcos, are planning to take over the churches of those towns sometime next week."[15]

Like the Methodist pastor in Mexico, many of these priests and nuns are supported in whole or in part by money raised in more prosperous countries like the United States, Holland, and Germany. This money is given by faithful Catholics and Protestants who think they are supporting traditional missionary work. They would be appalled to learn that their money is sometimes helping to undermine the faith.

The problem is that many missionaries in Latin America have come to define their work as primarily helping to bring about a secular revolution. Many of them are not conscious Marxists. Many, perhaps most, are not aware of Marxist efforts to infiltrate and subvert the Church in the countries in which they work. Nevertheless, when these missionaries turn to European and American agencies that have traditionally financed mission work, they argue that it is not possible to preach the gospel to the poor unless economic and political change occurs first. The agencies often find this argument convincing, and the monies they give are channeled into programs that further advance left-wing secular revolutions. The growth of the "basic Christian community" movement in this regard is filled with ambiguity. Obviously the Church desperately needs a proliferation of grass-roots ways of experiencing and living genuine Christian community. At the same time, though, many of these communities, at least in Latin America, seem to be used mainly as devices to organize the poor to exert political pressure, rather than as ways of developing balanced Christian life in which social concern finds its proper expression.[16]

The claim that political change must precede evangelism is preposterous. Evangelical Protestants and pentecostals have enjoyed outstanding success preaching the good news to the Latin American poor, often in the very same barrios where secularized Catholic priests and nuns are insisting that you cannot preach the gospel to the poor until the revolution comes. As a result of conversion to Jesus, the power of the Holy Spirit, and the sustaining power of the Christian Church, those poor are better able to work together for social change. Cardinal Léon-Joseph Suenens of Belgium pointed out the fallacy of the "you can't preach the gospel to the poor unless you first improve their economic situation" approach as long ago as 1957 in his book, *The Gospel to Every Creature*. He reiterated that stand in his contribution to the book *Charismatic Renewal and Social Action*.[17]

Explicit Marxist infiltration of the churches is hardly restricted to Latin America. Other Third World countries are undergoing the same onslaught. In one of these, hundreds of priests and nuns and even bishops are members or sympathizers of Marxist front movements designed to spearhead the revolution. Many of the country's national and regional "peace and justice" and "social apostolate" organizations are controlled by members or sympathizers of the Marxist fronts. Some of these "social apostolate" organizations have set up broader "renewal" programs that are being used to "conscientisize" (indoctrinate) Catholics in such a way that they will support the hoped-for revolution. Organizations of priests and nuns have been set up, including one for major superiors of religious orders, to give an impression of strong Church support for the Marxist program.[18]

Situations like this one have spurred John Paul II to warn against the ideological subversion of religious education and Christian teaching. He warns of danger in

> the temptation to mix catechetical teaching unduly with overt or masked ideological views, especially political and social ones, or with personal political options. When such views get the better of the central message to be transmitted, to the point of obscuring it and putting it in second place or even using it to further their own ends, catechesis then becomes radically distorted. [Truly Christian catechesis] goes beyond any kind of temporal, social or political "messiaism." It seeks to arrive at man's innermost being.[19]

Many in the Church today have succumbed to this temptation to subvert the gospel with ideology. We are seeing the "radical distortion" of Christian truth, and, often enough, the basic gospel message is "obscured," "put in second place," and used to further secular ideological ends that are foreign to the gospel.

CHAPTER SEVEN

The Secular Humanist Influence on the Church

THE GOSPEL IS BEING TAMPERED with and eroded not just in countries where the Church is being infiltrated and subverted by Marxist agents and ideology, but also in the United States and Western Europe. Here, the thinking and action of many Christians—including many priests, nuns, and even bishops—is being radically influenced not so much by Marxism as by a collection of anti-Christian ideologies known as "secular humanism."[1]

From a purely human point of view, the accelerated de-Christianization of the United States and much of Western Europe in the last thirty years or so can be attributed to many factors. I would like to draw attention to two of them. First, affluence and an increasingly secularized higher education have contributed to a growing religious and moral lukewarmness and indifference on the part of many of the Christian people in the Catholic and the major Protestant Churches. Secondly, a relatively small group of committed and knowledgeable anti-Christian secular humanists have been extraordinarily successful in gaining control of key institutions and organizations and in changing both national laws and the minds of the people to reflect their goals.

Secular humanism has most of the characteristics of a religion.[2] Broadly speaking, secular humanists place man at the center of all things, apart from God. Most secular humanists have a profound—and to a Christian, a profoundly naive—faith in the perfectability of man by his own efforts. Contrary to all evidence, they believe that man is making progress toward a more humane society. They believe that further progress comes as man shakes off the fetters of religious and moral beliefs. Another tenet of the secular humanist creed is the idea that men and women should be free to behave in any way they wish, constrained only by the vague qualification, "as long as it doesn't hurt anybody else."

A good way to capture the religious flavor of secular humanism is to read the "Humanist Manifesto II," a statement of humanist beliefs written in 1973 by a group of humanist intellectuals. This document provides an insight into the ill-founded optimism and faith secular man must possess if he believes in his own ability to "fulfill himself." In essence, the "Humanist Manifesto II" gives extraordinary testimony to man's stubbornness and resistance to the Good News and to an accurate perception of reality itself.

The first Humanist Manifesto, published in 1933 by leading intellectuals, proclaimed man's ability to perfect himself, both on an individual and a societal level. It described Christianity as an obstacle to progress because it distracts mankind from the real work at hand and gives him illusory hopes. In 1933, the humanists noted many hopeful signs that mankind was indeed making extraordinary social, political, and economic progress. The preface to the second Manifesto, published in 1973, puts the best possible face on the horrors of the subsequent forty years:

> It is forty years since Humanist Manifesto I (1933) appeared. Events since then make that earlier statement seem far too optimistic. Nazism has shown the depths of brutality of which humanity is capable. Other totalitarian regimes have suppressed human rights without ending poverty. Science has sometimes brought evil as well as good. Recent decades have shown that inhuman wars can be made in the name of peace. The beginnings of police states, even in democratic societies, wide-spread government espionage, and other abuses of power by military, political, and industrial elites, and the continuance of unyielding racism, all present a different and difficult social outlook. In various societies the demands of women and minority groups for equal rights effectively challenge our generation.

In the face of this bleak picture, the 1973 humanists propose a leap of "faith":

> As we approach the twenty-first century, however, an affirmative and hopeful vision is needed. Faith, commensurate with advancing

knowledge, is also necessary. In the choice between despair and hope, humanists respond in this *Humanist Manifesto II* with a positive declaration for times of uncertainty.

As in 1933 humanists still believe that traditional theism, especially faith in the prayer-hearing God, assumed to love and care for persons, to hear and understand their prayers, and to be able to do something about them is an unproved and outmoded faith. Salvationism, based on mere affirmation, still appears as harmful, diverting people with false hopes of heaven hereafter. Reasonable minds look to other means for survival.[3]

The "Humanist Manifesto II" rules out Christianity as unscientific. Yet, on the grounds that "an affirmative and hopeful vision is needed," it declares belief in man's ability to perfect himself and to solve the world's problems without God. This assertion bears all the earmarks of a religious creed with no scientific foundation whatsoever. In fact, the evidence mounts daily that secular humanism is illusory. With Christianity eliminated as an option, the alternatives are despair and blind hope. Humanists opt for the blind hope, based not on God's Word, but on wishful thinking.

Indeed, secular humanism is not scientifically established at all. Rather, it is a "faith" based on the rejection of God and the affirmation of man's autonomy. Of course, this is precisely the root dynamic behind man's original fall into darkness and disaster. It cannot possibly repair the consequences of man's fall, but assures they will continue.

Secular humanists view orthodox Christianity as an enemy and an obstacle to their program. Since the Church cannot be destroyed immediately, some secular humanists use the same strategy as the Marxists: they attempt to subvert the Church. They try to win Church leaders over to a secular humanist program which will ultimately lead to the demise of the Church. Just as Marxists set up front organizations to enlist Christian support for Marxist causes, so do secular humanists establish fronts to lure religious support. For example, Catholic groups supporting abortion function like front organizations. Also, like the Marxists, secular humanists attempt to discredit Church authority and divide Catholics from their pastors and the pope. They consciously employ tactics meant to break the will of the Church to resist and to render it ineffective. They make special efforts to gain control of key communications media in society at large and within the Church. This strategy is working. The secular media have little respect for Church authority. Even Catholic publications are affected by this influence.

The secular humanist tactics follow a now-familiar course. First, a plea is issued for a dominantly Christian society to "tolerate" what appears to be deviant behavior. Then pressure is applied to place the deviant behavior on an equal footing with traditional Christian values.

Secular humanists argue that a pluralist society cannot do otherwise. They then try to make the deviant behavior seem normal and behavior governed by Christian values seem abnormal—a threat to a pluralist society. The last step is often to use the legal system to protect immorality and to undermine what Christians have always considered righteous behavior. A well-known Catholic historian pointed to the role of the media in this whole process:

> The media's alleged commitment to "pluralism" is at base a kind of hoax. The banner of pluralism is raised in order to win toleration for new ideas as yet unacceptable to the majority. Once toleration has been achieved, public opinion is systematically manipulated first to enforce a status of equality between the old and the new, then to assert the superiority of the new over the old. A final stage is often the total discrediting, even sometimes the banning, of what had previously been orthodox.[4]

This final step is now underway in the United States and in many areas of Western Europe. Societal and legal support for marriage as it has been lived in the Judaeo-Christian tradition is being stripped away. Education is being used as a tool for secular humanist indoctrination. As laws supportive of Christian morality disappear, as the place once allotted to the Christian people in society severely narrows, we can see the first signs of punitive laws and social pressure against Christians. Even the rights to live the Christian life freely and to educate one's children according to Christian principles are coming under attack.

For example, a new law in Sweden makes it a crime for parents to discipline their children, even in non-corporal ways. Another law is being proposed in Sweden that would allow children to "divorce" their parents. In the United States, action is being taken to require that mandatory sex education programs in public schools present pre-marital sex, homosexuality, and masturbation as valid "lifestyle options." Certain features of these programs encourage sexual experimentation by requiring children to "role play" different types of sexual behavior. In some schools, active homosexuals have won the right to teach children and even present their lifestyle in a positive way.

Secular Humanism in the Church

Today the vacuum created by the attack on the authority and sufficiency of scripture and the tradition of the Church has left the way open for a secular humanist mentality to pervade the life of the Christian people. The secular humanist call to fulfill oneself, to achieve individual happiness, to place one's faith in the inevitability of human progress has a powerful hold on the minds of many Christians today.

For many Christians the desire for worldly happiness and success has become the driving force in their lives. They may go to church, but the creed that really shapes their lives is not the one they recite on Sunday but is the secular humanist creed. A fundamental tenet of this worldly creed is the right to pursue individual "happiness" at the expense of many values that are central to Christian living—for example, fidelity to commitments, service to others, self-sacrifice for the common good and even for one's own good.

The rapidity and ease with which Catholics as a whole are matching the divorce and abortion rates of society in general show how deep this indoctrination has gone. How many times in recent years have Catholics faced with situations requiring a painful moral choice, (concerning divorce, abortion, fornication, adultery, or homosexual activity, for example) heard the following refrains: "You deserve to be happy." "You have it coming to you." "It's impossible to think of living so unfulfilled." "You've got to be you." "You deserve to remarry." "Don't stifle your capacities for happiness." "Think of yourself." "Don't conform yourself to the expectations of others." Or even worse: "God doesn't want you unfulfilled." "If God gave you those desires he wants you to express them." "The Church has changed in its thinking." "Be an adult Christian, decide for yourself." "You've got to do what you think right."

This situation is all the more tragic in that many people and institutions within the Church are actively supporting the secular humanist cause. Many of these people still view themselves as sincere Christians, and are perhaps still praying regularly and frequenting the sacraments, but their hearts are mainly committed to making the Church into an instrument for accomplishing certain secular humanist goals. For some, these goals are socialism, gay rights, or feminism. For others, it is "save the whales," "peace and justice," "disarmament," or "pro-choice." Only secondarily—if at all—do they consider it important to bring all men to explicit repentance, conversion, faith, and incorporation into the new society which is the body of Christ. Of course authentic Christian social concern may coincide with certain secular humanist positions on particular issues, but in a totally different context and in a way that respects the totality of the Christian message of salvation.

Scripture says, "Wherever your treasure lies, there your heart will be" (Mt 6:21). Some secular "ethical" causes have so won the hearts of modern Catholics that, as John Paul II warned, they "get the better of the central message to be transmitted, to the point of obscuring it and putting it in second place or even using it to further their own ends."[5]

Sometimes Church leaders support causes that may be at heart inimical to Christianity because they may be naive or ignorant about what is really at stake. Naivete may explain why some American Church leaders have eagerly lent Church support to certain socially popular causes in American society.

For example, the bishop chairman of a U.S. Bishops Committee on Women in Society and the Church recently testified in favor of the Equal Rights Amendment, even though the American bishops decided to remain neutral on the issue. The bishop, testifying simply "as an individual," told a Congressional committee that "I feel it is very necessary for us to secure passage of the ERA so that all of us can feel secure in our own hearts that women are not second-class citizens. It's even more important for women themselves to know this."[6]

The bishop said it was "absolutely essential" to separate the issue of abortion and the issue of the Equal Rights Amendment. His reason was that "ERA touches only those concerns which both men and women share, and since men cannot bear children, the ERA does not concern abortion." He also denied that the amendment would affect what he called "that very special area, the personal relationship between husband and wife."[7]

Without getting into a detailed discussion on the merits of the Equal Rights Amendment, a few comments about the bishop's testimony are in order. Professor John Noonan, professor of law at the University of California at Berkeley and an expert on the legal questions surrounding abortion, thinks that abortion and ERA go closely together:

> The chief problem about ERA and abortion is that ERA would be interpreted by federal judges who in a great number of cases have shown tremendous sympathy for the ideology of abortion. With this amendment in force, these judges might well go on to, say, compel the funding of abortion. The Catholic sympathizers of ERA seem to read the amendment in the air, abstractly without sensitivity to the great political battle that is now going on about abortion and without awareness that the majority of the federal judiciary are members of what can fairly be described as the pro-abortion party. It would, I think, be a great mistake to give this party a new legal tool with which to promote the abortion cause.[8]

Since Professor Noonan gave his warning, a court ruling in the State of Massachusetts, which has a state ERA law, verified his prediction that the judiciary would use the ERA concept to protect and extend the practice of abortion.[9]

The bishop did not seem to be fully consistent about his claim that ERA would not affect the relationship between husband and wife. When asked why many of his fellow bishops opposed ERA, he responded by saying that some bishops are worried that ERA will change the role of husband and wife. "But, as I see this," the bishop said, "I think that it's going to be changed anyway."[10]

This remark illustrates a common and troubling attitude in the Church: the Church had better get on the bandwagon because modern society is inevitably going in a certain direction. This bishop was able to cheerfully contemplate a piece of legislation that may have profound repercussions on basic relationships between husbands and wives without, apparently, deeply considering the natural and Christian truths pertinent to this area. He did so partly on the grounds that this is the inevitable direction of modern culture.

If naivete and ignorance are behind some of the positions some modern Catholics take, pride may be behind others. Certain segments of the modern Church seem to be ruled by a desire to be highly regarded by the secular media-academic-governmental secular world. To win such acceptance, there is a tendency for Christians to grow silent about their beliefs and support what the secular world supports. In the process, a spiritual blindness creeps in. The Church is misled into supporting secular causes that are hostile to God and destructive to his people. At times the words of scripture are coming to pass, that he "is marked out as God's enemy if he chooses to be the world's friend" (Jas 4:4).

Signs of this deterioration are everywhere. Catholic universities seem especially hard hit. Having dedicated themselves to "academic excellence"—in itself, of course, a good thing—and to winning the approval of secular institutions, Catholic universities are now beginning to wonder what their unique and specific identity is. Their efforts to define a Catholic identity often lack substance. Catholic identity is talked about almost exclusively as something that allows the formation of humane, ethically sensitive graduates who are able to bring an ethical dimension to bear in their occupations. There is little evidence that this actually happens. More seriously, such statements ignore the specifically Christian aspects of life: namely, the redemption through the death and resurrection of Jesus, and the implications of the gospel for evangelization. Without this explicit foundation, Catholic universities are adrift. They reaffirm their Catholic identity in ethical terms that are virtually identical to the conventional ethical wisdom of contemporary ideologies.

For example, consider one issue of *Notre Dame Magazine*, the alumni magazine of a Catholic university in the United States that aspires to be the best Catholic university in the world.[11] A brief review of its tone and contents is instructive.

The magazine as a whole exudes the sentimental, vaguely ethical vision of Catholicism that characterizes many "updated" Catholics today. One of the articles explains how faculty members of this university are granted tenure. The criteria do not include any consideration of the professor's Catholic life and beliefs, or lack thereof, but only teaching, research, and service to the university. (A subsequent issue of the magazine reported that eighty-six percent of the faculty said that Catholic beliefs should not be considered in tenure and promotion decisions. Sixty-two percent said it should not be a factor in hiring faculty.)[12]

Another article, on "Friendship," was written by a priest who left the ministry to marry.[13] The next article, on "Women Friends," was written by the divorced wife of a former faculty member. The writer begins her article this way:

> We were sitting on the beach at Michigan City a few years ago, my friend and I, talking as we often do about all the changes in our continually rearranging lives: our divorces, our children, our ideas, our work and our men.[14]

Another article profiles a graduate of this university who has been successful in pro football. It casually mentions that he is already into his second marriage, with no further explanation.[15]

Also featured in this issue are extracts from the journal of the renowned priest-president of this university, a priest who visited the People's Republic of China as the head of a United Nations delegation preparing a conference on Science and Technology. In his journal, at least in the published extracts, the priest makes an exceedingly feeble and unfocused attempt to view the trip with a Christian perspective. He does not mention redemption and evangelization. He ends with this feeble desire: "I guess there is hope for peace in the world, if *somehow* we can liberate the basic human impulse to work together for peace and justice in a world that badly needs both."[16]

A fully Christian perspective would hold that this "basic human impulse" can only be liberated if certain realities—sin, Satan, and the Fall, the sacrificial death of Christ on the cross, his resurrection, Pentecost, repentance, faith and baptism—are clearly grasped and lived. But nowhere in the journal extracts, nor for that matter anywhere in the magazine, are these truths clearly stated.

One of the most influential Catholic educational systems in the world is the Jesuit network of schools, colleges, and universities. Many critics, both inside and outside the schools, doubt that these institutions succeed in producing fervent and apostolic Catholics. One of the doubters is Fr. Pedro Arrupe, the superior general of the Jesuit order, who confessed to disappointment that Jesuit-trained graduates had failed to exert an apostolic influence on their environments. A recent international gathering of representatives of Jesuit graduates underlined the secularization of much of contemporary Catholic thought.

The main resolutions of the gathering concerned the dominant secular ethical causes: economic and social justice, the arms race, the society of consumerism, and so on. These matters are worth a Catholic's careful attention, of course, but the absence of specifically Christian content is very troubling.[17]

Indeed, the Jesuit order as a whole is plagued by efforts of some of its members to reinterpret Christianity almost exclusively in terms of secular ethical causes that are sometimes at variance with the gospel. A corresponding problem is silence among many Jesuits about redemption and direct evangelization. American Jesuits have been in the leadership of the Catholic groups pushing for tolerance of active homosexuality and the ordination of women.[18] These do not seem to be just isolated incidents, but parts of a larger picture among some influential Jesuits which sees Christianity being bent to the service of secular humanist goals. For example, one American Jesuit document proposed some "Aims for Those Whom We Teach" as follows:

1. Jesuit graduates are to be highly skilled, humane technocrats.
2. Who are able and hopeful of the technological world and have integrated technology into their personalities.
3. Who have experienced, affectively and effectively, creation and man's evolution as intelligible, beautiful and moral.
4. Who have developed the facility for and the habit of examining their beliefs, convictions, and commitments in the light of more mature thinkers, of their peers, and of the great value systems of mankind.
5. Who—wherever feasible—are familiar with Jesus Christ, faithful to Him, and (where appropriate) faithful to His Church.[19]

Fr. Arrupe, encouraged by John Paul II, has ordered a review of the order's state of spiritual and doctrinal health throughout the world. John Paul II's concern for the Jesuits was shared by Paul VI and John Paul I. In the fall of 1981, Pope John Paul II directly intervened in the problems affecting the Jesuits by suspending aspects of their constitution and appointing a personal delegate to take charge.

Jesuit institutions and Notre Dame are not the only institutions of higher learning that have allowed their treasure to tarnish. Many Catholic colleges and universities are affected similarly.[20]

Ideological subversion of the gospel takes different directions in different countries. Its direction in a particular country is determined by the nature of the prevailing ideological currents. In the United States, the gospel of salvation and repentance is transformed by the sentimental optimism of "selfist" psychology and the unfounded hope of secular humanism. In Europe, with its strong Marxist left, elements of Marxist rhetoric are combined with secular humanism.

For example, France's Young Christian Workers have for many years consciously and explicitly promoted class struggle along Marxist lines. In 1979, a congress of eighteen Belgian youth organizations promised as its goal for the year "to organize on the national level a vast campaign of action against the conditioning and oppression of youth."[21] The groups represented at this congress also vowed "to wage campaigns of solidarity with the oppressed peoples of the world," and "to struggle against discrimination." The groups also vowed "to work for peace," "to provide a chance for the full blossoming of one's personality," and "to become committed to the protection of the environment."

While many of these values are indeed worthy of Christian support, to focus on them exclusively, as is so often done, is to neglect the truly unique contributions of Christianity, namely, its full message of salvation in Jesus Christ, which necessarily involves faith, repentance, and incorporation into the Church.

True and False Christian Humanism

Historically, secular humanism has always challenged Christianity. Whether the humanism of the Greeks and Romans, the humanist revival in the Renaissance, the Enlightenment "humanism," or the radical secularism of our own day, secular humanism has been no friend of Christianity. Secular humanists have regarded Christianity as oppressive, and as neglectful of man in this world. They are fundamentally hostile to the authority contained in Christianity—the Word of God itself and the teaching leadership of the Church. When secular humanists try to remold Christianity so that it can be compatible to humanist causes, they attack its sources of authority.

Throughout the ages, Christians have countered these attacks on the Church by stressing the profound truth of how Christianity is really "for" man. This line of thinking, called Christian humanism, has made significant contributions to the work of apologetics and evangelization. Christian humanists have emphasized that Christianity is "for" man and not against him, that it favors the full development of persons and the fulfillment of man's whole potential. Christian humanists maintain that man's fulfillment was precisely what Christ came to accomplish, and that a faithful following of Christ's way will lead to the true fulfillment of the human race.

Today we are seeing a renewed emphasis on secular humanism and in response a corresponding deepening of insight into authentic Christian humanism. Recent popes, including the current pope, have stressed how mankind is fulfilled only through the gospel, and that only Jesus Christ liberates men and women from the bondage of sin and allows them to live as the people God created them to be. Such Christian humanism allows modern men and women to perceive the value and beauty of the gospel; it allows the gospel to be preached more effectively. Christian humanism also redresses an imbalance that had crept into certain thinking in the Church that was sometimes perceived as being hostile to authentic human values and to what was fundamentally good in creation.

Pope John Paul II has clearly delineated the content of an authentic Christian humanism. At its heart must be a firm and clear understanding that human beings can be "themselves," "reach their potential," and become "fully human" only insofar as they become new creatures "in Christ," born again of water and the Spirit. Anything else, stresses the pope, will ultimately end in disaster:

> The man who wishes to understand himself thoroughly . . . must with his unrest, uncertainty and even his weakness and sinfulness, with his life and death, draw near to Christ. He must, so to speak, enter into him with all his own self, he must "appropriate" and assimilate the whole of the reality of the Incarnation and redemption, in order to find himself.[22]

For John Paul II, the greatest tragedy of human history is not any particular economic, social, or political problem; it is that "Jesus Christ is not known and therefore loved."[23] He views the turmoil and disarray of the current age in terms of fundamental truths that man must acknowledge: the human race is fallen and needs a redeemer. God has acted to give him salvation through Jesus Christ. This salvation must be accepted by human response in repentance, faith, and baptism.

However, the Christian humanism exemplified by the pope is often misunderstood and distorted in the Church today. Some claiming to be "Christian humanists" are actually using Christian language but distorting its meaning under the influence of secular humanism. For example, consider this revised "Creed," which was actually used in the liturgy of the eucharist in a Catholic parish:

> I believe in man, and in a world in which it is good to live for all
>   mankind; and that it is our task to create such a world.
> I believe in equal rights for all men, in love, in justice, brotherhood
>   and peace.
> I must continually act out these beliefs. . . .
> And I believe in the resurrection, whatever it may mean. Amen.

It is often difficult to sort out the conflicting and confusing elements that thwart authentic Christian humanism. For example, consider these reflections on the meaning of Vatican II by a leading figure in American Catholicism:

Once upon a time, not too long ago, we gloried in our power and importance. We thought that, as American Catholics, we were at the cutting edge of the church's engagement with the modern world. During the council we were naive enough to believe that, drawing upon our American inheritance of personal freedom and political democracy, we had something of value to contribute to the church universal. . . . Understandably following Vatican II, we sometimes lost that confidence. . . . In disappointment, we turned away too quickly from our earlier liberalism and Americanism to take ideas and approaches to change which had little or no basis in the pastoral and political experience of American Catholics. . . . We lost that sense of mission and purpose which our deeply held faith in the promise of America had long given us. We let the banner of a liberal, progressive, democratic Catholicism drop and have not yet picked it up.

I believe that the time has come to pick up that banner once again—the banner of an authentic Christian humanism, the apostolate of the laity, the social mission of the church, and all the truths of "the American proposition," as John Courtney Murray called it. We must recapture something of the optimistic confidence in the human enterprise, in reason, in democracy, in social progress, which informed preconciliar humanism and found its crowning point in [Vatican II's] *Gaudium et Spes*.[24]

This statement is a confusing mixture of contradictory elements: concepts from the Council are combined with such ideas as "personal freedom," "political democracy," "a liberal, progressive democratic Catholicism," and "optimistic confidence in the human enterprise, in reason, in democracy, in social progress." The statement smacks of that groundless optimism in the human enterprise which is the secular humanist faith.

Such secular optimism seems to have replaced genuine Christian hope in large sectors of the Church today. Authentic Christian hope is based and anchored in Christ, who is now "at the right hand of God," and who will return again in glory to judge the living and the dead. Therefore, the only hope for the human race is for men and women to repent and believe the good news and be joined to Christ's community, the Church. Apart from Christ, progress is not only illusory; it can also frequently be yet another manifestation of rebellion against God and his plan. As such, God will judge it, not commend it.

Another distortion of Christian humanism is confusion revolving around the notion of being "fully human." Christians today suggest it is possible to be "fully human" without Christ, and that to be fully "human"—whatever that means—is already to be Christian.

As one theologian put the question represented by this position:

> If the purpose of the Church is to provide the experience of community and opportunities for the celebration of that experience and if we find that other people, outside of the Church, also experience and celebrate community, then why should we worry about their relationship to the Church or even to Christ himself?[25]

A revealing expression of this aspect of "Christian humanism" is found in the following statement by an American Catholic priest, the director of his order's media evangelization efforts. This priest is also president of the Human Family Education and Cultural Institute, an organization which awards a "Humanities Prize."

> God wills our humanization. He wills our growth and fulfillment, the complete flowering of our humanity. This is the central thrust of Jesus' mission. It is also the preoccupation of the authentic evangelist. Christian values and human values converge and strengthen each other. Any time we help our fellow human beings understand what it means to be human, challenge them to take charge of their lives and affirm their dignity, responsibly exercise their freedom by protesting unjust social conditions and by reaching out in love to one another, we are doing what Jesus did. We are revealing his continuing presence, building his kingdom, preaching his Good News. We are evangelizing.[26]

The first point about this statement concerns the excessive ambiguity of its language. Such recasting of the gospel into jargon makes the gospel hostage to contemporary humanism. Our secular culture defines terms like "growth and fulfillment" and "complete flowering of our humanity." By using them, the priest risks having his listeners read something into the statement he did not intend to say. Besides, how can such terms ever adequately communicate the aspects of repentance, death to sin, and self-denial that are integral to the gospel?

But this statement has more problems than ambiguity of language: it is a wholly inadequate statement of authentic Christian humanism. By no stretch of the imagination is it true to say that "any time we help our fellow human beings understand what it means to be human" we are doing what Jesus did. A Christian understanding of what it means to be human must include the Fall, the need for repentance, forgiveness of sin, freedom from bondage to the devil, rebirth in Christ, and the Church. If we are as vague on this point as the above formulation, then preaching the Good News becomes virtually identical to the directives in the Humanist Manifesto.

The Mission of the Church

The humanist and Marxist "gospels" exert a powerful appeal to man's imagination; they promise redemption without the Redeemer, salvation by man's own hands. Many Christian and Catholic organizations and institutions have become so weakened in their understanding, living, and proclamation of the Christian gospel that the Marxist and humanist gospel of salvation sweeps the gospel away or subordinates its language to their ends. Significant segments of the Church are preaching salvation, not by the cross of Jesus Christ, but by the works of man: by class struggle and armed revolution; by psychological health; or by sociological, economic, and political progress. Although a Catholic piety or flavor may be in evidence, a predominantly humanist or Marxist view of reality frequently predominates in Catholic life and institutions today. The vision of authentic Catholicism and Christianity has become so dim in some places that prominent Christians are regularly making statements that betray profound lack of comprehension about fundamental Christian truths. One well-known theologian succinctly summarized a question raised by many Christians working for social justice,

> If the purpose of the Church is the pursuit of peace and social justice, and if we find that there are many people outside of the Church who are already involved in that struggle and perhaps more *effectively* than the Church, why should we worry about their relationship to the Church or even to Christ himself?[27]

This mentality underlies much of the confusion manifested in the current distortions of the gospel. It is hardly adequate to describe the purpose of the Church as a merely temporal human fulfillment or as the pursuit of an earthly peace and social justice, as important as these may be in the overall mission of the Church. As Walter Kasper, the German theologian, expressed it:

> An important feature of them [Jesus' miracles] is the absence of any planned or systematic attempt to improve the world. Jesus did not systematically heal all the sick or drive out all the demons; he simply gave isolated signs, which cannot be separated from the total context of his work, the message of the coming Kingdom of God. Jesus is not interested in a better world, but in the new world. But according to his message, man and the world can only become really human

when they have God as their Lord. Anything else would not be human, but would lead to superhuman efforts and very easily to inhuman results.[28]

Or as Avery Dulles, the American Jesuit theologian, put it in an essay:

> The Church does not exist to help any particular group, whether "haves" or "have-nots," to achieve their own special interests. It exists for the sake of the kingdom of God, and in service to the kingdom it must invite all persons and collectivities to repentance and conversion. Not satisfied with a reshuffling of power and wealth, to be accomplished by social revolution, the Church looks forward to a total transformation of man and creation, to be accomplished by the power of God. A reshuffling of earthly resources may at times be called for, but it will not achieve justice in the long run unless human hearts are renewed by God's grace in Jesus Christ.[29]

Anyone with even a rudimentary grasp of the faith can understand why we should be concerned about the relationship of human beings to Christ and the Church. The frightening thing is that many Christians—even leaders exercising significant control of Church institutions and organizations—seem to reveal confusion regarding this basic understanding. Because of this state of affairs, large segments of the Church's efforts at mission are in disarray and bear amazingly little fruit that abides.

CHAPTER EIGHT

The Undermining of Sexual Morality

CHRISTIAN MORALITY FLOWS from the basic truths of creation and salvation as taught by the scripture and the Church. Once these truths have been discredited or stripped of their authority, morality is also displaced from its sure foundation and set adrift to "dialogue" with modern culture.

Scripture makes clear that there is a deep link between knowing and adhering to the basic Christian truths and living a life of moral righteousness. The source of righteousness is Jesus. He gives those who believe in him and keep his word the ability to live righteously through the power of the Holy Spirit.

The first chapter of the Epistle to the Romans points out the connection among the rejection of fundamental truths about God, spiritual blindness, and perverse moral behavior. Consider this passage carefully. It is a key to understanding why there is moral decay and confusion of basic truth in today's world—and today's Church.

The wrath of God is being revealed from heaven against the irreligious and perverse spirit of men who, in this perversity of theirs, hinder the truth. In fact, whatever can be known about God is clear to them; he himself made it so. . . . Therefore these men are inexcusable. They certainly had knowledge of God, yet they did not glorify him as God or give him thanks; they stultified themselves through speculating to no purpose, and their senseless hearts were darkened. They claimed to be wise but turned into fools instead. . . .

115

In consequence, God delivered them up to their lusts to unclean practices; they engaged in the mutual degradation of their bodies, these men who exchanged the truth of God for a lie and worshipped and served the creature rather than the Creator—blessed be he forever, amen!

God therefore delivered them up to disgraceful passions. Their women exchanged natural intercourse for unnatural, and the men gave up natural intercourse with women and burned with lust for one another. Men did shameful things with men, and thus received in their own persons the penalty for their perversity. They did not see fit to acknowledge God, so God delivered them up to their own depraved sense to do what is unseemly. They are filled with every kind of wickedness: maliciousness, greed, ill will, envy, murder, bickering, deceit, craftiness. They are gossips and slanderers, they hate God, are insolent, haughty, boastful, ingenious in their wrongdoing and rebellious toward their parents. One sees in them men without conscience, without loyalty, without affection, without pity. They know God's just decree that all who do such things deserve death; yet they not only do them but approve them in others!

(Rom 1:18-19, 20-22, 24-32)

Paul emphasizes the connection between a refusal to acknowledge and obey God and a subsequent degeneration of morality. False worship, pride in one's own wisdom, and futile speculation cause spiritual blindness. These subject man to the destructive and degrading drives of his fallen nature—particularly in the area of sex, especially perverse expressions of sexuality including homosexuality, but also in rebelliousness and a general lack of loyalty and human dignity. People who have fallen into such spiritual blindness and moral decay not only sin grievously themselves, but also encourage others to do so.

This passage from Romans describes our situation today with remarkable accuracy. Of particular interest is the link between rejection of God's truth and disordered sexuality. Our sexual identity as male and female is a fundamental dimension of the way God has created us. Thus, rejection of God logically issues in rejection of mankind created in the image of God—male and female. Modern man's rebellion against God is today strikingly expressed in rebellion against our fundamental God-given sexual identity. The growing number of men and women today who are troubled about and resent their sexual identity and try to blur or deny it testifies strikingly to the link between rejection of God and rejection of our humanity created in the image of God. The area of sexual morality, of course, is not the only important area of Christian morality under attack today, but it is one attack that is particularly intense at this time and which in some way affects nearly all of us. For these reasons I would like to devote this chapter to an in-depth analysis of the attack in this area.

While rejection of truth can cause moral decay, scripture also teaches that it can work the other way: a previously existing moral disorder can cause people to reject the truth simply because they want to continue in their perversity:

> The judgment of condemnation is this: the light came into the world, but men loved the darkness rather than light because their deeds were wicked. Everyone who practices evil hates the light; he does not comes near it for fear his deeds will be exposed. (Jn 3:19-20)

The only way men and women can truly be "themselves" and experience the full potential of their created natures is by living their lives in, through, and with Jesus Christ. He is the perfect human being, the source of healing, restoration, and fulfillment for human beings. A humanism that starts by rejecting him inevitably ends up rejecting man and betraying the human race, at first selectively, as in abortion in many of our countries, or in the elimination of the Jews in Nazi Germany, but eventually in a totalitarian oppression of all of life and the breakdown of civilization. The only authentic humanism is an explicitly Christian humanism.

God's Word is clear: knowing God and living lives of holiness are connected. Belief and behavior are deeply bound up with our fundamental "heart" disposition toward God. When fundamental Christian truths are denied or doubted, there inevitably follows rejection of the life of holiness and morality that these truths call forth, demand, and make possible.

We see this today in many Christians' restless search for the canon within the canon, for the magisterium within the magisterium, for the "enlightened" theologian, for the "sensitive" confessor. This happened in New Testament times too. Paul warned Timothy to stand firm against people seeking "teachers" and "teachings" to suit their own fancy:

> I charge you to preach the word, to stay with this task whether convenient or inconvenient—correcting, reproving, appealing— constantly teaching and never losing patience. For the time will come when people will not tolerate sound doctrine, but, following their own desires, will surround themselves with teachers who tickle their ears. They will stop listening to the truth and will wander off to fables. (2 Tm 4:1-4)

Today, tragically, some Christian theologians and teachers can only be called false teachers. They are leading Christians to sin and, in some situations, even to see sin as virtue.

Human Sexuality

A book titled *Human Sexuality* gives striking evidence of how authentic Christian morality is being subverted in the Church today.[1] This study is particularly significant since it was commissioned by the Catholic Theological Society of America and published with its assent, even though the book's contents were not necessarily endorsed by the society as a whole. The authors all held—and still hold—positions of responsibility in Catholic seminaries and theological faculties. After extensive checking, as of this writing, four years after initial publication, I have found no indication that any of the authors have retracted the substance of their views put forward in this study. The book was published by a Catholic publishing house run by a Catholic religious order. It was translated and published in other countries and continues to be used widely.

The study asserts that the teaching of scripture, tradition, and the Church about sexual morality are no longer sufficient guides to moral behavior. The book claims that because modern man faces new situations and now knows much more about sexuality than the scriptural authors did, scripture becomes just one source of input about moral decisions. The findings of contemporary "experts" in the social sciences are another source. Since scripture and its authoritative interpretation and clarification in tradition and contemporary Church teaching are no longer sufficient, the authors claim, modern man needs a new set of principles to judge the morality of sexual behavior.

The authors proceed to formulate such principles.

We maintain that it is appropriate to ask whether specific sexual behavior realizes certain values that are conducive to creative growth and integration of the human person. Among these values we would single out the following as particularly significant:

(1) Self-liberating. . . .
(2) Other-enriching. . . .
(3) Honest. . . .
(4) Faithful. . . .
(5) Socially responsible. . . .
(6) Life-serving. . . .
(7) Joyous. . . .

Where such qualities prevail, one can be reasonably sure that the sexual behavior that has brought them forth is wholesome and moral. . . . By focusing on the many-splendored values of wholesome sexuality and avoiding absolute categorizations of isolated, individual sexual actions, one can arrive at a much more sensitive

and responsible method of evaluating the morality of sexual patterns and expressions.[2]

One immediately suspects that such criteria are not so much "moral
principles" as ambiguous slogans employing the jargon of modern
social science. Used "creatively" and willfully, such principles can
justify virtually any sexual behavior, even behavior that scripture and
tradition clearly regarded as sinful. Consider, for example, the authors'
treatment of adultery. After reviewing the reasons why confessors and
counselors may frown on adulterous relationships, the authors say
this:

> These facts, however, do not rule out the possibility that there may
> occasionally arise exceptions, when such relationships can truly be
> "creative" and "integrative" for all involved, and therefore morally
> acceptable. Extreme caution is imperative in arriving at such conclu-
> sions in particular cases.[3]

With this loophole, almost any adulterous relationship can be justified.
To be moral, adulterers and their confessors must only exercise "extreme
caution."

The effect of the moral principles proposed in *Human Sexuality* is to
overthrow the real authority for Christian moral behavior and to replace
it with the opinion of the secular "experts." These experts prove
themselves unable to offer much useful moral guidance at all. Let us
consider three examples of this failure from the book.

The first example is the authors' consideration of the morality of
certain "therapeutic" practices common today in "sex clinics," organizations which counsel people with sexual difficulties. The sex clinic
therapies that draw the attention of the authors are the practice of
masturbation and the use of "surrogate partners" for "therapeutic"
intercourse. This is how they analyze the ethics of these practices:

> Applying the ethical norm adopted in this study, namely that sexual
> expression to be moral must be "creative and integrative" for the
> parties involved, it might seem on first reflection that the sexual
> activity prescribed in serious therapy would present no moral diffi-
> culty. Self-stimulation oriented to healthy sexual intercourse fits the
> norm without difficulty. Sex partners truly intent on being the means
> of making the other whole and capable of relating sexually to his or
> her beloved would also seem to be engaged in a moral use of genital
> sex. Theoretically, this would be true whether they be married cou-
> ples, unmarried lovers, surrogates or volunteer partners of unmar-
> ried patients. In fact, however, there is serious doubt within the

experienced scientific community that sexual "stand-ins" really help overcome, in any effective way, the sexual difficulties that affect an existing relationship. Their use does, in fact, risk weakening an ailing relationship further. Since it is not at all clear that the use of surrogates is necessary even to achieve the limited objective of erotic arousal and may be counter-productive in achieving the long term therapeutic objectives of curing a sexual dysfunction in the context of a specific human relationship, the use of stand-ins does not seem morally justified at this time.[4]

The authors also consider the morality of therapists engaging in "therapeutic" sexual activity with their patients:

Apparently the practice is not uncommon and is defended by some psychiatrists and lay-therapists. Officially the professional societies continue to condemn it for reasons of law, public confidence and therapy effectiveness. (The American Psychiatric Association specifically prohibits it. However, the American Psychological Association code of ethics does not mention it, and a resolution prohibiting sexual activity with clients failed to pass at the 1975 convention of the association.)

Applying the norms adopted in this study, we would have to say that in a hypothetical case wherein erotic expression between therapist and patient in fact results in making the patient whole without harm to the other relationship of therapist and patient, such direct involvement of the therapist might be moral. However, the overwhelming majority of professionals in the field deny the possibility of such an outcome. The burden, therefore, would be upon the therapist to justify morally the risks attendant on such practice, considering the individual and social dimensions in each case.[5]

The authors also discuss the specific forms of adultery involving "threesome" sexual relations and "mate swapping":

Much is being written about this dimension of sexual experience today. Some authors have advocated this form of human interrelatedness as a truly Christian response to the problems and needs of particular groups of society, such as the elderly and the "unhappily single." . . . As suggested previously, the empirical data does not as yet warrant any solid conclusions on the effects of such behavior, particularly from the long-range point of view. Traditional Catholic teaching considers all such cases unjustifiable, as contrary to the nature and purpose of marriage. Others would acknowledge at least the theoretical possibility that such an arrangement could uphold the principles of true human growth and full integration. In practice, however, such relationships would seen to contradict many of the characteristics of wholesome sexual interrelatedness, and, above all, to compromise the "covenant fidelity" presented by Scripture as an ideal. Thus, while remaining open to further evidence from the empirical sciences, we would urge the greatest caution in all such matters, lest they compromise the growth and integration so necessary in all human activity.[6]

Notice the method of analysis in all these three cases. The authors acknowledge that scripture and tradition would regard these situations as instances of fornication or adultery—forbidden by God's Word. Yet these traditional Christian moral views are only one element the moralists must consider. It turns out that it is a subordinate element. The decisive criteria for judging the morality of sexual behavior are the views of "professionals in the field" and "evidence from the empirical sciences."

One of the many problems in this choice of criteria is the fact that scientists rarely ever consider an issue finally closed; social scientists almost never do. The nature of the scientific method compels scientists to remain forever open to new data, to always admit the possibility of an exception. In the area of sexual morality such an approach ends up subverting the Word of God.

Nevertheless, the authors of *Human Sexuality* continue to form the priests and religious educators of the future from their teaching positions at Catholic seminaries and theological faculties. Their book is still distributed by its Catholic publisher, and large numbers of Catholics have been influenced by it and the widespread thinking that it represents in their approach to sexual behavior.

It is interesting to note that one of the authors of *Human Sexuality*, shortly before its publication, published an article attacking Pope Paul VI and the charismatic renewal for reaffirming the existence of the devil and the presence of his work both within the world and the Church.[7] It is astounding to see how little the reality of Satan and his ways of working are taken into account in what can only be called false teaching and immorality in the Church today. Scripture views this as an area of demonic activity and influence *par excellence*.

> The Spirit distinctly says that in later times some will turn away from the faith and will heed deceitful spirits and things taught by demons through plausible liars. (1 Tm 4:1, 2a)

The ideas contained in *Human Sexuality* and articles and lectures like it are finding their way into the broad life of the Catholic Church.[8] One

article, written by a Catholic "marriage and divorce adjustment counselor" found that the Church's prohibition of sexual acitivity to divorced
people was not "relevant" to the "experience" of the six million divorced
American Catholics:

> [Divorced Catholics] cannot be told that intercourse is a "wrong"
> way of loving. They know better. They know that intercourse cou-
> pled with love can be enriching and stabilizing—even outside of
> marriage. . . . The more mature among them do not reject help in
> making decisions, but they will not leave such decisions to another
> person or institution, especially if that institution's stated position
> seems to have little relevance to their experience.[9]

The author credits this revolution in Catholic attitudes to "Vatican II,
with its profound emphasis on the role of informed and individual
Christian conscience, and in a negative sense, *Humanae Vitae*." The
result? "Faithful Catholics, quietly and without much ado, rejected
magisterial control not only over their sexual relations but over the
meaning of Christian marriage."[10]

This article illustrates the now-familiar distortion of the teaching of
Vatican II, in this case the Council's teaching on religious liberty and
the role of "individual conscience." The Council in fact taught that
Catholics must form their consciences by the teaching of the Church
and give "religious assent" to those teachings, that is, to accept them
wholeheartedly.[11] That is precisely what being a Catholic means. We
are to conform our mind to the mind of Christ, not to the mind of the
world. We are to "bring every thought into captivity to make it obedient to Christ," in accordance with the Church as the authentic inter-
preter of His Word (Rom 12:2; 2 Cor 10:5).

The article also illustrates the manipulation of public opinion that has
become common in the Catholic communications media. In this author's
vocabulary, a rebellious attitude toward authority is "maturity." By
implication, those who obey the Church's teaching must be immature,
stupid, or ill-informed.

Even worse are the effects of the media's outright misrepresentation
of the Church's teaching and of the views of Church officials. Catholics
who have not really studied the Council documents and the scriptures
depend largely on the media for information about these things. The
fact is that the Council did not teach what many in the media say it
teaches. Consider, for example, the way this Catholic "marriage and
divorce adjustment counselor" characterized the Church's reception of
the book *Human Sexuality*:

> Perhaps the closest the teaching church has come publicly to open
> discussion of sexual activity outside of marriage is found in *Human*

Sexuality (Paulist Press), the study commissioned but not endorsed by the Catholic Theological Society of America. Its findings, repudiated by some of the hierarchy, were seized upon with relief by many priests involved in counseling.[12]

Without making an explicitly false statement, this writer conveys the false impression that the most thoughtful and responsible members of the American Catholic Church generally welcomed *Human Sexuality*. To the contrary, many were shocked at the book. The writer does not mention that the American Bishops' Committee on Doctrine repudiated the book and issued a detailed statement pointing out its numerous deficiencies. For its part, the Vatican commended the American bishops for clarifying their stand on the Christian truths in question. Yet the Vatican also voiced concern:

> At the same time, the Congregation cannot fail to note its concern that a distinguished society of Catholic theologians would have arranged for the publication of this report in such a way as to give broad distribution to the erroneous principles and conclusions of this book and in this way provide a source of confusion among the people of God.[13]

This was a polite way of expressing shock at what's happening among some Catholic moral theologians.

Do Moral Theologians Corrupt Youth?

Indeed, one respected Catholic philosopher at Notre Dame University, Dr. Ralph McInerny, wrote an article entitled "Do Moral Theologians Corrupt Youth?" He describes how the 1976 Vatican Declaration on sexual morality,[14] a document reaffirming scriptural and traditional teaching on sexual morality, was received on the campus of perhaps the leading Catholic university in the United States:

> Despite the fact that we were discussing a serious document from Rome, there was a widespread tendency to think that either the church or scripture or both have not condemned the kind of conduct mentioned or if either or both has done so, this has been on the basis of a primitive understanding of human existence long since surpassed by intellectual giants like ourselves.[15]

McInerny characterizes *Human Sexuality* as a "scandalous," "confused," and "bizarre" document, but notes that it is being taken seriously. He points out that at Notre Dame the book is being used to rationalize sin:

Some few months ago a self-professed homosexual invoked this book in a series of articles in the Notre Dame student newspaper, and it was abundantly clear that he took comfort and corroboration from the book. If the authors could not foresee that they were apparently issuing carte blanche not only to individual homosexuals but to the homosexual ideology, then they are incapable of understanding their own words. Of course I do not suggest that they would flinch from such apparent approval. . . . If in moral matters sound doctrine is not a guarantee of good conduct, it is surely true that when the wells of doctrine are poisoned, bad conduct is inevitable. . . . Nowadays, when the clear doctrine of the church is muddied and confused by theologians allegedly speaking in her name, we run the risk of adopting the pagan morality of the world as if it were the fulfillment of the Christian ideal.

One thinks of millstones.[16]

McInerny makes a crucial point, one which must stay in the front of our minds as we survey the crisis of truth in the Catholic Church. The point is that the poisonous ideas in books such as *Human Sexuality* have the gravest possible practical consequences. They jeopardize the salvation of millions of Catholics. These are not interesting ideas, plausible or implausible, possibly true, possibly false, to be analyzed at leisure in a graduate seminar on moral theology. They are powerful ideas which lead people into real sin. They are used to justify contraception, masturbation, fornication, adultery, divorce, homosexuality, abortion, and other distortions of God's plan for sexuality as revealed to us in scripture, witnessed to in tradition, and reaffirmed by the pope and bishops teaching in union with him today.

The moral relativism that is increasingly espoused is often a strong component of official training programs, workshops, and seminars set up to "equip religious educators." Typical is the advice 1,200 religious educators were given by a featured speaker:

We have to allow for diversity in our moral teaching. . . . Honesty means that theology is an exercise of the intellect, not an exercise of the will. We can't expect everyone to be uniform in what they believe or say on moral issues. . . . [The Church] should enter a conversation not to say the last word but to say one of the words that will help the truth to be discovered. . . . The important thing about morality is to be with people as they make decisions and mistakes.[17]

There can be no doubt that poisonous moral ideas are not restricted to graduate seminars and campuses. They are heard frequently in

Catholic life today. For example, one issue of *Today's Parish* magazine, a popular journal aimed at active lay people, contained two articles which praised immorality.[18] One article, which we discussed in Chapter Two of this book, promoted bisexuality. Another promoted the moral legitimacy of active homosexuality. Consider the reasoning used in this article to justify homosexual activity.

> But doesn't the Church teach that *active* homosexual persons are sinning? Yes and no. The Church teaches that sex is for having children. This part of the Church's message rings as true as it ever did, and as it always will. But the Church also teaches that sex is for loving. It's for loving in marriage, and nowadays, the Church is not so sure that *all* sex-for-love outside marriage is sinful. Surely it is when new life is likely to be generated. People who play around with sex, and then find themselves with an unwanted pregnancy, often get abortions. This is the reason the Church opposes sex outside marriage—family stability for the security of offspring. It's a good reason. Let's hold on to it, you and I who are the Church. But this is not a problem in sex between two people of the same gender. . . . But doesn't the Bible condemn homosexual acts? That it surely does, and roundly. Genesis condemns the men of Sodom and Gomorrah for wishing to have sex with Lot's male guests—by raping them. It is not the homosexuality of mutual respect and sacrifice that Scripture condemns here.
>
> But what about Leviticus, and the Epistle to the Romans? Do they not call homosexuality "an abomination to the Lord?" Yes, but the outcry is heavily culturally conditioned. . . . Well, we've multiplied and filled the earth, and Jesus the Messiah is already here. Can it be that childless sex is no longer an abomination?[19]

This sort of gratuitous dismissal of clear scriptural teaching as "culturally conditioned" and therefore non-binding, this "reinterpretation" of scripture to justify immoral conduct, is a travesty of genuine scholarship. This author grossly misrepresents the teaching of the Catholic Church in an area where this teaching is crystal clear and totally consistent. The teaching of the Catholic Church today, as always, is that all sexual activity outside of life-long marriage is a violation of God's Word; this specifically includes masturbation, premarital sex, extra-marital sex, and the active practice of homosexuality. The Church distinguishes between homosexual inclinations and tendencies, and homosexual acts; only the latter, of course, are sinful. It expects the person with homosexual tendencies to resist temptation with the help of an active Christian life, and if unmarried, to live a godly single life, just as it expects the unmarried person with heterosexual temptations to resist them also and live a godly single life. The smug tone of this article and the condescending picking and choosing from among Church teaching and scriptural teaching is characteristic of what can only be called the active propaganda effort being made today to open Catholics and other Christians to false thinking and immoral behavior. Sadly, the scholarly community is often strangely silent in the face of such a mockery of scholarship.

The author of the *Today's Parish* article is a reputable Jesuit moral theologian. Perhaps because the article was perceived to be shocking, the editors seem to have made a special effort to list his "impeccable credentials" in detail:

Father Springer is Professor of Sexual Ethics and Bioethics at Maryknoll Seminary, New York. He holds the doctorate in Moral Theology from the Gregorian Pontifical University, Rome, where he was Instructor in Moral Theology before transferring to Fordham University, and a full professorship in Moral Theology at Woodstock, then the New York Jesuits' major seminary. Dr. Springer is the author of a score of articles on ethical and moral matters in the *New Catholic Encyclopedia, Theological Studies*, and elsewhere.[20]

Fr. Springer has much company in his effort to reinterpret the scriptural teaching on homosexual activity. There is a widespread effort today to win acceptance for the active practice of homosexuality as a viable Christian lifestyle. In recent years, many articles and books have been published pleading for the acceptance of active homosexual practice as permissible for Christians in certain circumstances. This effort seems to be particularly strong right now in the Catholic Church but is going on as well in the major Protestant churches[21] and even in conservative evangelical Protestant circles.[22]

The type of "reinterpretation" of scripture offered in Fr. Springer's article has provided a rationale for the founding of certain Catholic "ministries" to homosexuals that actually justify homosexual activity.[23] A new Protestant denomination, called the Metropolitan Community Churches, was recently founded on the basis of the acceptance of the active practice of homosexuality. This is a quote from a report on a sermon given at a local Metropolitan Community Church, meeting in facilities provided by a Presbyterian and Episcopal church:

Brothers and sisters . . . scripture has been turned around, misinterpreted in the area of homosexuality for years. . . . Their sin [Sodom and Gomorrah] was not that there was homosexuality there, but that the people were not hospitable, were not open to others.

The sermon went on to extol the virtues of being open to others.[24]

Just in the past few years, popular Catholic periodicals such as *U.S. Catholic*, *Commonweal*, *New Catholic World*, *Today's Parish*, *National Catholic Reporter*, and the *Notre Dame Magazine* have all published articles sympathetic to the active practice of homosexuality. Full-length books have also appeared justifying homosexual practice.[25] The arguments used are frequently similar. They are summed up well in an article in *Commonweal* by Fr. Edward Vacek, S.J., who taught at the Jesuit School of Theology in Chicago at the time the article appeared. He is now a member of the Jesuit faculty at Weston Theological Seminary in Cambridge, Massachusetts.

My own approach tries to discover the relevant biological, psychological, rational, and religious values. It then tries to weigh these values and make a judgment within an ethics of proportionality. In examining homosexuality, I find myself confronted by Jesus' demand (Lk 12:57) "Why can you not judge for yourselves what is the right course?" Stated briefly, my judgment is this. Homosexual actions are biologically deficient, but they may be psychologically healthy, the best available exercise of one's interpersonal freedom, and may even be a form of authentic Christian spirituality.[26]

Shortly after this article appeared, the theology faculty at Catholic University of America voted to invite Fr. Vacek to apply for a teaching position in their department. Fr. Vacek declined so as to be able to continue teaching in a Jesuit institution.[27]

"Reasoning" like Fr. Vacek's is often combined with emotional appeals to be "compassionate." The definition of "compassionate" in these instances usually means not disturbing somebody's peace by pointing out to them that they are sinning.[28]

These arguments for homosexual activity and other immoral acts do not appear in publications primarily directed toward specialists. They are published in popular magazines and in widely circulated books. Proponents of these views want to reach the widest possible audiences. Moral theologians give press interviews, deliver lectures, write articles, appear on television, and do all they can to influence the thinking and behavior of the Catholic population in directions that profoundly undermine God's Word.

In a public talk at a Franciscan renewal center, a leading moral theologian, on the faculty of a leading Catholic university, is reported as saying that extra-marital sexual relations in certain circumstances may be morally permissible in the sight of God. He repeated his views when questioned about them in a subsequent interview.[29] Another priest travels around the country attacking the scriptural and Church teaching on divorce and remarriage, as he "ministers" to the divorced. His message:

> If the marriage sacrament has to involve a loving relationship, if there is no longer a loving relationship, there is no marriage and the people are not bound by it.[30]

This atmosphere of moral relativism is so pervasive that one American bishop has stated that, "It is very difficult to find a professor of moral theology in the Roman Catholic Church today who is not affected by consequentialism, situationism, or some 'ism' of that kind."[31] While there are undoubtedly many faithful theologians today serving the Church, it seems very often that the dominant tone in many institutions and programs is set by those giving out an "uncertain sound" or outrightly undermining God's Word.

Catholics listen to this false teaching and act on it. Millions of Catholics are having abortions, divorcing and remarrying, engaging in homosexual activity, adultery and fornication, masturbation and artificial contraception, all of this with a "good" or at least not a seriously troubled conscience. It would be foolish to think there is no link between the great increase in recent years of Catholic acceptance of immoral practices and the corruption of teaching and counseling in the area of sexual morality.

The Focus on Feelings

Exhortations to "be adult," to "decide for yourself," and to "follow your conscience" are common in the Church today. Unfortunately, they are often invitations to take feelings and secular ideologies as one's primary moral guides. Adult Catholics are encouraged to engage in a "dialogue" between the teaching of the Church and that of contemporary society. But more often than not, the dice are loaded: secular society is almost always the dominant partner in this discussion. The ordinary "educated" Catholic's experience has become too weak and subject to criticism to stand up to it. Contemporary society voices its views loud and clear. It is particularly insistent on the importance of "doing your own thing." In practice, this often translates into "follow your feelings." In many circles, it is deemed a positive advance in human maturity to abandon rationality and "let go."

Increasingly, many people decide what is right and wrong on the basis of subjective opinion which is heavily based on what "feels" right, good, or pleasurable. One of the greatest goods many suppose one human being can do is to make another person "feel good"; one of the greatest wrongs is to make someone else "feel bad." The focus in much of pastoral practice is increasingly on whether one "feels" guilty about a particular action. Less frequently do pastors consider the objective morality of the matter or the possibility that the Lord has clearly revealed his mind about it. One pastoral center in Canada works with unmarried couples living together. Its rationale: "We work with couples who are living together . . . that's their decision. We try to help them deal with their conflicts."[32]

"Guilt" is generally regarded today as a neurotic state that should almost always be done away with by "affirmation." Of course, neurotic guilt which is not based in actual wrongdoing should be relieved by suitable effective methods. But it is seldom asked whether there is a concrete basis for the guilt, whether the guilty party should repent, make restitution, and undergo moral change. The presumption seems to be that "guilt" feelings are regrettable, and that the unfortunates who find themselves in this state need help getting over it.

This modern focus on feelings greatly diminishes the range of human freedom and dignity. Today's pastoral care often exclusively focuses on subjective questions of blame and "mitigating" circumstances, rather than on the objective rightness or wrongness of specific actions. The fact is that all actions have two dimensions—one dealing with the objective order of reality and God's Word, the other with subjective responsibility and blame. When pastoral care becomes a form of therapy that deals with feelings and subjective states rather than objective right and wrong, it neglects a dimension crucial for moral guidance and human freedom and dignity.

The scriptures and the tradition of the Church insist on the importance of this objective, moral dimension. They teach that, while subjective mitigating factors are indeed relevant in gauging responsibility, there remains a wide range of freedom in which human beings are held responsible for their actions.

Indeed, sinners instinctively deny responsibility for their actions. Adam and Eve were the first to show this very human characteristic. Adam tried to shift the blame to God and to the woman: "The woman whom you put here with me—she gave me fruit from the tree, and so I ate it" (Gn 3:12). Eve blamed the serpent: "The serpent tricked me into it so I ate it" (Gn 3:13). But God rejected these excuses and held them accountable for their decisions and actions.

Scripture even warns that we may be responsible not only for those actions whose moral consequences we know, but also for those we commit in ignorance of God's Word. Jesus said that "the slave who knew his master's wishes but did not prepare to fulfill them will get a severe beating, whereas the one who did not know them and who nonetheless deserved to be flogged will get off with fewer stripes" (Lk

12:47-48). Jesus indicates that the punishment will be less for those who do wrong in ignorance but they will be held responsible nonetheless. Jesus was not ignorant of the psychological depths of human beings (cf. Jn 2:25); he participated in their creation! Both scripture and the Church teach that it is the creature's responsibility to seek out God's will and Word in a particular matter. We are not to passively drift into action presuming that God has no opinion or that his opinion is not accessible to us.

Even our own human laws can illustrate the point. If you disobey driving laws in a foreign country because you are unfamiliar with them, you are still responsible in the eyes of the law. Ignorance is no excuse. Everyone is responsible for learning the law of the land in which they live.

The same holds true for the teaching of the Church. We have a responsibility to form our consciences soundly. Before we act, we must seek out a reliable source to help us determine the teaching of Christ and the Church.[33] As genuine Christians, we are committed to act in situations as Christ would.

This approach is all too rare today. Christians are urged to follow their consciences, and to shape them according to the propaganda of secular ideologies and to the sway of their feelings. For example, one survey of divorced churchgoers in California found that only nine percent of the men and twenty-seven percent of the women were abstaining from sexual activity. Some of the comments of these individuals justifying their behavior reveal the extent to which subjective feelings are replacing the Word of God in the area of sexual morality:

> "I don't feel condemned by God."
> "My personal faith affirms God's laws for the whole of man, not unreal, antiquated rules."
> "Christ wants us to live abundant lives; to me that includes sex."[34]

Or consider this remark by a Catholic layman:

> I was uneasy when my oldest daughter left for California to live with her friend. Later I realized my chief problem was with family, friends, and neighbors, whom I thought might be critical of my ability to maintain family stability. After examining the situation, I realized my daughter's relationship was monogamous and in no sense living in "sin." . . . Such "arrangements" may be the solution for divorced and widowed people who need companionship and intimacy that is not constant and continual.[35]

The moral elements of human actions are increasingly being diminished in moral theology and pastoral practice today. They are being reduced to matters requiring either a therapeutic adjustment of "hang-ups," or "inner healing." Of course therapy and inner healing can be useful adjuncts in pastoral care, but they cannot replace the need to take responsibility for one's actions. We can be forgiven for our sins—but only if we first repent and confess what we have done. Today, however, forgiveness is considered somewhat superfluous. Why should we seek forgiveness if one is hardly ever free as a moral agent, or if God is so merciful that he overlooks all sin? These ideas make a mockery of the sacrifice offered for us on the cross; they are blasphemous, presumptuous affronts to the mercy of God. As Ralph McInerny comments:

There is nothing we can do that God is unwilling to forgive. . . . There is, however, a sentimental understanding of the divine mercy which would have it that, since God will forgive anything, there is nothing to forgive. It is suggested that since Christ did not avoid the company of thieves, adulterers, prostitutes, and the like, there is nothing wrong with the conduct from which one is denominated a thief, an adulterer, a prostitute. But, of course, Christ does not love the sinner *as a sinner*. He wants us to repent, to amend our lives, and to sin no more.

How radically Christian morality is trivialized by the suggestion that sins are not sins, that moral wrongs are somehow all right, acceptable as such! Mercy loses its meaning if there is nothing to forgive, and it is a profound disservice to the sinner to persuade him that he has nothing to be sorry for, that he can even flaunt his sin and be thereby noble and admirable. The one thing some moral theologians seem sure of is that condemnation of immorality is somehow immoral. If their point is that it is the sin and not the sinner who is condemned, the English language provides a variety of ways of making it clearly.[36]

The focus on feelings in pastoral care and education is not simply an emphasis affecting individuals. It is also changing the whole tone of Church life. For some, Christian life is now focused on psychological states: the search for "affirmation" and "empathy"; the emphasis on "vulnerability," with its consequence of always being "hurting"; the quest for and addiction to "intimacy" (often with its barely submerged coy sexual innuendo); the celebration of "authentic personhood," which is accompanied by orchestration of cooing affirmation and affectionate stroking.

This feeling-centered "spirituality" has convinced many people that they are not functioning as normal human beings unless they are constantly "affirmed" in their "vulnerability" and "unique personhood." A school of Christian professionals has grown up to serve these new emotional needs. Many of them are receiving their training in Catholic seminaries dominated by the feeling-centered psychology. A prominent Catholic psychiatrist has expressed his concern about the impact of this training on the psychological condition of today's seminarians and recently ordained priests:

> In my opinion, current anxieties about seminary training in America are well grounded indeed. Not only is theology slowly being replaced by psychology, but what makes it even worse, by psychology of the worst kind. It is the kind that has spawned a life—in and out of the seminary—outlined in the perverse pastoral guidelines advocated by the theologian-authors of *Human Sexuality*.
>
> Having spoken with large numbers of seminarians and priests— and religious men and women—in the privacy of the consultation room and on my many lecture tours throughout the North American continent these past 30 years, I would be the last one to deny the urgent need for changes in seminary formation in the Western world. But that is not to say that just any change will do. In fact, the impact of the psychologism and theological quicksand of the Seventies on the psyches of the graduates of these deteriorating seminaries, promises to be far worse than that of the repressive climate of our pre-Vatican II seminaries. These future priests can be expected to develop a new type of psychic disorder resembling, in greatly magnified and intensified form, the psychic state of the spoiled child. The child who, because of premature gratification of all his desires and unrestrained expression of his emotions, has lost the capacity to find delight in all that is good, true and beautiful. The child who, because of immature or misguided educators, lacks the harmonious integration of his psychic powers, and thus the necessary inner order and self-restraint of the truly mature person.
>
> Such a "spoiled" priest will not be able to move others to the Source of all good because he himself cannot be moved. He will not inspire young men to a priestly vocation. Moreover, his disordered psychic state will be less likely to respond to therapy than that of the pre-Vatican II seminarian and priest, whose scrupulosity, obsessive-compulsive neurosis, or deprivation neurosis can now be treated successfully, and, of course, prevented.
>
> . . . Not many Catholics, not even members of organizations dedicated to the promotion of priestly vocations, seem to be aware of the extent of the on-going deterioration of American seminaries, much less of the negative forces directing it.[37]

A particularly disturbing development in the education of our future priests is the growing popularity of "sexuality seminars" designed to "desensitize" seminarians to all kinds of disordered sexual behavior, helping them to get in touch with their "feelings" about sexuality and become "empathetic and non-judgmental" in their ministries and personal lives. In one seminary, a sexuality seminar used color films which explicitly depicted perverse sexual behavior. Heavy pressure was exerted on the seminarians to attend the seminar and to view and discuss the films. When this scandal became public, it was further discovered that the films had been produced and supplied by a sex center in San Francisco that has developed materials explicitly designed to break down moral inhibitions and to present sexual immorality as attractive and desirable. Some members of the board of the center are well-known opponents of Catholic morality.[38]

The Media and the Redefinition of Sin

The destructive effects of this undermining of morality are illustrated by the way the media discusses the Catholic Church. I am going to discuss in some detail an article on the Catholic Church in Australia that appeared in a secular Australian magazine. Written by a Catholic and based on interviews with "leading Catholic spokesmen," the article shows how deeply rooted the moral chaos has become in a country far distant from the centers of progressive theology in the United States and Europe. Some of the Australian Catholics' "leading spokesmen" appear to be consumed by a desire to be in line with the "latest thinking" and the "latest findings," no matter how suspect or corrupt these may be. Indeed, Catholics' desire to be perceived as "up-to-date" is one of the most powerful forces contributing to the undermining of Christian morality in the Church today, not only in Australia but in many countries.

The Catholic writer of the article uses emotional, political language to describe the change he sees in the Australian Church:

> The freer society of the 70's has shaken the once-rigid Irish-Australian Church and produced an institution which is more liberal, more relaxed about sex and more aware that religion should aim to help people live their lives, not oppress them by inflexibly laying down the law.[39]

The article points out that statistics show that Australian Catholics are having proportionately as many divorces and abortions as the rest of the Australian population. No longer is there a significant difference between the moral behavior of Catholics and non-Catholics in two areas where Catholic teaching has been clear and consistent. The writer declares that the Australian Church has undergone a "moral reformation." The change, however, is not uniform throughout the Church.

Some "problematic" conservative bishops oppose it, in contrast to the "good" liberal bishops and dioceses who welcome it. But the writer expresses hope for the future, since much of the change is embodied in what is now the Church's dominant theology. It is embodied too he claims "in the training of priests and in the teaching of religion in schools."[40]

Several points here are especially noteworthy. The writer accurately notes that the widening discrepancy between official Catholic teaching on sexual morality and actual practice among Catholics exerts a great pressure on bishops and other leaders of the Church. The response to this problem in certain quarters of the Church has been to narrow the gap between teaching and practice by changing the teaching. In this case this "solution" is no solution at all. It is unfaithfulness to the teaching of Christ and distortion of His Word. The real solution lies in the other direction, namely, in helping people live according to the teaching of Christ.

Another striking feature of this article is the association of "conservative" with bad, and "liberal" with good. "Conservative" bishops are portrayed as "repressive" and "rigid," while "liberals" are judged "understanding" and "compassionate." This tactic of the secular press and the secularized Catholic press has formed the thinking of post-conciliar Catholics far more profoundly than we have perhaps realized. The media now influences the way Catholics think about Church policy far more strongly than the Church itself does.

The writer of the article also claims that the new situational morality has become entrenched as the de facto "official" teaching in many seminaries and Church schools. That this morality stands in opposition to the true teaching of the Church seems to make no difference. The article goes on to discuss the intellectual roots of the "moral reformation":

> An important factor in this "moral reformation" has been the Church's recently-gained ability to rid itself of its irrational fear of psychology, psychiatry, sociology and other social sciences. For the past decade or so the Church has been drawing on the insights of these disciplines. This, together with the influence of some American theology, has helped the Church evolve a new concept of sin. The changed idea of sin underlies the shift in attitudes toward sexuality.[41]

This "changed idea of sin" consists mainly of inventing euphemisms for immorality. With the help of the social sciences, of psychiatry, and of certain American theologians the language of sin is changed. We are said to no longer commit sin. Rather, we have "learning experiences" or "inevitable life transition experiences." We are exonerated by our innocent "immature behavior" and our "doubtfully free acts."

Applauding this shift in the Australian Church, the Catholic author of the article reflects on changes in the traditional distinctions between mortal and venial sins:

> Happily, the Church's thinking has progressed. According to moral theologian Dr. John Hill [who teaches moral theology at Sydney's St. Patrick's Seminary] the concept of sin now centers on whether one's relationship with God has been shattered—not on the mere committing of specified acts. . . . In the new concept mortal sin is seen as being fairly hard to commit. . . . Hill said moral theologians were expanding the idea of venial sin and shrinking the notion of mortal sin. . . . "Sin is a personal thing," he said. "The question is: how grave does an individual human act have to be to rupture a relationship with God?"[42]

The Church has already answered this question: specific sinful acts when they involve serious matters are seriously wrong. Yet this "shrinking of the concept of mortal sin" now being undertaken by some moral theologians is having its effect on millions of Catholics. Many now believe that perhaps only great sinners like Hitler have done anything serious enough to actually "rupture" a relationship with God, and perhaps even Hitler was too troubled and unbalanced to be able to act freely. While Christians must certainly pay primary attention to the quality of their underlying relationship with God, they should not commit seriously wrong acts on the doubtful assurance of some moral theologians that a "mortal sin is almost impossible to commit." Scripture and the Church clearly point out that people who indulge in certain specified acts are excluded from the kingdom of God. Christians ignore this, reinterpret it, or dismiss it at their eternal peril. As Paul told the Corinthians:

> Can you not realize that the unholy will not fall heir to the kingdom of God? Do not deceive yourselves: no fornicators, idolaters, or adulterers, no sodomites, thieves, misers, or drunkards, no slanderers or robbers will inherit God's kingdom. And such were some of you; but you have been washed, consecrated, justified in the name of our Lord Jesus Christ and in the Spirit of our God.
>
> Do you not see that your bodies are members of Christ? Would you have me take Christ's members and make them the members of a prostitute? God forbid! Can you not see that the man who is joined to a prostitute becomes one body with her? Scripture says, "The two shall become one flesh." But whoever is joined to the Lord becomes one spirit with him. Shun lewd conduct. Every other sin a man commits is outside his body, but the fornicator sins against his own

body. You must know that your body is a temple of the Holy Spirit, who is within—the Spirit you have received from God. You are not your own. (1 Cor 6:9-11, 15-20)

Nevertheless, Christians today, encouraged by some moral theologians, are seriously distorting the whole concept of sin. The casual treatment of certain "specific" acts assures that more and more people will commit them. Witness this statement from the moral theologian quoted above: "Premarital sex is something that is very often excusable. One has to be sympathetic to young people."[43]

The large number of marriage annulments which have been granted by diocesan marriage tribunals in recent years exemplifies the change in the Church's pastoral practice. One Church official quoted in the Australian article was encouraged by the fact that his diocese has processed a greatly increased number of requests for annulments and that, in 1979, had granted more than ninety percent of them. The factor usually cited to explain this dramatically soaring rate of annulments is a new definition, drawn from the modern social sciences, of what constitutes maturity and freedom. Fr. Hill commented that "Canon law is conditioned by psychological and sociological opinions of the time."[44]

Is this always progress, we might ask, or is it using the contemporary "traditions" of men to subvert the law of God? Are we using "modern thinking" in some cases to obscure the true nature of something that God has joined together and will judge accordingly? Are the increasing numbers of annulments granted by diocesan marriage tribunals all reflecting the teaching of the Church as expressed by John Paul II?

> Our Lord Jesus Christ himself insisted on the essential indissolubility of marriage. His Church must not allow his teaching on this matter to be obscured. She would be untrue to her Master if she did not insist, as he did, that whoever divorces his or her marriage partner and marries another commits adultery (Mk 10:11-12). The unbreakable union between husband and wife is a great mystery or sacramental sign in reference to Christ and the Church. It is by preserving the clarity of this sign that we will best manifest the love that it signifies: the supernatural love that united Christ and the Church, that binds together the Savior and those whom he saves.[45]

The pope has expressed concern about the increase in annulments:

> If, among the evils of divorce, there is also that of making the celebration of marriage less serious and binding, to the extent that

today it has lost due consideration among a good many young people, it is to be feared that also the sentences of the declaration of matrimonial nullity would lead to the same existential and psychological perspective, if they were multiplied as easy and hasty pronouncements.[46]

In a talk to university students, he boldly called for clear thinking and truthfulness in this critical area:

Learn to think, to speak and to act according to the principles of simplicity and evangelical clarity: "Yes, yes, no, no." Learn to call white white, and black black—evil evil, and good good. Learn to call sin sin, and do not call it liberation and progress, even if the whole of fashion and propaganda were contrary.[47]

Have some significant segments of moral theology and pastoral practice in the Church reached the point today where the words of the prophets are again fulfilled? Are some priests no longer distinguishing between what is clean and unclean, between what is holy and unholy? Are false prophets strengthening those who do evil, saying "peace, peace," where there is no peace?

We have had ample warnings about what is happening. The pope and other bishops have deplored the deadening of the sense of sin, the minimizing of its gravity, and the discounting of the grave importance of specific acts of sin. In the words of John Paul II:

Modern man experiences the threat of spiritual indifference and even of the death of conscience; and this death is something deeper than sin; it is the killing of the sense of sin. Today so many factors contribute to killing conscience in the men of our time, and this corresponds to that reality which Christ called "sin against the Holy Spirit." This sin begins when the word of the cross no longer speaks to man as the last cry of love, which has the power of rending hearts.[48]

Cardinal William Baum, former chairman of the U.S. Bishops Committee on Doctrine and now Prefect of the Congregation for Catholic Education and Seminaries, has said that

the sacramental or symbolic relation between man, God and the world makes it tragically possible for the human person to violate his vocation and dignity by means of single acts, not just by a "whole-life's orientation" or corruption of his "fundamental option."[49]

Cardinal Baum quoted this section of *Persona Humane*, the Declaration on Sexual Ethics by the Congregation for the Doctrine of the Faith:

> According to the Church's teaching, mortal sin, which is opposed to God, does not consist only in formal and direct resistance to the commandment of charity. It is equally to be found in this opposition to authentic love which is included in every deliberate transgression, in serious matters, of each of the moral laws. . . .
>
> A person therefore sins mortally not only when his action comes from direct contempt for love of God and neighbor, but also when he consciously and freely, for whatever reason, chooses something which is seriously disordered. For in this choice, as has been said above, there is already included contempt for the divine commandment: the person turns himself away from God and loses charity.[50]

In other words, serious wrongdoing is not merely a matter of "lifelong intention" or change in one's "fundamental option." Specific acts, freely chosen and involving serious matters, are mortal sins. This teaching of the Church faithfully reflects the New Testament teaching as well as the Old Testament emphasis on individual responsibility and the significance of specific acts in determining one's destiny:

> As for you, son of man, tell your countrymen: The virtue which a man has practiced will not save him on the day that he sins; neither will the wickedness that a man has done bring about his downfall on the day that he turns from his wickedness. . . .
>
> Yet your countrymen say, "The way of the Lord is not fair!"; but it is their way that is not fair. When a virtuous man turns away from what is right and does wrong, he shall die for it. But when a wicked man turns away from wickedness and does what is right and just, because of this he shall live. And still you say, "The way of the Lord is not fair!"? I will judge every one of you according to his ways, O house of Israel. (Ez 33:12, 17-20)

Many in the Church seems to be rushing headlong into the arms of the spirit of the age. "I think the Church's attitude reflects the trends of the society we're in," claims an unidentified suburban priest, quoted in the article on Australian Catholicism. "The 50's were much different from the 70's, even in common standards of sexual behavior. The Church is part of society and its attitude has changed, too."[51] This betrays an all too common lack of clarity regarding what it means to be "in the world, but not of it."

The Future of Catholic Morality

Where, we might ask, are many in the Catholic Church heading with this "evolution" of thinking about morality, with this "redefinition" of sin? A glimpse of the future can be found in the disintegration of Christian truth and morality in Christian denominations that have vigorously pursued this course before the Catholic Church did. We have set out on a path other Christians have taken before us, and the fruits of their choice are already apparent if we care to look. Will we listen to the Archbishop of Canterbury, as he worries about the flood of divorces in ostensibly Anglican England?

It will take hard thinking and serious action on the part of a great many of us if the present landslide is to be stopped. . . . A country whose divorces have multiplied by four in the space of 30 years is a country in danger.[52]

As relevant as the Archbishop's words are, it is ironic to note that segments of the worldwide Anglican communion have in many ways led the way in the moral decline we are now seeing even within God's people. In 1930 the Anglican Church became the first Christian Church to officially reverse the traditional Christian teaching against the use of artificial contraception. In 1973, the Episcopal Church in the U.S. abandoned the Christian teaching on the dissolubility of Christian marriage and allowed the remarriage of divorced people whose first marriages were valid. In 1976, the same church reversed the long standing Christian teaching against abortion. In 1981, it approved the ordination of divorced and remarried Christians.

Have we considered the implications of the "life-journey" of one of the founders of the Methodist American University Christian Movement— a woman who is continuing to work on revealing "heterosexism as an institution that politically restricts women," and who left her husband to live in a commune with lesbian feminists? Despite her activity in Christian institutions, this woman's commitment had obviously shifted to certain movements and values originating outside Christianity. As her "life-journey" progressed she came to view her Christian work as a tool for promulgating secularist feminist theories:

I also started to use my church connections to travel around speaking about feminism; and through the Mobilization Committee To End the War in Vietnam, I was sent to Hanoi to represent the growing feminist movement—and that was in 1970. . . . In 1971, I started to work on a special issue of *Motive*, a Methodist student movement magazine, on lesbian feminism.[53]

Perhaps another "life-journey" story—this one from an official in the Methodist Church—will give us pause. A Catholic reporter covering a "Conference on Women and Religion" gave this report of the woman's testimony:

> They agreed that male images of God and male rules of religion must be replaced. But by what?
> United Methodist Church official and author _____ took a step toward answering this question by calling for a new "feminist ethic." She then took on the most frustrating and divisive ethical question of our time: abortion. . . . She described abortion in a moving, personal way. . . . [and] provided the conference's most dramatic moment when she described publicly for the first time the abortion she herself had after she conceived a child by a man who is not her husband. She is married and has two children, which added to her anguish:
> "For weeks before the abortion I lay around in a torture of fear, guilt, anger and self-doubt. How could I, a woman in mid-life, a professional with graduate degrees, a woman who knows all about birth control and abortion, a Christian who promised when she married to be faithful to her husband, a feminist who should have gotten beyond letting her emotions run away with her body—how could I have gotten into such a mess?"
> She and the man—who went with her to the hospital—mourned together "the cutting off of possibilities for life which in other times and circumstances might have been able to be fulfilled." After the abortion _____ said she felt tremendous healing. "Next to my childbirths . . . this I can truly say is the holiest experience of my life! . . . Feminist ethics, I think, must begin with the telling of our stories. When the experiences of over half the earth's population have gone unexpressed, unexamined, how can anyone presume to set up an ethical system purporting to judge according to some universal standard, motivation and human behavior?"

The Catholic reporter ends her story with a very good question:

> What is the new feminist ethic? Who can honestly say? The question has only been asked. . . . As women confront our religious and ethical systems, demanding that our experiences be taken into account, that our stories be heard, it is hoped, but not automatically assured,

that the outcome will be a better—or even a more compassionate—world. At this point women know what we are going *from*. Exactly where we are headed is not yet clear.[54]

It is indeed clear where women influenced by the feminist ethic and others who have rejected God's Word are going from; they are leaving behind the one, true God, and the truth of His Word. We have before us the terrifying experience of growing numbers of Christians substituting their personal experiences, feelings, and anti-Christian ideologies for the Word of God, and coming to call "holy" what God calls an abomination, and calling an abomination what God calls "holy."

In some circles, the tragic violation of God's Word and will is even ennobled with religious ceremonies. Consider this portion of a religious ceremony used to "solemnize" a divorce between two Christians:

Officient: Dearly beloved, we have gathered here to solemnize the end of one time in Matthew's and Anne's lives and the beginning of another. We are so made that we cannot live in isolation from our fellow men, but neither can we live too closely joined with them. We are social beings, but also individual selves, and it is the rhythm of union and separation that enables us to live in the communion which sustains our selves, and in the solitude which nourishes our community. . . . Let us pray. Almighty and loving God, who has ordered that seasons shall change and that human lives shall proceed by change, we ask thy blessing upon thy children who now, in their commitment to thee, have severed their commitment to each other. Send them forth in the bond of peace. When they meet sustain them in their liberty. Keep them both reminded that thy love flows upon and through them both. Sanctify them in their lives, deaths, and resurrections, by the power of thy Holy Spirit, and for the sake of thy Son, Jesus Christ our Lord. . . . Go in peace.[55]

The words of Ezekiel come to mind:

Her priests violate my law and profane what is holy to me; they do not distinguish between the sacred and the profane, nor teach the difference between the unclean and the clean; they pay no attention to my sabbaths, so that I have been profaned in their midst.
(Ez 22:26)

For the very reason that they led my people astray, saying, "peace!' when there was no peace, and that, as one built a wall, they would cover it with whitewash, say then to the whitewashers: I will bring down a flooding rain; hailstones shall fall, and a stormwind shall break out. And when the wall has fallen will you not be asked: Where is the whitewash you spread on? (Ez 13:10-12)

I believe we can avoid God's judgment on false teaching and morality only by responding to Pope John Paul II's reaffirmation of Catholic truth with something like Church-wide repentance and change, and by Church-wide discipline of such wisdom and courage that it effectively deals with what can only be described as established corruption. May God help us and give us strength!

Part Two

What Should We Do?

IN THE FIRST PART of this book we have considered certain aspects of the Church's current situation. We have particularly attempted to answer the question "Where are we?" as it pertains to matters of basic Christian truth. In so doing we have especially discussed the widespread undermining of basic Christian beliefs that touch on the foundations of faith, morality, and mission. Many other topics of course are relevant to the Church's situation today, but these are the ones this book is primarily concerned with.

Part II will attempt to provide help in answering the question "What should we do?" in response to the crisis of truth in which the Church now finds itself. Again, we will consider only a few of the relevant factors. A complete analysis would involve many other factors and would be considerably beyond the scope of this book. In order not to be misunderstood I want to clearly say that I am fully aware that the Church confronted important and serious problems before the Second Vatican Council. Indeed, only in the context of these problems is it possible to fully understand some of the post-conciliar overreaction. I especially have in mind problems such as the exercise of authority by individuals in a truly oppressive manner without adequate safeguards; the exclusive identification of the Church with the hierarchy and not the whole people of God; the pride and triumphalistic attitudes that made it difficult, if not impossible, to exercise certain forms of humble service in relationship to other Christian bodies and the world at large; the restriction of theological and philosophical inquiry to models from previous ages; and perhaps an overemphasis on institution and rules and not enough on the Church as the body of Christ and the Holy Spirit as the effective power enabling Christians to live the Christian life.

When I discuss certain aspects of the post-conciliar period in the following chapters, I do so to identify elements that have contributed significantly to the current confusion over basic Christian truths. This does not mean that I consider other factors and dynamics irrelevant and unimportant. However, in a book of restricted scope, I have chosen to concentrate on those issues I consider to be most relevant to the matter at hand.

CHAPTER NINE

Seeing and Not Seeing

THE CATHOLIC CHURCH will not be able to respond adequately to the crisis of truth unless Catholics—especially those with pastoral responsibilities—parents, lay leaders, priests, religious superiors, bishops— face the current situation squarely. I do not want to deny that some aspects of the Church's situation today are encouraging. The Church is blessed with many men and women of great faith and talent. In some regions, even in some entire nations, the Church is relatively healthy and vigorous. There are bright spots and great opportunities. However, as we have attempted to show in this book, the Church is embroiled in a crisis. Broad currents and trends inside and outside the Church are weakening it. Great masses of Catholics have not been properly evangelized, formed in the faith, and incorporated into local church bodies, and are particularly vulnerable to being blown about by "every wind of doctrine."

A statement like this may well have been true of the Catholic people in almost any time in the history of the Church. Today, however, the general lack of cohesion, unity, and commitment among Catholics leaves them vulnerable to anti-Christian forces that are worldwide in scope and growing stronger. Modern secular culture has a stronger hold on the minds of many Catholics today than does the teaching of the Church. In the Third World, the Church is under growing pressure from Marxist, right-wing, and Islamic governments and movements. The secularized states of the developed countries are expunging all traces of the Christian culture which once provided protection and support for the Christian life.

More seriously, the Church's strength is eroding from the inside.

Catholics are cooperating with, and even welcoming, political and intellectual forces that are hostile to the Church. This has happened because many Catholics have begun to lose their grasp of and commitment to basic Christian truths. A very real corruption of basic doctrine, moral behavior, spirituality, and mission is now apparent in many places, not just in isolated instances.

The Church's prospects would be difficult enough if it had to contend with only a continuation of the current unhappy situation. However, the Church must also face the probability that the pressures on it will intensify and the environment it inhabits will become more hostile. Sober men and women today predict major dislocation in the world economy. Resource shortages, media manipulation, punitive social and legal measures, political terrorism, social upheaval, and even war are happening now and may well worsen later. Many Catholics today do not have the organization, commitment, and loyalty to cope with this challenge and come out as effective witnesses to Christ.

Unless God intervenes in response to the cry of his people, large segments of the Christian population may for all practical purposes abandon the faith. If there is a serious intensification of hostility toward the Church, or a political and economic collapse, hostile ideologies, anti-Christian governments, and evil spiritual forces could well decimate a lukewarm, uncertain Church. At stake is nothing less than the continued existence of the Catholic Church in anything like its present size or strength.

The first step toward dealing with the Church's situation is to face it squarely. To do so, however, those responsible must remove and overcome obstacles to a clear and accurate assessment of the Church's situation.

Obstacles to Seeing

When they ponder the Church's severe problems, many Catholics almost automatically declare themselves to be optimistic. Among some leaders, optimism is almost an official policy. This optimism sometimes flows from genuine Christian hope and trust in Christ's promise to be with the Church through all time. Often, however, this official optimism misunderstands both Christian hope and Christ's promise. It operates as a defense mechanism that blocks clear seeing, permitting "business as usual" while masking the radical adjustments that the actual situation and God's Word truly demand.

Authentic Christian hope is the confidence that Jesus' victory foreshadows the victory of those who are faithful to him (Heb 6:17-20). Christian hope does not excuse negligence. We deal with our sin by acknowledging it and repenting, not by pretending it isn't there or presuming on forgiveness. Refusal to face sin only makes matters worse. As the psalmist prayed:

As long as I would not speak, my bones wasted away
   with my groaning all the day,
For day and night your hand was heavy upon me;
   my strength was dried up as by the heat of summer.
Then I acknowledged my sin to you,
   my guilt I covered not.
I said, "I confess my faults to the Lord,"
   and you took away the guilt of my sin.
For this shall every faithful man pray to you in time of stress.
                                            (Ps 32:3-6)

What often passes for Christian hope these days is presumption. Many optimistic Christians are blind to the actual requirements for God's blessing. A false understanding of Christian hope keeps many from seeing that our situation requires repentance.

Christ's promise to be with the Church till the end of time has been similarly misunderstood and abused (Mt 28:20). The Catholic Church commonly understands this promise to mean that in the final eventuality the pope and the bishops teaching in union with him will be preserved from error when officially teaching on faith and morals, and that the true understanding of the gospel will therefore be maintained. Christ's promise does *not* mean—as many think—that the Church as we know it will be preserved. The pope and the bishops teaching in union with him will be preserved from error in their official teaching, but the Church that they govern may well yield to infidelity, confusion, and decay. Indeed, this has happened to the Church before. In the fourth century, whole segments of the Church—including many bishops and priests—were led astray by Arianism, a heresy which denied the true divinity of Jesus. The heresy was so powerful that secular authority was invoked to exile Pope Liberius and other orthodox bishops.

It is also quite possible for the Church to virtually disappear from whole regions of the world where it was once powerful. This happened to the strong churches of North Africa after the time of Augustine and to the Pauline churches of Asia Minor. Nothing in Christ's promise to remain with the Church assures that large regional, national, or international expressions of the Church cannot disappear through lukewarmness, infidelity, or persecution.

Persecution can strengthen the Church, but it can also reveal and exploit its weaknesses. For example, the French Revolution first split the French Catholic Church, and then, through persecution, provoked widespread apostasy among bishops, priests, and people. One historian described the consequences of persecution this way:

> With a sound instinct those who thus sought to destroy the Church concentrated their attention upon the priests. . . . Of the eighty-five bishops of the Constitutional Church, twenty-four abdicated their office, while a further twenty-three specifically apostatized, renouncing their faith. . . . If more than half the episcopacy thus bowed to the storm, the proportion of the lower clergy who did so was probably even larger.[1]

God's treatment of his chosen people under the Old Covenant offers a relevant and sobering parallel. God's eternal covenant with the Hebrew people did not mean he overlooked their sin, negligence, lukewarmness, immoral behavior, corruption of worship, and accommodation to the surrounding pagan cultures. When his people failed to repent, he punished them. His chosen people suffered economic difficulty and military defeat, long-term exile, oppression at the hands of brutal powers like Assyria and Babylon, and finally the destruction of Jerusalem itself and dispersal and exile throughout the world. Many of these chastisements were specifically directed against the negligence of the leaders of the people, especially their failure to diligently uphold the Word of God and administer discipline. The Israelites were guilty of presumption about their status as God's chosen people. Their misunderstanding of his eternal covenantal promises blinded them to the facts of their infidelity. They failed to do what was necessary to correct their sins and avoid judgment.

The same psychological blocks that exist among Catholics today plagued the leaders of the Israelites. The prophet Jeremiah lamented that his people indulged in false optimism:

> Woe is me! I am undone,
>   my wound is incurable;
> Yet I had thought:
>   if I make light of my wound, I can bear it. (Jer 10:19)

By the time Jeremiah spoke these words, it was too late. The time for repentance had passed. It was time for judgment. As disaster approached, the prophet laid bare the defense that had prevented the people from seeing and responding to the situation facing Israel from within and without: "My wound is incurable; yet . . . if I make light of my wound, I can bear it."

The same dynamic is at work within the Church today. Many Catholics think, "If I minimize the seriousness of these problems, I can bear them." Such an attitude is, I believe, behind much of the "Christian optimism" and even the "Catholic pride" within the Church today.

Catholics, especially Catholic leaders, have good reason to fear the problems facing the Church and to doubt their ability to cope with them. Yet a policy of minimizing problems is self-deluding. If it breeds passivity and prevents repentance and the seeking of God's will, it can be a sin that must itself be repented of.

Reductionist Analysis

Self-deluding optimism often functions along with other attitudes that block a realistic assessment of the Church's condition. Optimistic Catholics and their pastors tend to look for reasons to be optimistic. They often find these reasons through modes of reductionist analysis that replace moral and spiritual considerations with secular social science.

Analyses of the Church's position become reductionist when they leave out spiritual and moral criteria and reduce problems to sociological, psychological, and aesthetic categories. For example, reductionist analysis would say that widespread adultery, homosexual activity, and other sexual immorality among Catholics represent "a swing of the pendulum." The implication is that the pendulum will one day swing back through normal social processes. A thoroughly Christian perspective would more accurately label immorality as "sin," and would not presume that the pendulum will swing back. The social sciences rightfully try to avoid value judgements. Thus they cannot detect the most important forces at work in the Church today: namely, the spiritual and moral elements involved in the interplay between the Spirit of God and the spirit of the age, the works of the flesh, and the work of evil spirits.

This kind of sociological analysis has a psychological counterpart. Disdain for authority is explained as an "understandable reaction." Rebellious behavior is "acting out." Acceptance of immorality is termed a "predictable heightened interest in sexuality." There is often value in psychological analysis, but not if it lulls Christians into the posture of the "disinterested observer" who ignores the spiritual and moral considerations that an effectively Christian response requires.

The great danger of over reliance on sociological and psychological analyses is that they can leave the distinct impression that the Church's life is essentially deterministic, an ebb and flow of trends which we watch as passive participants. Determinism eliminates accountability and responsibility: people are held to be not really responsible for their actions, and leaders are said to be unable to lead a Church on a pendulum swing.

A reductionist tendency is also evident in the way many Christians employ aesthetic categories in their interpretation of the Church's situation. For example, many Christians cherish a certain "don't-get-too-excited" serenity when pondering what to do about unfaithfulness and decay in the Church. Their priority is "balance." In this way of thinking, a response to a problem must above all be "balanced and proportionate," even if the problem itself represents something highly unbalanced in terms of Christian orthodoxy. Some of the problems facing the Church call for strong measures—corrective action that may well appear to be unbalanced and disproportionate to those who do not understand the spiritual and moral depths of the situation. Yet a Christian leader whose desire is to preserve an aesthetically pleasing "serenity" and "balance" will avoid them.

Indeed, the whole business of being a Christian who is faithful to the gospel and who desires to do the Lord's work is neither serene nor balanced as these categories are often understood in the Church today. A "sense of history" is very valuable, but not if it functions to instill indifference or passivity about the need for us to take responsibility before God for how we act in *our* historical situation. St. Francis Xavier, the great Jesuit missionary to the Orient, expressed something of the awfulness of this false serenity when viewed in the light of eternal truths:

Many times I am seized with the thought of going to the schools of your lands [Europe] and there cry out like a man who has lost his mind, and especially at the University of Paris, telling those in the Sorbonne who have a greater regard for learning than for willing so that they might dispose themselves to produce fruit with it: "How many souls fail to go to glory but instead to hell through their neglect. Would that they were as diligent in studying how much God our Lord will demand of them as they are in studying letters, and what will be expected of them for the talent which they have received; then they would be greatly moved . . . and they would say: "Lord, here I am! What would you that I should do? Send me wherever you will, and, if necessary, even to the Indians!" With how much greater consolation would they then live; and they would have great hope in the divine mercy of the hour of their death when they encounter that particular judgment which no man can escape, saying for themselves: "Lord you gave me five talents, behold, I have gained another five."[2]

We need this zealous Christian perspective today. If we truly share in the mind and heart of Christ and if his Spirit dwells in us, should we not also expect to share Jesus' anger when he saw his Father's temple defiled?

> In the temple precincts he came upon people engaged in selling oxen, sheep and doves, and others seated changing coins. He made a whip of cords and drove sheep and oxen alike out of the temple area, and knocked over the money-changers' tables, spilling their coins. He told those who were selling doves: "Get them out of here! Stop turning my Father's house into a marketplace!" His disciples recalled the words of Scripture: "Zeal for your house consumes me."
>
> (Jn 2:13-17)

Today too, the temple of God is being defiled—the very body of Christ, the people of God, the Church. Is not a false "serenity," a false "balance" in response to this situation, in itself something of a defilement?

Our response to the crisis of truth in the Church must begin with a candid look at the inner nature of our response to the situation facing the Church. Those of us who bear Christ's name should be consumed with zeal for the purity of his body, the Church. Those of us who have some degree of responsibility for the Church must be honest about the way we view what is happening to those under our care. If our people are being misled, if they are behaving unfaithfully to God and to each other, do we slip into ways of thinking that tend to make these facts seem less painful and less serious? Worse, do we think about what is happening to the people under our care in a way that tends to lessen our own responsibility for changing the situation?

It can be difficult to discern God's will for his people, and even harder to faithfully and consistently implement it in the midst of the pressures, cross-currents, and difficulties that plague the Church today.

Nevertheless, we must not let our discernment of the real situation of the Church and God's will for it to be lulled by a false optimism, serenity, and balance, or by our acute sensitivity to the ways social forces act on institutions and psychological dynamics operate on individuals and groups. This is not to say that sociological, psychological, aesthetic, and historical perspectives cannot be helpful in pastoral work. They can be helpful in their proper place. However, these modes of analysis are limited and subordinate. They are essentially "natural" ways of seeing and thinking. If employed exclusively or excessively they will squeeze the spiritual and moral components out of our vision and deny us the means to make a response appropriate to the magnitude of the problem. Today, as always, the words and deeds of God are "madness" and "foolishness" in the eyes of the world.[3]

Catholics—especially those who share in pastoral responsibility for the Church today, which in some measure is all of us—should be no less zealous for the Word and the way of God than those who preceded us. Increasingly today, the right attitude toward the corruption of faith and life that is going on in the Church is indignation. And indignation should characterize our response to it.

CHAPTER TEN

Powers, Principalities, and Organizations

IN ORDER TO BE ABLE to adequately respond to the crisis of truth confronting the Church today we need to realize the significant extent to which our struggle is not just with "human weakness" and "well-meaning mistakes" but with powers, principalities, and organized centers of hostility. Jesus and the apostles warned about the pervasive activity of Satan, the methodology of his operations, and the desire of his heart. The "whole world is under the evil one" (1 Jn 5:19), who is "prowling like a roaring lion looking for someone to devour" (1 Pt 5:8). "Satan, the seducer of the whole world" (cf. Rv 20:8), is luring human beings to destruction and ruin, getting them to believe the ruinous lies of plausible liars who are often within the Church. His compelling motivation is a murderous hatred of God and men.

Modern men and women often lack this spiritual perspective. The contemporary opinion of secular society, shared by many in responsible positions of Church leadership, view today's struggle as simply a clash of human ideas, movements, and trends. They completely ignore the often hidden, but sometimes open, work of Satan and the evil powers under his control. The fact is that the influence of ideologies and trends on society and the Church is not simply a matter of "flesh and blood." It also involves an encounter with "powers and principalities" working brilliantly and deviously to bring the human race to spiritual, moral, and physical destruction. The precise elements of evil spiritual influence often cannot be clearly distinguished from human

153

contributions. But often they can be, and discerning them is a valuable skill. If we become more aware of this dimension, we will better understand the struggle we are engaged in and be better equipped to resist and counter it.

Much of the rest of this chapter will be devoted to a description of Satan's often hidden work in various movements in society and the Church. Of course we must here guard against the danger of seeing Satan's activity everywhere and undervaluing the significant contribution of human sin and malice to our present situation. But in the present climate of the Church, in which Satan's reality and activity are often ignored and even denied, some attention to this reality is essential.

It is well to remember that Satan inspired man's original turning from God and spurred his drive for autonomy and for knowledge apart from God. He continues to inspire the human race's rebellion against God, a rebellion visible in many contemporary forms.

This primordial satanic temptation of man—to be "like God" apart from him and in opposition to him—appears again and again in the history of the development of modern thought and modern man. For example, studies of the Renaissance have shown that the desire of man at that time to be liberated from religious restraints was combined with involvement in various forms of "magic." Drawing on "esoteric knowledge" and "powers," leading Renaissance figures attempted to control their destinies and manipulate the physical world through their access to "knowledge" and "powers."[1]

A significant element of the Enlightenment—that upheaval of learning and change which profoundly shaped the modern world—was an explicit rejection of God, the Church, and revelation. What Voltaire, a leading figure of the Enlightenment, said about the Church, *Ecrasez l'infame!*, probably comes close to reflecting the sentiments of Satan on the subject: "Crush the accursed thing!"

This overt hostility toward Christianity and the Church manifested itself unmistakably in the French Revolution, a revolution that became something of a prototype for the political upheavals that have characterized the modern world. Along with its hostility to Christianity, the French Revolution ushered in an idolatrous worship of "reason," a conscious and deliberate exaltation of man above God. Yet this esteem for reason was coupled with irrationality, and produced something like an anti-religious religion. A "feast in honor of reason," held on November 10, 1793, in Notre Dame Cathedral in Paris, graphically illustrates the point.

> On the top of a scaffolding, placed in front of the choir, was erected a temple dedicated to philosophy, and to crown all was installed, in

place of "inanimate images," an actress from the Opera, chosen for her beauty, as a "masterpiece of nature," but entitled, without very evident cause, the "Goddess of Reason."[2]

This "abomination of desolations" in a holy place focuses and symbolizes that murderous hostility toward God that constitutes the center of Satan's activity and works. His hostility is directed toward man's own destruction.

If we can see some satanic purposes being achieved in the French Revolution, they are much more evident in the more recent unfolding of the Marxist revolutions, even though these revolutions have protested, like the French Revolution before them, real injustices. Marxists display the same opposition to God and the Church, the same conscious exaltation of man in place of God. However, they impose their hostility more ferociously and explicitly, more systematically. Recent research into the life of Karl Marx has found the seeds of the wider revolution in Marx's personal life. Apparently converted to Christ while a teenager, Marx soon rejected him. Marx's miserable personal life and relationships, and the subsequent suicide of his daughters, all witness to the victory of Satan, the enemy who lies and deceives in order to bring man to ruin and damnation.[3] In many ways, Marx's own life became an anti-sign of the "new man" his revolution was supposed to produce.

Our understanding of human history will always be inadequate unless we realize that, as Paul puts it, "our battle is not against human forces but against the principalities and powers" (Eph 6:12). To the solidly instructed and spiritually sensitive Christian, the role played by satanic principalities and powers in the lives of certain "great" men and "great" events is unmistakable.

Jesus identified Satan as one who is seeking to deceive and blind the human race, to direct it down paths that will lead to murder and death now, and damnation forever (Jn 8:43-47). Satan accomplishes his will through human instruments, just as God does. A view of history that does not take these spiritual realities into account is of necessity partial, blind, and distorted.

Sometimes we can surmise only by external signs and indications that a satanic element is at work in certain historical movements and figures. Other times, however, the evidence is fairly direct. Such a case is that of H.S. Chamberlain, a writer whose racial theories were hailed by the Nazis as the "gospel of the Nazi movement." Chamberlain's ideas found a hearing, inspiring the people who destroyed six million Jews. H.S. Chamberlain openly acknowledged a significant demonic element in his life and work:

Hypersensitive and neurotic and subject to frequent nervous break-downs, Chamberlain was given to seeing demons who by his own account, drove him on relentlessly to seek new fields of study and get on with his prodigious writings. One vision after another forced him to change from biology to botany, to the fine arts, to music, to philosophy, to biography, to history. Once, in 1896, when he was returning from Italy, the presence of a demon became so forceful that he got off the train at Gardone, shut himself up in a hotel room for eight days, and abandoning some work on music that he had contemplated, wrote feverishly on a biological thesis until he had the germ of the theme that would dominate all of his later works: race and history.

Whatever its blemishes, his mind had a vast sweep ranging over the fields of literature, music, biology, botany, religion, history, and poli-tics. There was, as Jean Real has pointed out, a profound unity of inspiration in all his published works and they had a remarkable coherence. Since he felt himself goaded on by demons, his books (on Wagner, Goethe, Kant, Christianity and race) were written in the grip of a terrible fever, a veritable trance, a state of self-induced intoxica-tion, so that, as he says in his autobiography, *Lebenswegt*, he was often unable to recognize them as his own work, because they surpassed his expectations.[4]

We can observe a continuum of evil. The Renaissance Magus' role as a secular messiah, who attempts to control human life through knowl-edge and power assisted by magic, becomes full-blown in Adolf Hitler, who built his Third Reich on the foundation of Chamberlain's racial theories. The doctrines designed by demons for the blinding and destruc-tion of the human race are successfully promulgated through a plausi-ble liar and applauded by "great men" and "leading intellectuals" of the day. "Liberation" from divinely-ordered restraints becomes slavery to the infernally evil genius who roams the world seeking for opportu-nities to deceive, blind, and destroy.

Closer to home, the remarkable career of Elisabeth Kübler-Ross pro-vides another insight into how apparently very "gifted" people can themselves be misled and mislead others in what appears to be at first very innocent ways.

A psychiatrist, Kübler-Ross published a book in 1969, *On Death and Dying*, in which she outlined five phases of death and responses to death, ranging from angry denial to ultimate acceptance. The book became immensely successful and was adopted by many Chris-tians and widely used in counseling and ministry to the dying. *Ladies' Home Journal* named Dr. Kübler-Ross as one of the eleven "women of the decade" for the seventies.

Kübler-Ross gave numerous seminars, many of which were attended and sponsored by church people. In them, often in response to questions, she would tell of her admiration for Mother Teresa and then go on to explain that her research with the dying indicated there was no "judgmental" God. Without necessarily calling into question her early research with the dying, I think it is fair to say that over a period of time her work has tended to lead people away from orthodox Christian faith. Now she explicitly does so.[5]

As her fame and influence grew, Dr. Kübler-Ross began to talk about a "pleasant state" that existed beyond death, one into which everybody entered irrespective of religious belief or of the moral quality of one's life. She also became involved in spiritualism and attempted to communicate with the dead. At a seminar given at a Catholic center for relgous education in a Midwest diocese, Dr. Kübler-Ross told the story of what happened to her after visiting a spiritualist center in California. (The following account was given by a participant at the seminar.)

> After she spoke to this group she was led downstairs into a dark basement room where she was told someone wanted to speak to her. She waited and was approached by a very large man whose presence was almost overwhelming. He told her she must continue her work. There was much to be done and she was needed and must continue. . . . He commissioned her to go and continue her work.

In 1979, the depth of Kübler-Ross' bondage to "spirits" became public when she declared herself to be an "immortal visionary and modern cartographer of the River Styx," and defended her deep involvement with a spiritualist group called the Church of the Facet of Divinity. A regular feature of this group's sessions was the invocation of spirits, who then materialized and ministered to the participants' various problems. (Sometimes they were purported to give back rubs.) Kübler-Ross bought land near this spiritualist center, naming it Shanti-Nilays (Sanskrit for "Home of Peace") and making it a center for workshops on death and dying.[6] In recent appearances and interviews, Kübler-Ross openly admits that she has had contact with "spirit guides" for nine years and that they have told her that there is no such thing as damnation, judgment, or hell.[7]

Although now professing disillusionment about her heavy dependence on a particular psychic, her non-Christian occult views remain unchanged:

> There is no such thing as good or bad. If we don't learn what we're supposed to in this life, we'll learn it in another.[8]

Participants at seminars run by Kübler-Ross often describe her as "peaceful," "gentle," "wise," "like an angel." This can serve as a reminder, once again, that sometimes theories which most deeply undermine Christian truth are often attractive and presented by spokesmen who appear to be "angels of light." The most diabolical and murderous "wisdom" can appear "life-enhancing" and "liberating." We need to be alert enough today to recognize the spiritual forces at work in certain contempory theories, spokesmen, and movements. We need to ponder God's Word of warning about angels of light, and be firmly rooted in the objective truth of His Word.

> For even if we, or an angel from heaven, should preach to you a gospel not in accord with the one we delivered to you, let a curse be upon him! (Gal 1:8)

> For even Satan disguises himself as an angel of light. (2 Cor 11:14)

To be successful, deception must deceive. It must include much truth and it must appeal to what appears noble, positive, creative, and just. Chamberlain intertwined with his demon-inspired racial theories many references to Christ and Christianity. Kübler-Ross' gentleness, peacefulness, and "respect for religion" put her in an excellent position to lead people to doubt or to be silent about important aspects of God's Word to us.

> The Spirit distinctly says that in later times some will turn away from the faith and will heed deceitful spirits and things taught by demons through plausible liars. (1 Tm 4:1-2a)

It is not uncommon that a polite, reasonable desire to "purify" Christianity of its belief in the reality of the devil goes along with doing the devil's work. For example, as we have seen, one of the authors of the *Human Sexuality* study, discussed in Chapter Eight, berated Pope Paul VI and leaders of the charismatic renewal for reaffirming the reality of Satan as a basic truth of Christian faith:

> All the more incongruous, therefore, is the fact that Pope Paul should feel pressed into delivering a defense for the existence of a personal devil at this time. . . . If there are demons to be exorcized in the Church, their twin names are dogmatism and fundamentalism.[9]

Is it coincidence that this theologian participated in the writing and publication of a study which undermined the authority of God's Word in the area of sexual morality and in effect invited many to embark on the "broad road that leads to destruction?" As of this writing this theologian is on the theology faculty of the Jesuits' St. Louis University.

The spiritual roots of secular humanism are especially evident in certain organized segments of the feminist movement. Gloria Steinem, editor of the influential *MS* magazine, has written that "Feminism is the path to Humanism, and it is Humanism which is the goal." Ms. Steinem went on to say: "By the year 2000 we will, I hope, raise our children to believe in human potential, not God. . . ."[10] Betty Friedan, a leading feminist and founder of the National Organization of Women, is a signer of Humanist Manifesto II.

Certain feminists express intense, open hostility to the Christian view of sex and the family. Dr. Mary Jo Bane, associate director of Wellesley College's Center for Research on Women declared: "We really don't know how to raise children. . . . The fact that children are raised in families means there's no equality. We must take them away from families and raise them."[11]

Some feminists have rejected God and Christ and call for a return to witchcraft and the worship of pagan gods and goddesses. As one feminist document put it: "All of history must be rewritten in terms of the oppression of women. We must go back to ancient female religions."[12] The *Los Angeles Times* described one such feminist worship service:

> SANTA CRUZ—Nearly 400 women picked different notes and held them, catching their breaths at different times so the sound droned unabated for five minutes. The eerie monotones from this congregation of sorts reverberated against the angular outside walls of the Theater of Performing Arts and filtered through clumps of tall pines on the UC Santa Cruz campus. The hymnic call was to the Goddess. Later in the day, encouraged by the beat of bongo drums, spontaneous groups of circling women danced barebreasted in scenes suggestive of frolicking wood nymphs. . . .
>
> More than a successful university extension course, however, the event was indicative of a burgeoning spiritual dimension of the women's movement in America. . . .
>
> Christine Downing, head of San Diego State University's religious studies department, estimates that many—if not most—spiritually sensitive women in the women's movement are willing to replace the biblical God with a frankly pagan and polytheistic approach. . . . A Santa Cruz woman, Ebon of the Mountain, 38, said, "Some of the women think of themselves as witches, but not all."[13]

Unfortunately, such profoundly anti-Christian trends are finding a welcome within Church institutions and publications and among Church personnel. As one Catholic theologian put it:

Through him [an anti-Christian college professor] I discovered the meaning of religious symbols not as extrinsic doctrines but as living metaphors of human existence. . . .

I knew that Ba'al was a real god, the revelation of the mystery of life, the expressions of the depths of being which had broken through into the lives of the people and gave them a key to the mystery of death and rebirth. . . . As for the defects of Ba'al, were they more spectacular than the defects of the biblical God or Messiah, or perhaps less so? . . .

I could not give allegiance to any "jealous god" on the level of historical particularity. . . .

I could not tell her [a nun] that my devotion to Mary was somewhat less than my devotion to some more powerful females that I knew: Isis, Athena, Artemis.[14]

Another Catholic theologian's book carries the message in its title: *Beyond God the Father*. This book introduces the subject of going beyond God the Father with a somewhat incoherent melange of references to lesbianism and the occult.[15] As of this writing, this theologian is still teaching at Boston College, a Jesuit institution.

The feminist movement attacks some genuine injustices and some of its goals, especially some pertaining to economic injustices, can be supported by Christians. Nevertheless, the militantly anti-Christian heart of this movement, at least as revealed in many of its leaders, should make Christians cautious, and even suspicious. One can only see naivete and lack of discernment when a Catholic bishop boldly proclaims without qualification that the feminist movement is a movement of the Holy Spirit.[16]

The Secular Humanist Assault on Life

The denial of the reality of Satan and his activities are often associated today with a wider doctrinal and moral decay. In the name of God and of life, "reasonable" people have wreaked terrible havoc on humanity. A book written by a Yale University psychiatrist asks how German physicians, "heirs to Europe's proudest medical tradition," could participate in mass slaughter and grisly human experiments in the Nazi death camps. The problem, of course, was not restricted to German doctors; most of the educated professional classes in Germany were also implicated. The author of this study concludes that the German doctors participated in a self-chosen delusion:

Doctors were the embodiment of Nazi political and racial ideology in its ultimate murderous form. The killing came to be projected as a medical operation. . . . "If you have a gangrenous growth, you have to remove it." . . . If you view the Jews as death-tainted, then killing them seems to serve life. . . . *Most killing is not done out of sadism, not even most Nazi killing. . . . The murders are done around a perverted vision of life enhancement.*[17] (italics added)

The Nazi Holocaust was carried out by men who believed they were "enhancing life." The similarity to today's silent holocaust of abortion is numbing.

There is a particular link today between often satanically inspired rejection of God and His Word and sexual sin and disorders. The rejection of God's Word regarding sexuality and its purposes in the name of "fulfillment" not only assaults Christian values but produces a harvest which is miserable in simply human terms. In the name of "life," secular humanists bring death and disease through abortion and venereal disease, broken relationships through massive infidelity and divorce, and psychological problems through attacks on commitment and fidelity.

Organized groups are working skillfully to push contemporary societies in this direction. Often they enlist Church personnel to help them. The International Planned Parenthood Federation is one such group.

With international headquarters in London and local affiliates in more than ninety countries, Planned Parenthood is dedicated to freeing sexual experience from any link with procreation or family life. It pursues an active program of promoting contraception, abortion, sterilization, and sex education, using blatantly anti-Christian materials. In recent years the international organization has received about forty percent of its budget from the U.S. government through the Agency for International Development and through U.S. contributions to the United Nations Fund for Population Activities. In the U.S. alone, Planned Parenthood affiliates operate more than 729 clinics. In 1978, the national organization received half of its stated $117.5 million budget from the U.S. government.[18]

Planned Parenthood groups in the United States target their efforts especially at the poor and at teenagers. For example, the Planned Parenthood affiliate of the Mohawk Valley area of New York State declared that it wants "6,000 more contraceptive users in 1980, with continued emphasis on teens."[19] Planned Parenthood's favored method of contraception for the poor is often sterilization. It has been remarkably successful in places such as Puerto Rico, where as many as thirty-five percent of the child-bearing age women have been sterilized; and among native American Indians.[20]

The Planned Parenthood program is advanced with appeals to patriotism and "enhancing the quality of life." Newspaper, radio, and television advertising campaigns promote the Planned Parenthood vision and services under the slogan: "Planned Parenthood. Helping Build a Strong America By Helping Build Strong American Families."[21]

Margaret Sanger, the founder of Planned Parenthood, was a woman dedicated to the overthrow of the Judaeo-Christian morality, and openly advocated and practiced premarital and extra-marital sex. Sanger's followers today seldom mention some of her other beliefs. She frequented seances, and wanted to weed "bad stock" out of the race by manipulating the poor into using contraceptive devices and getting them sterilized.[22]

Another organized effort to push society and the Church in the direction of secular humanistic values and lifestyle is the development and promotion of many sex education programs now required in public schools, and even adopted by some Catholic schools. Many of these programs are designed to break down the Christian approach to sex and family life; they encourage children to be open to a multitude of sexual experiences. The issue here is not whether children should have sex education. Obviously they should. Rather the issue is, by whom, in what context, with what values, and by what methodology.

There are some useful sex education curricula available that are respectful of Christian values. But many are subtly or blatantly undermining of Christian belief. They seek to break down resistance to sexual activity even among very young children. While often pretending to be "value neutral" programs which simply help students "clarify" their values, these programs are in fact designed to open a wedge between the student and any authority, including the Church and parents, and to encourage them to independent action in the area of sexuality. They present various forms of sexual activity in an allegedly "neutral" way so students can examine their feelings about them. Of course, the "value free" claim is often a hoax. The underlying value is relativism, the belief that truth and morality are what you make them, and what you wish.[23]

The proponents of value clarification programs sometimes reveal their secular humanistic and anti-Christian presuppositions clearly. Sidney Simon, a leading developer of value clarification programs, once said this:

> The old "shalt nots" simply refuse to maintain relevance. . . . We certainly do not need more moralizing and preaching on the right and good values.[24]

Simon went on to say that his own value clarification system is a method by which teachers can change the values of students "without being caught."[25]

Another description of a value clarification program in use in certain schools begins like this:

It's OK to lie—It's OK to cheat—It's OK to steal—It's OK to have premarital sex—It's OK to kill—if these things are a part of your own value system and you have clarified those values to yourself.[26]

Advocates of "value neutral" sex education often argue that the only way to overcome such problems as unwanted teenage pregnancies is to equip young people with a good knowledge of sex and of the ways to prevent pregnancy. The programs usually include outright propagation of views about sexual behavior which are contrary to Christian teaching. Many of these programs also include positive presentations of homosexuality and lesbianism, proposing them as alternate lifestyles which students can choose if they wish.[27]

The claim that such "value free" sex education will decrease teenage pregnancies is not supported by the facts.

In her study, "Illegitimacy" (University of California Press, 1975), Shirley Foster Hartley noted that in Sweden—where sex education became compulsory in 1956—the illegitimacy rate (the number of illegitimate births per thousand females of child-bearing age), which had been declining, subsequently rose for every age group except the older group which did not receive the special sex education. Swedish births out of wedlock now amount to 31 percent of all births, the highest proportion in Europe, and two and a half times as high as in the United States.[28]

Lacking evidence for their views, proponents of "value free" sex education usually fall back on secular humanist rhetoric. They say that such programs will produce a "fuller life," a "more fulfilled and sexually integrated personality." These claims also depend on ignoring other facts, such as the well-documented increase in the rate of impotency and other sexual dysfunction in modern society. The proponents of sexual freedom are actually making a spiritual statement, and have a "vision" of human life. It is one based on a rejection of God and scripture, and a hostility to the Church.

It is thus imperative that Christians responsible for various aspects of sex education exercise great care and discernment. Sadly, many of them display an astounding naivete—or worse. For example, one of the most militantly anti-Christian secular humanistic organizations dedicated to breaking down Christian morality is the Sex Information and Education Council of the U.S. (SIECUS). It assists in the production of sex education films which explicitly depict heterosexual and homosexual intercourse, masturbation, group sex, and other sexual behavior, and presents them in an attractive, desirable light. The purpose of these films is to "desensitize" the viewers so that they approach such behavior in a sympathetic non-judgmental manner. These films have been used in sex seminars sponsored by Christian groups. At least one Catholic seminary has used these films to prepare their students for ministry.[29]

Was it naivete or lack of discernment or something else that led the United States Catholic Conference representing the Catholic bishops in the United States to join a coalition with groups that included Planned Parenthood, National Gay Task Force, Zero Population Growth, American Association of Sex Educators, Counselors and Therapists, and the National Alliance for Optional Parenthood, to present a "united front" on family life during the White House Council on the Family? Fortunately, the Catholic delegation withdrew from the coalition when the Conference had almost reached its final stage, but not before the Christian witness on family issues had been significantly muted.[30]

Dr. Armand Nicholi, a Christian psychiatrist affiliated with the Harvard Medical School, has commented on the disturbing trends in our increasingly de-Christianized society, their implications for the future, and the passivity of the Churches in giving effective guidance to their members.

The trend toward quick and easy divorce and the ever-increasing divorce rate subjects more and more children to physically and emotionally absent parents. The divorce rate has risen 700 percent in this century and continues to rise. There is now one divorce for every 1.8 marriages. Over a million children a year are involved in divorce cases and 13 million children under eighteen have one or both parents missing. . . .

The family is also affected by the lack of impulse control in our culture today. . . . The deep moral confusion we have observed over the past decade seems to have lifted all restraint. During the past ten years, I have noticed a marked change in the type of problems that bring people to a psychiatrist. Previously, a great many came because of their inability to express impulses and feelings. Today, the majority come because of an inability to *control* their impulses. (People in my field relate this lack of control to the declining influence of the father in the home.)

The steady rise of violent crime in this country most clearly demonstrates our inability to control aggression. In Boston, where more people pursue higher education than perhaps any place on earth, a murder occurs about every third day. Aggression in the home has been increasing steadily. . . .

Even more prevalent in society is the failure to control sexual impulses. The number of illegitimate births in this country continues to rise. . . . I have also noticed an increased incidence of homosexuality among young people and also much greater freedom in expressing it. . . . A home in which both parents are available to the child emotionally as well as physically has become the exception rather than the rule. . . .

What about the future? What can we expect if these trends continue? First, the quality of family life will continue to deteriorate, producing a society with a higher incidence of mental illness than ever before. Ninety-five percent of our hospital beds may be taken up by mentally ill patients.

This illness will be characterized primarily by a lack of self-control. We can expect the assassination of people in authority to be a frequent occurrence, as well as events like the sixteen-year-old girl who recently began shooting people "for the fun of it."

Crimes of violence will increase, even those within the family. . . . The suicide rate will continue to rise . . . In the past twenty years, however, the suicide rate in ten to fourteen-year-olds has tripled. We already are producing an enormous number of angry, depressed, and suicidal kids. . . .

As sexuality becomes more unlimited, more separated from family and emotional commitment, the deadening effect will cause more bizarre experimenting and widespread perversion. Jean O'Leary has written in the National Organization for Women publication that lesbianism should be taught in our schools and that school counselors should take courses "to teach a positive view of lesbianism." And a group in Boston called the Boston Boise Committee has been trying to convince the public that there is nothing "inherently wrong with sex between men and boys," to lower the age of consent to fourteen, and to change the child molestation laws to reduce legal barriers against such relationships."[31]

Dr. Nicholi points out that the Christian Churches have been responsible for much of this disorder by their passivity, silence, and ambiguous teaching.

As a nation we appear to be more confused morally than at any time in our history, and the church has failed to give leadership. Perhaps we need to hear a little less about self-fulfillment and a little more about self-denial. Could it be that denial is the key to fulfillment? . . . The church should spell out clearly the Christian sexual ethic. The church's reluctance to speak out clearly on this issue has resulted in confusion within many homes. So many voices in our society point in opposite directions, and enormous stress falls upon the young person who has no clear guidance in this area.[32]

Finally Dr. Nicholi points out the embarrassing fact that the conclusions to which even the social scientists are coming merely confirm what the Christian Church has known all along but has sometimes become too confused and compromised to teach clearly and confidently.

> Social scientists have recently been trying to clarify scientifically through large surveys what constitutes happiness and fulfillment. These studies describe the most significant prediction of fulfillment and happiness to be family relationships and love within those relationships. Yet we have known this for 2,000 years. If the scriptures are what they claim to be, "inspired by God . . . useful for teaching the faith and correcting error" . . . the comprehensive equipment for resetting the direction of a man's life and training him in good living . . . then we might expect to find in them guidelines on how to live on this planet with a sense of fulfillment.[33]

A Spiritual Perspective

We need a spiritual perspective on this aspect of the crisis of truth. How many of those that the world calls "great"—how many "great leaders," "innovative thinkers," "distinguished jurists"—will be found, on the day of judgment, to have been instruments of Satan's purposes? How much of the world's wisdom will be revealed to have come, not from "on high," but from below, to have been satanic in its origins and its purposes? (Jas 3:13-18). As John Paul II put it:

> For then, there is revealed—with an almost implacable necessity— this second alternative: only the earth, which for a certain time accepts the dominion of man, turns out to be the master in the last analysis. Then the cemetery is the place of man's final defeat. It is the place where a final and irrevocable victory of the "earth" over the whole human being, rich as he is, is manifested; the place of the dominion of the earth over him who, in his own lifetime, claimed to be its master.
>
> These are the inexorable logical consequences of the view of the world which rejects God and reduces the whole of reality exclusively to matter. At the moment in which man, in his mind and in his heart, makes God die, he must consider that he has condemned himself to an irreversible death, that he has accepted the programme of man's death. This programme, unfortunately, and often without reflection on our part, becomes the programme of contemporary civilization.[34]

The evidence is all around us, for those who have eyes to see and ears to hear. Christian eyes and ears should be able to recognize and identify the workings of the world, the flesh, and the devil in the midst of our fallen, blinded society. It is a society which, in the words of John Paul II, has set out on "the programme of man's death."

Many Christians today think nothing of breaking solemn commitments, wantonly expressing their urges, and threatening the human life and happiness of others—all in the name of "fulfillment." A deep-seated rebellion against God and a rejection of Christ and his Word lurks behind phrases like, "I want to be a humanly fulfilled Christian," or, "I feel God will understand what I've done."

How different are the words of Jesus:

Enter through the narrow gate. The gate that leads to damnation is wide, the road is clear, and many choose to travel it. But how narrow is the gate that leads to life, how rough the road, and how few there are who find it! (Mt 7:11-14)

Whoever would save his life will lose it but whoever loses his life for my sake, will find it. (Mt 16:25)

If your hand is your difficulty, cut it off! Better for you to enter life maimed than to keep both hands and enter Gehenna with its unquenchable fire. If your foot is your undoing, cut it off! Better for you to enter life crippled than to be thrown into Gehenna with both feet. If you eye is your downfall, tear it out! Better for you to enter the kingdom of God with one eye than to be thrown with both eyes into Gehenna. (Mk 9:43-47)

Do not be afraid of those who kill the body and can do no more. . . .
Fear him who has power to cast into Gehenna after he has killed.
(Lk 12:4, 5)

The way to fulfillment is to live in holiness and obedience to God. We must lay down our lives, renouncing the distorted thoughts, feelings, and desires of our fallen natures in order to become new creatures. We must follow him to his cross, so that we may follow him in his resurrection and be found acceptable in his sight on the day of judgment.

It is far better to be poor and unfulfilled in the eyes of the world than to risk eternal condemnation, from an unrighteous pursuit of earthly good or "fulfillment." It is far better to enter eternal life without having entered into an unrighteous second marriage, without having selfishly pursued that full expression of our potential, without purchasing that "integrated personality" at the price of obedience to God and His Word, without have "gained the whole world" but suffered the loss of our soul. Such self-denial ultimately leads to a fulfillment that passes all understanding, to a life of eternal joy and fullness of life with God and with those who have followed and obeyed him. Those who have unrighteously pursued their own fulfillment in this life will live to eternally regret it, in a union of misery, hatred, and resentment with those who have based their lives on the lies of the Evil One and have accepted his invitation to disaster.

Only in the light of eternity can we really make wise choices about how to live life in this world. Only God's Word tells us the purpose for which we have been created and the manner in which we can fulfill most fundamentally and lastingly our "potential" for life and happiness. The work of the power, principalities, and organizations dedicated to the silencing of the gospel and the destruction of the Church, and indeed, of the whole human race, can only be countered by Christians properly defending themselves and taking up appropriate arms to counter these forces. In the words of scripture:

> Finally, draw your strength from the Lord and his mighty power. Put on the armor of God so that you may be able to stand firm against the tactics of the devil. Our battle is not against human forces but against the principalities and powers, the rulers of this world of darkness, the evil spirits in regions above. You must put on the armor of God if you are to resist on the evil day; do all that your duty requires, and hold your ground.
>
> Stand fast, with the truth as the belt around your waist, justice as your breastplate, and zeal to propogate the gospel of peace as your footgear. In all circumstances hold faith up before you as your shield; it will help you extinguish the fiery darts of the evil one. Take the helmet of salvation and the sword of the Spirit, the word of God.
>
> (Eph 6:10-17)

CHAPTER ELEVEN

Pastoral Passivity

EVERY INSTANCE OF CORRUPTION of Christian truth and life we have considered in this book has occurred under the pastoral oversight of someone in authority in the Church. Every Catholic theologian who has attacked the authority of God's Word in scripture, tradition, and the magisterium is under the authority of a bishop, religious superior, or seminary rector. The Catholic publishing houses that publish the flood of false teaching and contradictions of Church teaching in their books, magazines, and newspapers are under the authority of local bishops or religious superiors. The Catholic Church is constituted in such a way that the pope takes responsibility for the soundness of life and teaching of the bishops, the bishops for the priests, and the priests for the people, and parents for their children. Superiors care for religious orders and oversee the soundness of life and teaching of everyone in the order. The orders themselves are under the authority of either or both officials in Rome and the local bishops of the dioceses where they are active.

Thus an immense amount of false teaching has been propagated in this post-conciliar period by people who are under pastoral authority. Yet, for the most part, they have not been corrected. Even today, as we have seen, professors of theology and priests who openly write and teach against the teaching of the Church on sexual morality and other areas continue to teach in Catholic seminaries and schools of theology. They continue to form the priests and religious educators of tomorrow.

How are we to understand this considerable problem of pastoral passivity? In order to do so we must take a look at the purpose of the Second Vatican Council and the confusion that followed in its wake.

Vatican Council II

Vatican Council II was an attempt by the Church to get its own house in order and to adopt a stance toward the modern world that would overcome unnecessary alienation. Pope Paul VI summed up the objectives of the Council in these terms: "to make the Church of the twentieth century ever better fitted for proclaiming the Gospel to the people of the twentieth century."[1]

To renew itself internally, the Council adopted a concept of the Church that was expressed in more biblical terms, took a concern for liturgical renewal, encouraged lay people to consider themselves full and active members of the Church, called for renewal of priestly and religious life, and completed the interrupted work of Vatican I by affirming the important role of bishops and their co-responsibility with the pope to care for the Church.

The Council moved in several ways to change the relationship of the Church with the world at large. Its *Decree on Ecumenism* established better relations with non-Catholic Christians by trying to create a positive climate in which Christian unity might move ahead. Its *Declaration on Religious Liberty* affirmed the Church's respect for the freedom of people to choose their own religion without undue interference from civil authorities. It also tried to establish more productive relationships with non-Christian religions by expressing a willingness to dialogue with them to find areas of mutual collaboration for the welfare of mankind, and to establish an atmosphere in which the claims of Christ might be presented more effectively. In the *Pastoral Constitution on the Church in the Modern World*, the Council endeavored to overcome once and for all the Church's reputation as an enemy of mankind and an opponent of even the good elements of modern culture and civilization such as scientific and political progress, and human, social, and economic development. It did so by forsaking unnuanced condemnations of modern culture and by affirming those elements of modern culture that are compatible with Christianity. The Council also strived to present the Church as the true friend of mankind. It portrayed the Church as the only institution in a position to care for all man's needs and to help him develop all his potentialities. At the same time, the Council made very clear in numerous references, particularly in the *Decree on Missions*, that the Church's primary aim in all this "dialogue" and "openness" was to win again a hearing for the gospel it was entrusted to proclaim to all mankind, and to work more effectively for the incorporation of all men into Christ and his Church.

Unfortunately, there is little evidence that the Church has adequately realized the internal renewal that the Council hoped for. Neither has it achieved the successful evangelism that the Council wanted to flow from the new "positive" attitude toward the modern world. We need to ask "what went wrong?"

In the space we have available, we can only quickly survey some of the factors that have led to the confusion that has followed in the wake of Vatican Council II. Those interested in studying this question more thoroughly should consult the full-length studies that are available.[2]

Since theologians made such a major contribution to the Council, their status was greatly enhanced afterward. People looked to them as the "definitive" interpreters of the Council. Bishops frequently did not feel qualified to interpret the Council. Moreover, they often tended to wait for other bishops to say something first. As a result of these factors, theologians quickly became the primary interpreters of the Council.

From the very beginning of the post-conciliar period, and indeed, even during the Council itself, a small but influential group of theologians—along with some priests, lay leaders, journalists, and even a few bishops—worked to push the Council to "go farther" than it did. They were active during the Council. After the Council, they were among its most prominent interpreters, and they often interpreted it as having gone "farther" than it actually did. We have already seen how they influenced crucial choices in the translation of Council documents, and gave a certain slant to the explanatory footnotes in the more widely used editions of these documents. We have also seen how some pushed the interpretation of such favorite Council documents as *Gaudium et Spes* to make openings for the "new morality" and for the narrowing of Church mission to the embrace of transitory popular social and political causes.

Interpretation of the Council was necessary of course. After the Council, the vast majority of Catholics did not comprehend its significance for their lives. Theologians and journalists were willing to explain what the Council meant, but they often distorted its meaning in a more "progressive" direction. The Catholic and secular press played a crucial role in coining labels: "progressive" forces prevailed over "reactionary" ones; "liberals" influenced some documents, "conservatives" won other rounds. ("Liberals," of course, were good and "conservatives" were bad.)

Many Catholics, including bishops, formed their understanding of the Council from the media's interpretations. In these interpretations, the Council was often presented as one more step on the progressive road, a road the Church would inevitably take, a road leading to ever-greater openness to the world and appreciation of its values. People who wanted to interpret the Council as authoritative and binding were made to feel as though they would be left behind in a few years if they did so. In order not be be left behind, they were encouraged to move "beyond" the Council. Often they were encouraged to disregard its actual texts in favor of what was called the "spirit of Vatican II."

Of course there is nothing intrinsically wrong with wanting to move beyond the Council if this means discussion of issues not treated by the Council, elaboration of issues the Council did not treat fully, or a deeper understanding and appropriation of conciliar teaching. However, those wanting to move "beyond" the Council often meant an effort to move beyond the boundaries of Christian truth and morality. They wanted to *change* Christian teaching, not merely develop or adapt it.[3]

The windows opened by Pope John XXIII and the Council allowed other spirits besides the Holy Spirit to move more freely in the Church. Many Catholics were caught up in a heady sense of freedom and new frontiers. Many theologians, as well as many "progressive" priests and lay people, began their work and theology in the Spirit, but ended up as victims of their own pride, rebellion, and sense of importance. Some people used the new freedom to justify the works of the flesh. Other people, slowly and almost imperceptibly, came under the domination of "the spirit of the age." Unsound theological theories were irresponsibly and widely promulgated as reliable truth to thousands of priests, religious, and lay people. This weakened Catholics' allegiance to the teaching of scripture and the Church. Instead, they gave their allegiance to theological speculation, which was often unsound.

Along with this, many Catholics, particularly priests and religious, indulged in a certain naive and adolescent delight in "rediscovering the world and its goodness." Since many had abandoned basic truths in their theological speculation, they no longer possessed adequate criteria for judging what was appropriate and what was inappropriate. Consequently their new freedom and openness was often indiscriminate, and frequently overtly sinful. Infidelity to vows of celibacy and marriage commonly occurred in the name of the new "openness" to the world.

One of the most notable trends in the Church, even among the leaders of the Church, was a headlong rush to embrace certain secular causes and to incorporate into the Church the latest findings of secular research. Many equated "newer" with "better," whether it meant catching up with advanced theories of biblical exegesis or social action, or adapting moral theology to Marxist or Freudian insights. The desire to be respected by the secular world and accepted by secular experts often led to indiscriminate affirmation of their findings and adoption of their methodologies, which often were based on hidden anti-Christian presuppositions.

Many Catholics tried to develop a "contemporary, relevant spirituality." This often meant equating doing God's will with doing what one pleased. Many people gave up prayer, self-denial, and self-discipline, further weakening their ability to discern the Spirit of God from the human spirit, the spirit of the world, or the evil spirit. The lack of clear criteria of objective truth, coupled with the abandonment of authentic spiritual life, led many to become spiritually blind. They could no longer distinguish the true from the false, the things of God from the things of the world, the flesh, and the devil.

The effects of this spiritually weakened condition were noticeable as Catholics developed a preoccupation for responding to the Council on the structural level. Their efforts to set up structures that would "facilitate co-responsibility" usually followed secular political and organizational models. These models often proved unsuitable for a spiritual organism like the body of Christ, with its distinctive modalities of life. This, in turn, produced little spiritual, evangelistic, or even organizational fruit.

The Assault on Authority

Implementation of the Council also involved a concerted effort to reinterpret authority so that no one in the Church would ever have to do anything he or she did not want to do. The Council, it was said, presented authority as "loving service." Thus those in authority were said to have an obligation to "affirm" those for whom they were responsible, and, by implication, never to correct, discipline, or order them to do anything. This reinterpretation of authority, of course, was contrary to the Council's teaching. At the same time, interpreters of the Council tried to intimidate those in authority so that, in practice, they would not use their authority. Bishops and other pastors were urged to adopt a passive, permissive silence as the theologians and experts went about their work of implementing the Council.

A Catholic theologian defined authority in this way: "Authority for a human may be defined as 'the ability to perceive and point out the good.' Authority here is suasive (*suavis* equals 'sweet') and for the good, (*kalos*). Authority exercises its own attractiveness and sweetly compels the human heart to its embrace."[4] Such definitions simply reduce authority to kindly advice, to be accepted or rejected as one pleases. In the end, people under this kind of authority are free to do as they please. As a result, unity is no longer possible, whether in family life or in wider Church life.

Of course, authority should be exercised in love. Decisions should be based on good information, and there should normally be a phase in which the one in authority discusses matters with those under authority. But this is only part of the authentic definition and exercise of authority. A person in authority also needs to be able to correct, admonish, discipline, and, ultimately, to exclude someone from a position of responsibility or from the community itself for serious reasons and as a last resort, with appropriate accountability and appeal procedures.

Another pressure on pastors and parents is a post-conciliar emphasis on authority as "service." This frequently involves serious distortion of what it means to "serve." Today this is commonly understood to mean that those in authority should let those in their care do what they want. However, authentic Christian service is based on fidelity to the truth. To "give the people what they want" is indeed to serve them very badly when it involves assenting to the obscuring of the Word of God.

The naive view of human nature implicit in these definitions of authority is typical of much of the distorted teaching that occurs in the Church today. It fails to fully take into account the depth of the Fall. Those concepts of the Trinity and of the Church which inadequately envision them as a democratic society or community fail to properly comprehend the nature of God or of the Church. These ideas contribute greatly to the foolishness that sometimes abounds today under the guise of Christianity and renewal.

This reinterpretation of authority has been accompanied by successful efforts to reward and publicize those bishops, priests, and parents who operate in harmony with this deficient concept of authority, and to punish those who do not. New "pastoral" bishops are praised in a way that conveys the impression that their main virtues reside in their ability to give good press conferences, to be popular in secular society, to present a good image, and to allow their subordinates to do as they please. "Pastoral" has often become a code word for "permissive" and "accommodating." Often, "pastoral" bishops are contrasted with "behind-the-times" bishops who are "doctrinally" oriented, as if there is an irreconcilable conflict between objective truth and actual life.

This blatant media promotion of "pastoral" bishops is accompanied by subtle and private intimidation. Bishops are sometimes confidentially and "caringly" told: "You don't really know much about this area, so why don't you leave it to the experts?" Parents are often told the same thing by religious educators. Often, bishops' unofficial "media advisors" will subtly manipulate their behavior by telling them what will "look good" and what will not "look good" in the eyes of the press. (Of course, forthright exercise of spiritual authority seldom looks good to the press.) At other times bishops are told: "The whole staff is in agreement over this draft of your speech. I'm sure you'll have no trouble accepting it." Bishops sometimes end up being managed by their staffs in the same way political candidates are managed by their campaign staffs.

Of course, attempts by those under authority to manipulate those in authority are as old as the human race. But seldom have such attempts been as successful as they have been in the Catholic Church today at every level.

Sometimes official statements issued in the name of whole episcopal conferences bear the marks of such staff management. On the occasion of the first direct elections for members of the European Parliament, the Bishops' conferences of Europe issued a joint message that went to unusual lengths to avoid a direct statement of the gospel. It even omitted specifically Christian words in a quote from John Paul II. This is a quote from the Statement of the Presidents of European Episcopal Conferences on the future of Europe:

> Europe must establish an opportunity of economic, cultural, and spiritual development for all. The words addressed by John Paul II to the whole world, on 22 October last, still ring in our ears and it seems to us that they should be applied to Europe itself: "Open the frontiers of States, economic and political systems, the immense fields of culture, civilization and development. Do not be afraid!"[5]

The actual words of the pope are as follows:

> Brothers and sisters, do not be afraid to welcome Christ and accept his power. Help the Pope and all those who wish to serve Christ and with Christ's power to serve the human person and the whole of mankind. Do not be afraid. Open wide the doors for Christ. To his saving power open the boundaries of States, economic and political systems, the vast fields of culture, civilization and development. Do not be afraid.[6]

Another tactic that effectively intimidates bishops and parents is to browbeat them with the authority of "experts." They are told that "the whole professional association (of theologians, canon lawyers, ecumenical commissions, vocation directors, or religious educators, etc.) is accepting this emphasis." Or, the bishop hears that "Bishop So and So has already agreed to such an emphasis and his people are very happy with the results." Or, "The best theologians no longer see things so black and white." Or, "I know a good summer program where you can update your thinking." Not only bishops but religious superiors, seminary rectors, parish councils, and parents are targets for such intimidation tactics.

Some of the people who would like to push the Church in a certain direction are banking heavily on the hope that the new "pastoral" bishops will move into positions of greater responsibility in the coming years. As one prominent Catholic priest said recently, "I look forward to unbelievable changes in the next five years when some of these men move up into important positions."[7]

Inadequate Criteria for Pastoral Judgment

Pastoral leaders today often fail to exercise their responsibility effectively because they have inadequate models for leadership and employ inadequate criteria to judge their own work and the work of others.

Pastoral passivity is often justified as an appropriate posture for leaders of a "pluralist" Church. Indeed, pluralism in the Church can be a very good thing. The life of the Church is enriched by a certain kind of diversity in cultural expression, pastoral approach, and even theological and philosophical expression of the faith. Yet pluralism is legitimate only if it involves diverse expressions of the *one faith* as definitively interpreted by the teaching authority of the Church over the centuries. Today, calls for "pluralism" are often pleas to abandon the one faith. Many of those who work for the "pluralistic" Church of the future, in contrast to the "monolithic" Church of the past, are actually working for the destruction of the Church and any meaningful measure of unity of faith. Pope Paul VI called this kind of indiscriminate pluralism, the kind that lacks any clear criteria, as "corroding and ambiguous." It is indeed at work in the Church today.

Often an uncritical pluralism is combined with a conception of the pastoral leader as someone who is a "unifier." Of course, those responsible for families, parishes, and other segments of God's people need to work to unify their people. But they should not achieve unity at just any price. The unity appropriate to God's people is a unity based on a common adherence to Christian truth and the person of Christ. Saying "yes" to the teaching of the Church in areas of faith and morals is to say "no" to those who undermine and challenge them. Unity is based on truth. Yet many pastoral leaders today are presiding over a "unity" which contains contradictory elements, a "unity" which includes both acceptance and rejection of Christ, His Word, and the teaching of the Church. To tolerate the corruption of Christian truth in the name of unity or pluralism is to make a mockery of the genuine function and role of pastoral authority. It is, in fact, to preside over that corroding of Christian faith which Paul VI warned about.

Sometimes such corroding pluralism is tolerated because of a muddled or vague understanding of the wheat and the tares parable and other scripture passages that talk of problems within the church. In this connection it is frequently said that: "The Catholic Church is a church of sinners, a broad church that includes everybody; it is not a sect." Besides often incorporating an imprecise and often incoherent use of the sociological categories of "church" and "sect," such formulations are, more seriously, based on a misinterpretation of such scripture passages. The point of such passages is often to describe actual or future situations that can never be remedied simply by human effort, but can ultimately only be fully resolved by an action of God himself. The point of such passages though is not to counsel the advocacy of a lukewarm, passive, indifferent vision of Church life, in which the corruption of Christian truth and God's people is benignly presided over.

Such false applications of the parable have been common previously in Church history to justify a distorted approach to Church life, and St. Augustine addressed this situation squarely.

> In answer to these persons I would say, first of all, that in reading the testimonies of Sacred Scripture which indicate that there is presently, or foretell that there will be in the future, a mingling of good and evil persons in the Church, anyone who understands these testimonies in such a way that he supposes the diligence and severity of discipline ought to be relaxed altogether and be omitted is not taught by those same writings but is deceived by his own conjecture. The fact that Moses, the servant of God, bore most patiently that mixture of good and evil among the chosen people did not prevent him from punishing many, even with the sword. . . . In our times, when the sword has ceased to be visible in the discipline of the Church, what must be done is pointed out by degradations and excommunications.[8]

Other reasons for pastoral inadequacy are in large part psychological. Many pastors and parents are so deeply troubled by the extent of the problems plaguing the Church or family that they tend to seize on any apparent positive sign as an indication that everything is really all right. This often leads to self-deception. Let us consider some of the "positive" signs that cause pastoral passivity and wishful thinking.

Sometimes those in pastoral authority assume that evidence of someone's "good motives" somehow excuses the objective wrong he or she is doing. It is not uncommon to hear someone who is damaging the Church described as "sincere" or "well-meaning," as "someone who loves the Church," as a "man of faith" or a "prayerful man." "Sincerity" can excuse the objective results of such a person's ministry, or cause them to be overlooked.

It is, unfortunately, all too possible to sincerely do evil. It is all too possible to show love for the Church on the affective level, yet speak, teach, and act in a way that weakens the Church. It is possible to appear prayerful—even pious and devout—and yet do evil; it is also possible to appear humble, and yet be proud and rebellious. It is not sufficient today to call someone a "person of faith"; it is necessary to ascertain if they are a person of *Christian* faith.

Increasingly, even mistaken sincerity seems in short supply. A complete lack of goodwill and even outright deception characterize some of what is happening in the Church today.

In those areas of Church life where one expects objectivity and fairness, one frequently discovers obvious political manipulation. A case in point is the Catholic Theological Society of America's manipulation of a committee it established to examine the question of the status of women in the Church and society. The Society chose as committee members only people who openly supported the ordination of women. Furthermore, when the committee called in consultants, it selected scholars who were also already on record as supporting this view. The Catholic Theological Society similarly manipulated the formation of the committee it set up to do the human sexuality study which we have already analyzed at some length. Fortunately, such tactics are beginning to attract attention.[9]

It is hard to detect goodwill and sincerity in statements like the one made by a young biblical scholar who praised several prominent colleagues after they had been criticized for using their scholarship to undermine faith and morals. He said, "If they ever know what some of the rest of us are doing, they'd have a heart attack."[10]

A "polite and reasonable" manner of presentation often cloaks the most destructive positions. For example, a Catholic theologian made the following "balanced" observation:

> The source of tension, especially today, is the question of authenticity. A lot that a bishop has received has not been received from the Lord, and it is painful to learn from a theologian that something he has been teaching is not authentic.
>
> The theologian, in his turn, is constrained by his love for the community, so that his judgment of inauthenticity is not reached lightly.[11]

Despite the language of "respect," this statement illustrates the usurpation of authority that is characteristic of some theologians' attitude toward the teaching authority of the pope and bishops. A person's ability to use the right Christian language is not an adequate indication of his Christian fidelity. One of the most notable ways in which the Church's faith and life is being undermined today is through the perverse twisting of Christian language to camouflage fundamentally secular and humanistic ideologies.

Another inadequate criterion for judging Christian soundness is the

notion of "popularity" or "effectiveness." If, for example, large numbers of young people are responding "positively" to a certain youth
leader or religious educator, pastors and parents are tempted to interpret this "success" as Christian success. Quite often, they should
examine more deeply the basis of the popularity and the exact nature
of the positive response. The failure to penetrate beneath the surface
only assures that, sooner or later, in large measure or small, many in
the flock will end up as food for wild beasts.

Some Church leaders and parents have become victims of the cult of
feelings that has infiltrated the Church at every level. The fear of
"hurting someone" has allowed many unsound programs, publications, and even institutions to obscure Christian truth. In the process,
many people's prospects for eternal life have been seriously damaged.

Sometimes a false sentimentality has allowed the faith and moral
lives of others to be undermined. This kind of sentimentality is exemplified in a mistaken allegiance to an old schoolmate or friend or family
member. A bishop will feel reluctant, for example, to discipline a priest
who went to the same school or seminary with him. A parent may
withhold needed discipline because of the emotional bond with a child.

The toleration of corruption of faith or morality poisons the atmosphere of a community, large or small. It breeds the indifference and
lukewarmness that allows evil to increase and others to be corrupted.
Prompt and unambiguous correction and discipline produce the kind
of healthy "fear of the Lord" that provides the community with a
bulwark against sin (cf. Prv 14:26; Ps 2:11).

The consequences of weak and vacillating pastoral authority are
clearly illustrated in the story of Eli and his sons, told in the First Book
of Samuel. Eli and his two sons were priests in the Temple. However,
the sons were corrupt; they took offerings for themselves and engaged
in immoral behavior with women who had come to serve the Lord. Eli
rebuked them, and even pleaded with them, but he did not exercise
effective discipline by actually removing them from their positions.
Because of this, a prophet revealed to Eli that his sons would die, that
the priesthood would be taken away from his family, and that his
family and all his descendants would experience humiliation and chastisement. "I will choose a faithful priest who shall do what I have in
heart and mind" (1 Sm 2:35).

Situations similar to that of Eli and his sons are not uncommon in the
life of the Church today. It is not uncommon for those with pastoral
authority to give one message verbally—correction or admonishment
perhaps—but then to negate it by giving another message non-verbally,
by doing nothing when those corrected do not respond to the correction. The consequences of this passivity are often clearly evident in
families. Parents who remain passive when children ignore their cor-

rection preside over the destruction of their own authority.

The same is true in the wider Church. For example, the American bishops admonished and corrected the authors of the *Human Sexuality* study that we discussed in Chapter Eight. Yet all of the authors of the study have persisted in their opinions. And, as of this writing, four years after initial publication of the study, all the authors continue to teach on the faculties of Catholic seminaries and theology schools. This has led many Catholics to draw the obvious conclusion that the bishops' do not think they have any real authority in the matter. They regard the bishops' correction of these scholars as only one of many theological opinions about sexual morality. The same bishops appear to be continuing to ordain and hire people trained by scholars who dissent from and undermine the teaching of the Church. Like parents who let children ignore correction, the bishops are in fact presiding over, indeed subsidizing, those who are undermining their authority and misleading God's people.

The Consequences of Pastoral Passivity

The pastoral passivity that can end up tolerating great evil often begins with very small acts of disobedience. Many people in pastoral positions fear "rocking the boat." They are reluctant to summon the personal effort that would be necessary to challenge a questionable direction. They avoid making the effort to actually become acquainted with a troubled situation. Religious superiors fear the unpleasant scene that may follow their denial of someone's request. A bishop fears the outraged protests that would greet his demand that a seminary professor submit his course outlines for a review. A parent wants to avoid the scene that would follow his request that his child inform the parent of what he is reading or where he is going. Yet small acts of pastoral passivity, laziness, and negligence have allowed very great evils to grow up and go unchecked.

The separation of an individual, an institution, or a whole people from the will of God is often a very gradual process that has quite modest and almost imperceptible beginnings. C.S. Lewis cast light on this process in one of the *Screwtape Letters*. The instructor devil Screwtape gives the following advice to a younger devil:

You will say that these are very small sins; and doubtless like all young tempters, you are anxious to be able to report spectacular wickedness [Auschwitz?]. But do remember, the only thing that matters is the extent to which you separate the man from the Enemy. It does not matter how small the sins are provided that their cumulative effect is to edge the man away from the Light and out into the

Nothing. Murder is no better than cards if cards can do the trick. Indeed the safest road to Hell is the gradual one—the gentle slope, soft underfoot, without sudden turnings, without milestones, without signposts.[12]

Cardinal Basil Hume made a similar point while speaking about the situation of Christianity in Great Britain:

The majority of people in Britain have not so much rejected God, but have rather drifted away from him and now find themselves at the mercy of fashions, forces and influences which they are not able to shape or to control.[13]

Indeed, those in positions of pastoral responsibility in the post-conciliar Church at every level have too often overlooked the significant and sometimes decisive influence and activity of the "powers and principalities" (Eph 6:12). The Holy Spirit has his plan for the authentic renewal of the post-conciliar Church. The "prince of this world" also has his own plan. I doubt whether the first plan can be implemented successfully unless the second plan is recognized and dealt with. As one prominent Christian recently said, "The diabolical strategy is still the same. . . . persecution; intellectual deception, including false teaching; and moral erosion, including sub-Christian ethical standards."[14]

Bishops, priests, ministers, religious superiors, and parents have occasionally been startled to find that passivity has created situations over which they can no longer easily exercise any control. It is not easy for a bishop to control a whole religious order which has become an advocacy group for secular causes. The membership of theologians and even some seminary professors in secular professional associations has, in certain cases, meant that the Church is no longer the master of its own house. Because of pastoral passivity, dissident Church members have quietly obtained the legal leverage or popular support that they need to protect their own status in these institutions. Similar situations often develop in families.

Some dissident individuals and groups get protection directly from passive pastors. For example, a leading Catholic feminist theologian in Europe stated that "critical" Catholics like herself will simply go on doing what they would like to do. She cynically explained, "Rome won't excommunicate people like us as long as an important cardinal . . . is our leader."[15]

The fact is that manipulation and intimidation are not the only causes for pastoral passivity. Some pastors have made plainly unwise pastoral decisions in dealing with very real pastoral problems. Pastors have sometimes closed their eyes to outright false teaching or even immorality among those in their care because it would be difficult to deal with the situation or to find a replacement for an errant teacher or pastor. Some bishops have knowingly allowed priests with serious personal and faith problems to pursue advanced theological training, and, upon their return, placed them in sensitive pastoral positions such as campus ministry or seminary teaching. Many bishops today are under great pressure to staff their existing institutions and keep them functioning. The fact that they can no longer find reliably Christian pastoral personnel to staff them presents a dilemma. But to overlook doctrinal and moral infidelity in order to "keep the ship going" is a very poor choice indeed.

Even when pastoral leaders act, the measures they take often stop short of really dealing with the problem. They administer discipline that only hides the bad fruit. They do not lay "the axe to the root," the action often required for real cleansing and change.

For example, a few years ago Jesuit superiors ordered a Jesuit priest to stop his direct involvement in efforts to have women ordained as priests. He had been leading a national movement for women's ordination, a view which is directly opposed to all of Christian tradition and to that of the direct teaching of the pope and bishops. The priest's superiors, however, assigned him to another position of influence and responsibility. The priest soon declared his intentions: "I sure won't be publicly advocating women's ordination, but I will be publicly advocating equality in the church."[16] Such discipline did not deal with the priest's rebelliousness, but only deterred him from publicly challenging the specific issue of women's ordination. Such discipline was too weak to even begin to get to the heart of the problem.

Sometimes the consequences of pastoral passivity can engulf a whole national Church. The disarray of the Catholic Church in the Netherlands presently is a case in point. The results of years of such pastoral permissiveness are now immense infidelity to the Church's doctrinal and moral teaching. The Dutch Church is now trying to sort out its very serious problems with the unusual direct help and intervention of the pope. The lesson for bishops and others with pastoral responsibilities is clear: letting little infidelities go uncorrected today assures that larger infidelities and far more serious problems will develop tomorrow.

The Lord expects those whom he appoints as shepherds of the flock—whether they be fathers or mothers, priests or bishops—to take effective measures to guard the flock by disciplining those who corrupt faith and morality. Pastors are not to be deterred by a close personal relationship with the erring individual. Throughout the New Testament, the apostles constantly exercise such discipline over matters of faith and morality.

Our modern sentimentality recoils from such measures. Yet in so doing we recoil from true love and mercy, and risk eternally damaging the destiny of the wrongdoer and of those members of the community who are being corrupted by him. We often overlook the fact that one of the chief concerns of the Holy Spirit in speaking prophetically to the early Churches in the Book of Revelation was that the Churches maintain a high level of purity in their faith and morality. The Holy Spirit specifically warns the Christian people against tolerating in their midst those who hold or teach false doctrine or encourage others to immorality.

> Nevertheless, I hold a few matters against you: there are some among you who follow the teaching of Balaam, who instructed Balak to throw a stumbling block in the way of the Israelites by tempting them to eat food sacrificed to idols and to practice fornication. Yes, you too have those among you who hold to the teaching of the Nicolaitians. Therefore, repent! If you do not, I will come to you soon and fight against them with the sword of my mouth.
> (Rv 2:14-16)

Those Churches that failed to maintain such discipline and to diligently exercise pastoral authority were warned in prophecy that the Lord would directly chastise their communities.

> Nevertheless, I hold this against you: you tolerate a Jezebel—that self-styled prophetess who seduces my servants by teaching them to practice lewdness and to eat food sacrificed to idols. I have given her a chance to repent but she refuses to turn from her lewdness. I mean to cast her down on a bed of pain; her companions in sin I will plunge into intense suffering unless they repent of their sin with her, and her children I will put to death. Thus shall all the churches come to know that I am the searcher of hearts and minds, and that I will give each of you what your conduct deserves. (Rv 2:20-23)

In short, pastoral authorities who tolerate doctrinal or moral corruption become implicated in the corruption. In some measure, they are responsible for corruption and its evil results.

Of course, as with so much of what we're discussing in this book, this pastoral passivity is not unique to the Catholic Church. Many Protestant churches are affected in similar ways.

In a previous chapter, we cited the case of the Methodist leader who gave a public testimony to the "holiness" of her adultery-abortion experience. Her Methodist superior, an executive of the Board of Global Ministries and an ordained clergyman, was asked for a comment. He replied: ". . . one does not always agree with positions or perspectives of one's staff."[17]

The Primate of the Anglican Church in Canada, in response to a question during a press conference about whether the Church considers active homosexual relations to be sinful, declared: "It is not my job or the job of the Church to be always defining or judging things."[18]

I know these words may be difficult for some to receive. Those in pastoral responsibility in the Church display immense goodwill and exert an often heroic effort to do the best possible job. I know of no bishop and few parents who take their responsibilities lightly. I myself have pastoral responsibilities, including responsibilities as a parent. I have had to struggle and continue to struggle with many of the factors contributing to pastoral passivity that I discussed in this chapter. It is difficult to be a parent today in the increasingly pagan environment our children are exposed to; it is difficult to be a pastor of a parish or a bishop of a diocese. I do not pretend to have all the answers or even to understand all the complexities that those in wider responsibility have to face. Yet, as difficult as it is to face the facts of pastoral passivity, and to repent of it, it must be done. I believe the welfare of God's people depends in some significant measure on it.

Pastoral passivity or negligence—whether in the diocese, the parish, the seminary, or the family—is an invitation for the world, the flesh, and the devil to play havoc with God's own people, whom he purchased at the price of his own blood. Pastoral passivity has been and continues to be one of the main contributing factors to the crisis of truth in the Church. An adequate response to the crisis of truth must include a response to the problem of pastoral passivity and negligence.

CHAPTER TWELVE

The Signs of the Times: Pointing Toward Judgment

THE JUDGMENT OF GOD is expressed in many different ways. He makes partial and preliminary judgments manifest in history, and will judge all of the living and the dead at the end of time, with the consequences being eternal reward or eternal punishment.

Within history, God judges individuals, groups, and nations, pagans and even his own people. These judgments sometimes appear to be simply the inevitable, natural unfolding of the consequences of unrighteousness and rebellion against God. Such is the judgment experienced by those who turn from God and come into bondage to lust and every kind of evil, as described in the first chapter of Romans (Rom 1:20-25). These judgments, while in some ways the natural consequence of infidelity, are truly judgments of God.

The dimension of judgment is an essential perspective for understanding the situation of the world and the Church today. In many ways, the world and the Church are beginning to experience the natural, inevitable consequences of numerous acts of rebellion against God. The world may be about to reap what it has sown over several centuries of progressive turning away from God and exaltation of the creature over the Creator. Significant segments of the Church, unfortunately, are to a considerable extent implicated in this turning away from God, this deafness to His Word and blindness to the signs of the times.

God has always judged his people severely for accommodating themselves to the prevailing worldly cultures. In the Old Testament he punished them for intermarrying with pagans, for intermingling with them in a way that led to infidelity to His Word and ways. Many in the Church today have intermingled with contemporary culture in a way that has led them to turn away from God and His Word. Even shepherds of the flock are implicated in this corruption and "false prophets" have told many Catholics to regard the unclean as clean and to identify the spirit of the age as the Holy Spirit. Unfaithful priests have allowed God's Words to become blurred and confused; they have not distinguished between the sacred and profane, the clean and unclean. Parents of families have timidly allowed their children to adopt the thinking and behavior of "the nations" around them with only pleading rebukes rather than effective discipline. Many have acted like Eli in relation to his sons.

In the Old Covenant, God always judged this syncretistic and unfaithful accommodation to the prevailing cultures of the day. This was God's complaint against his people in this prophecy of Ezekiel:

> Say to the whole house of Israel: Thus says the Lord God: This is Jerusalem! In the midst of the nations I placed her, surrounded by foreign countries. But she rebelled against my ordinances more wickedly than the nations, and against my statutes more than the foreign countries surrounding her; she has spurned my ordinances and has not lived by my statutes. Therefore thus says the Lord God: Because you have been more rebellious than the nations surrounding you, not living by my statutes nor fulfilling my ordinances, but acting according to the ordinances of the surrounding nations; therefore thus says the Lord God: See, I am coming at you! I will inflict punishments in your midst while the nations look on. Because of all your abominations. . . . (Ez 5:5-9a)

Today, there is little doubt that the Church is guilty of similar accomodation. Some sociologists have pointed out that accommodation to the prevailing secular culture has become a dominant factor in the decline of contemporary Christian life in the Western countries. John Tracy Ellis, a distinguished historian of the American Catholic Church, has said that the chief cause of the decline of Christian life has been the assimilation of Catholics into the mainstream of American life. This has brought an emphasis on the pursuit of material success and the collapse of religious morality into secular humanism.[1]

Even Christian leaders who often express optimism are beginning to express serious concern about the trial the Church may soon undergo. For example, Billy Graham reported a conversation he had with his wife:

Ruth reminds me often that we need to be preparing the church in America to go underground, because that may be where we're headed. It may not be too long before judgment comes upon America and upon Europe, leaving us to face hostility and oppression as Christians.[2]

Other respected Christian leaders are moving toward the same conclusions. Dr. James I. Packer, an Anglican scholar and former principal of Trinity College, in Bristol, England, comments: "I am forced to believe that the Church of England is under judgment these days for multiple unfaithfulness to the Gospel."[3] Michael Harper, an Anglican clergyman and well-known author, points out the danger of presuming that the Church will overcome difficulties in the future simply because it has done so in the past. He warns that historical conditions in the West have no precedent in the centuries since Constantine:

In the past the Church could indulge itself in the luxury of unitarianism, sexual permissiveness, lax spirituality and political activism. It was protected by the State and by public opinion. It was to a large extent in the driving-seat. But those days are nearly over. The storm clouds are gathering. The enemy is at the gate if not already within the camp. Most of what goes for Western Christianity is like a beast fattened for the slaughter but seemingly unaware of the fate which is about to overtake it.[4]

The day after his election as pope, as he addressed the cardinals in the Sistine Chapel, John Paul II chose to interpret the sudden and unexpected death of his predecessor and his own unexpected election as warnings from God to turn to sober reflection and prayer.

Brothers, dear sons and daughters, the recent happenings of the Church and of the world are for us all a healthy warning: how will our pontificate be? What is the destiny the Lord has assigned to his Church in the next years? What road will mankind take in this period of time as it approaches the year 2000?[5]

John Paul II views the time in which we live as one in which there is an epic confrontation between the gospel and the anti-gospel, the Church and the anti-church. It is almost as if there were a prophetic, providential significance to what is unfolding before us.

We are now standing in the face of the greatest historical confrontation humanity has gone through. I do not think that wide circles of the American society or wide circles of the Christian community realize this fully. We are now facing the final confrontation between the Church and the anti-Church, of the Gospel versus the anti-

Gospel. This confrontation lies within the plans of divine Providence; it is a trial which the whole Church . . . must take up.[6]

It is also worth noting that a remarkable convergence of vision is occurring in the realm of what might be called prophetic vision. Although prophetic words are not, of course, at all on the same level as scripture, tradition, and magisterium, some of these words are worth taking note of briefly before we move on. Let us consider the prophetic word of St. Nilus, a sixteenth-century Orthodox hermit who is highly regarded in the Orthodox Church. Responsible Orthodox publications report that he appeared in a dream in the nineteenth century to a monk and gave the following prophecy:

> After the year 1900, toward the middle of the 20th century, the people of that time will become unrecognizable. When the time for the advent of the Antichrist approaches, people's minds will grow cloudy from carnal passions, and dishonour and lawlessness will grow stronger. Then the world will become unrecognizable. People's appearances will change, and it will be impossible to distinguish men from women due to their shamelessness in dress and style of hair. These people will be cruel and will be like wild animals because of the temptations of the Antichrist. There will be no respect for parents and elders, love will disappear, and Christian pastors, bishops, and priests will become vain men, completely failing to distinguish the righthand way from the left. At that time the morals and traditions of Christians and of the Church will change. People will abandon modesty, and dissipation will reign. Falsehood and greed will attain great proportions, and woe to those who pile up treasure. Lust, adultery, homosexuality, secret deeds, and murder will rule in society.
>
> At that future time, due to the power of such great crimes and licentiousness, people will be deprived of the grace of the Holy Spirit, which they received in Holy Baptism, and equally of remorse.
>
> The Churches of God will be deprived of God-fearing and pious pastors, and woe to the Christians remaining in the world at that time; they will completely lose their faith because they will lack the opportunity of seeing the light of knowledge from anyone at all. Then they will separate themselves out of the world in holy refuges in search of lightening of their spiritual sufferings, but everywhere they will meet obstacles and constraints. And all this will result from the fact that the Antichrist wants to be lord over everything and become the ruler of the whole universe, and he will produce miracles and fantastic signs. He will also give depraved wisdom to an unhappy man so that he will discover a way by which one man can carry on a

conversation with another from one end of the earth to the other. At that time men will also fly through the air like birds and descend to the bottom of the sea like fish. And when they have achieved all this, these unhappy people will spend their lives in comfort without knowing, poor souls, that it is the deceit of the Antichrist. And, the impious one!—he will so complete science with vanity that it will go off the right path and lead people to lose faith in the existence of God in three hypostases.

Then the All-good God will see the down fall of the human race and will shorten the days for the sake of those few who are being saved, because the enemy wants to lead even the chosen into temptation, if that is possible. . . . Then the sword of chastisement will suddenly appear and kill the perverter and his servants.[7]

Apart from its notable predictions pertaining to this century, this prophecy takes up and repeats the biblical words of warning about the struggle for the gospel even within the Church, and the stress that will come on the Church and the world through the activity of the spirit of infidelity and evil.

This prophecy gives warnings similar to the stream of warnings given to the Church and society of our time through the messages associated with the various Marian appearances. These speak of the eternal destiny of men and women and of the grave consequences of turning from God and his ways. They draw a connection between the chastisement inflicted on the Church and the world by communism and the great turning away from God now going on in Western society and in the Church itself.[8]

One of the most remarkable developments in the Church since Vatican Council II has been the great outpouring of the Holy Spirit in the charismatic renewal. This has been accompanied by a restoration of some of the gifts of the Spirit commonly at work in the early Church, including the gift of prophecy. The most tested, mature prophetic word coming from this renewal movement in the Catholic Church brings a message remarkably similar to that of St. Nilus and to that of the Marian apparitions. From this unexpected direction, in a different manner and vocabulary, the Holy Spirit seems to be trying once again to communicate something of importance to the Church. It is a message as old as the Bible, but it is addressed *to us*, here and now, and it demands a response.

Let us consider one recent prophetic word delivered by a respected leader of this renewal:

The Lord God says: "Hear my word. The time that has been marked by my blessings and gifts is being replaced now by the period to be marked by my judgment and purification. What I have not accomplished by blessings and gifts, I will accomplish by judgment and purification. My people, my church is desperately in need of this judgment. They have continued in an adulterous relationship with the spirit of the world. They are not only infected with sin, but they teach sin, pamper sin, embrace sin, dismiss sin. . . . Leadership unable to handle it . . . fragmentation, confusion throughout the ranks . . . Satan goes where he will and infects who he will. He has free access throughout my people and I will not stand for this.

My people specially blessed in this renewal are more under the spirit of the world than they are under the Spirit of my baptism. They are more determined with fear for what others will think of them, fears of failure and rejection in the world, loss of respect by neighbors and superiors and those around them, than they are determined by fear of me and fear of infidelity to my word. Therefore your situation is very, very weak. Your power is so limited. You cannot be considered at this point in the center of the battle and the conflict that is going on.

So this time is now come upon all of you—a time of judgment and of purification. Sin will be called sin. Satan will be unmasked. Fidelity will be held up for what it is and should be. My faithful servants will be seen and will come together. They will not be many in number. It will be a difficult and a necessary time. There will be collapse, difficulties throughout the world but—more to the issue— there will be purification and persecution among my people. You will have to stand for what you believe. You will have to choose between the world and me. You will have to choose what word you will follow and who you will respect. And in that choice what has not been accomplished by the time of blessing and gifts will be accomplished. What has not been accomplished in the baptism and the flooding of gifts of my Spirit will be accomplished in a baptism of fire. The fire will move among you and it will burn out what is chaff. The fire will move among you individually, corporately, in groups, and around the world. I will not tolerate the situation that is going on. I will not tolerate the mixture and the adulterous treating of gifts and graces and blessings with infidelity, sin, and prostitution. My time is now among you. What you need to do is to come before me in total submission to my word, in total submission to my plan. In the total submission of this hour, what you need to do is to drop the things that are your own, the things of the past. What you need to do is to see yourselves and those whom you have responsibility for in light of this hour of judgment and purification. You need to see them in that way and do for them what will best help them to stand strong and be among my faithful servants. For there will be casualties. It will not be easy, but it is necessary. It is necessary that my people be in fact my people, that my church be in fact my church and that my Spirit in fact bring forth the purity of life, purity and fidelity to the Gospel."[9]

In light of what we have considered so far concerning the prophetic aspect of our situation, the letter that Archbishop Fulton Sheen wrote to John Paul II a few weeks before the archbishop's death is of interest:

Pray for Your Holiness? That I always do for the Vicar of Christ, but in this fourth cycle of a crisis which strikes the Body of Christ every five hundred years, I pray for Your Holiness as for another Gregory the Great, Gregory VII, Pius V, and for our times as the poet Slowacki put it: "A Slav Pope will sweep out the Churches and make them clean within."[10]

There is little room for pleading ignorance. We have eyes to see and ears to hear. We can look at the pattern of judgment established in the Old Testament, the warnings of the New Testament, the lessons of history, the current signs of the times, and the actual prophetic word being addressed to the Church and world today. What we need now is action.

The prophetic word is often conditional. If God's people hear his word, and respond in repentance and restoration, sometimes the chastisement and judgment can be withheld or lessened. Sometimes, the beginning of judgment produces a repentance and turning to God that leads to restoration. But sometimes, if God's people remain blind, the whole, awful judgment must unfold.

If I close heaven so that there is no rain, if I command the locust to devour the land, if I send pestilence among my people, and if my people, upon whom my name has been pronounced, humble themselves and pray, and seek my presence and turn from their evil ways, I will hear them from heaven and pardon their sins and revive their land. (2 Chr 7:13-14)

But if there is no repentance, the glory of the Lord eventually "leaves the temple" and there remain only judgment and captivity (2 Chr 7:19-22).

CHAPTER THIRTEEN

A Time for Repentance

THE SITUATION OF THE CHURCH today is so serious that an appropriate response to it must be rooted in a profound repentance and turning back to God. We as individuals and as a Church must repent and turn more wholeheartedly to God.

Each of us must face our individual situation and seek repentance accordingly. To some degree or another, virtually all of us have accepted or tolerated false teaching, half-truths, and unrighteous behavior in ourselves and in those for whom we have been responsible. Because we form the body of Christ together, our lives are intertwined. We bear a corporate responsibility for our common situation. Genuine reformers have usually identified in some real sense with the "sins of the people." Personal righteousness and holiness are not sufficient in themselves for thoroughgoing reform. There is also a need for corporate repentance. Because God deals with us as individuals and as a people, we must respond on both levels.

The prayer of Nehemiah provides an example of how the individual and corporate dimensions intermingled in one reformer's prayer for repentance:

O Lord, God of heaven, great and awesome God, you who preserve your covenant of mercy toward those who love you and keep your commandments, may your ear be attentive, and your eyes open, to heed the prayer which I, your servant, now offer in your presence day and night for your servants the Israelites, confessing the sins which we of Israel have committed against you, I and my father's house included. Grievously have we offended you, not keeping the commandments, the statutes, and the ordinances which you committed to your servant Moses. But remember, I pray, the promise which you gave through Moses, your servant, when you said: "Should you prove faithless, I will scatter you among the nations; but should you return to me and carefully keep my commandments, even though your outcasts have been driven to the farthest corner of the world, I will gather them from there, and bring them back to the place which I have chosen as the dwelling place for my name." (Neh 1:5-9)

In order to turn back to God in individual and corporate repentance, we must first deal with the question of "blame." As we have already discussed, often today we are so concerned with ascertaining the degree of subjective culpability that we never properly deal with and even overlook objectively wrong and unfaithful actions. The prophet Jeremiah spoke to such neglect of objective wrong:

To whom shall I speak?
    whom shall I warn, and be heard?
See! their ears are uncircumcised,
    they cannot give heed;
See, the word of the Lord has become for them
    an object of scorn, which they will not have. . . .
Small and great alike, all are greedy for gain;
    prophet and priest, all practice fraud.
They would repair, as though it were nought,
    the injury to my people:
"Peace, peace!" they say,
    though there is no peace.
They are odious; they have done abominable things,
    yet they are not at all ashamed,
    they know not how to blush.
Hence they shall be among those who fall;
    in their time of punishment they shall go down,
    says the Lord. (Jer 6:10, 13-15)

It is virtually impossible to ascertain the subjective degree of responsibility in many cases. The remedy is to make the question of blame a subordinate consideration, and leave that judgment to God. Our attention should be focused on the objective nature of our thinking and action and their objective consequences. Subjective culpability is not even a judgment that rests with men. It rests with God, and as His Word says: "When a man knows the right thing to do and does not do it, he sins" (Jas 4:17).

I believe the time has come for us to stop condoning objectively wrong behavior with excuses: "I didn't know"; "I didn't have enough training"; "Everybody was doing it and it looked like the Church had changed its teaching"; "It's difficult for me to face conflict situations so I just went along with the tide"; etc. Let us leave these questions in God's hands. It is time for us to stop investing our energies in white-washing crumbling walls and instead to rebuild from the foundations on the basis of a wholehearted return to God and His Word.

> For the very reason that they led my people astray, saying, "Peace!" when there was no peace, and that, as one built a wall, they would cover it with whitewash, say then to the whitewashers: I will bring down a flooding rain; hailstones shall fall, and a stormwind shall break out. And when the wall has fallen, will you not be asked: Where is the whitewash you spread on? (Ez 13:10-12)

It is time to stop echoing the false prophets, saying "peace, peace" where there is no peace and confirming people in lives of sin, luke-warmness, and corruption.

> But among Jerusalem's prophets
>   I saw deeds still more shocking:
> Adultery, living in lies,
>   siding with the wicked,
>   so that no one turns from evil; . . .
> For from Jerusalem's prophets
>   ungodliness has gone forth into the whole land. . . .
> They say to those who despise the word of the Lord,
>   "Peace shall be yours";
> And to everyone who walks in hardness of heart,
>   "No evil shall overtake you," . . .
> Had they stood in my council,
>   and did they but proclaim to my people my words,
> They would have brought them back from evil ways
>   and from their wicked deeds. (Jer 23:14, 15b, 17, 22)

The teaching of scripture is that we need to accept responsibility for the wrong we have done—be it active or passive, an action or an omission—and leave questions concerning the degree of guilt or blame in God's hands. As a Church and as individuals, we need to fully face the present situation of lukewarmness and widespread infidelity and seek God in repentance for mercy and forgiveness. For currently our situation is under judgment.

> See, I bring evil upon this people,
>   the fruit of their own schemes,

Because they heeded not my words,
  because they despised my law. . . .
See, I will place before this people
  obstacles to bring them down;
Fathers and sons alike,
  neighbors and friends shall perish. . . .
See, a people comes from the land of the north,
  a great nation, roused from the ends of the earth.
Bow and javelin they wield;
  cruel and pitiless are they.
They sound like the roaring sea
  as they ride forth on steeds,
Each in his place, for battle
  against you, daughter Zion. . . .
O daughter of my people, gird on sackcloth,
  roll in the ashes.
Mourn as for an only child
  with bitter wailing,
For sudden upon us
  comes the destroyer. (Jer 6:19-23, 26)

The fact is that millions of Catholics, men and women who are the Church's responsibility through baptism, are living lives that are greatly offensive to God and gravely injurious to their fellow man—lives of adultery and fornication, greed and lust, sorcery and idolatry, anger, hatred, jealousy, murder, homosexuality, disobedience to parents, oppression of the poor. There are many who are trying to serve both God and money, who are mixing the worship of God with the invocation of evil spirits, the love of God with the hatred of men. Among those exercising pastoral responsibilities in the Church, there are parents, priests, and bishops who are functioning as false prophets, giving assurance of innocence where there is in fact guilt; as false priests, who no longer truly teach the Word of God, no longer distinguishing between the clean and the unclean, the sacred and profane; as false shepherds, whose sin of negligence and passivity has left the flock scattered, a prey for wild beasts, who now roam at will through the dispersed flock "seeking whom they may devour."

For us as a Church and as individuals, the only appropriate response to this situation is thorough and deep repentance; given the wretched condition of God's people, questions of degrees of blame are secondary. We need to evaluate our situation, not by the standard of "what has always been the case" or what is the "statistical norm," but by the norm of God's Word, his standards, his criteria, as expressed clearly in the scripture and the teaching of the Church.

By this standard, we stand greatly in need of his mercy and forgiveness, greatly in need of repentance.

Preparation for Repentance

In order not to take as "nought, the injury to my people" (Jer 6:14), we need to approach repentance as individuals and as a Church by careful consideration of our unfaithfulness before God.

We must consider not only the objectively wrong things that we have done, but also the serious nature of what we have failed to do. Our failure has allowed evil to flourish and the Church to be corrupted. "When a man knows the right thing to do and does not do it, he sins" (Jas 4:17).

We need to consider not only the evil we have done, but also the "good" we have done that was not the will of God. What have we done under the impulse of the "flesh," of the desires of "natural man," that was in fact an obstacle to God's plan for his people? Sometimes even apparently very "worthwhile" Christian activities can be out of the will of the Lord.

None of those who cry out, "Lord, Lord," will enter the kingdom of God but only the one who does the will of my Father in heaven. When that day comes many will plead with me, "Lord, Lord, have we not prophesied in your name? Have we not exorcized demons by its power? Did we not do many miracles in your name as well?" Then I will declare to you solemnly, "I never knew you. Out of my sight evildoers!" (Mt 7:21-23)

How much of what has been done in the name of Church "renewal" has been simply the product of man's "natural" thinking or enthusiasm—not the will of God, and therefore bearing no lasting fruit, producing no life? How much apparent "service" of God has been disobedience, a manifestation of a failure to seriously seek to know God, his will, and His Word? How much of our activity has been in direct contradiction to God's will, word, and ways?

How many times have we been "busy about many things"—many good and useful things—while forgetting the "one thing necessary," namely, seriously listening to God, knowing His Word, and doing his will?

For all of this we need to accept responsibility and ask forgiveness in the measure appropriate to each.

Let us now examine particular areas that will help us to approach repentance.

Our Own Lives. These are some questions to ask:

Have I allowed myself to be seduced by false teaching? Have I been eager to believe things to satisfy the desires of my flesh, to satisfy my "itching ears?"

Have I been eager to believe teachers or advisors who told me what I wanted to hear?

Have I used the "freedom" of the post-conciliar Church as an opportunity to satisfy the lusts of the flesh?

Have I allowed myself to be formed in my thinking and acting by contemporary culture in a way that has choked off my life with God and clouded my Christian mind?

Avery Dulles suggests that confronting ourselves with the eternal perspective can help reveal ways in which we have wrongly adopted the thinking of the world:

> Few Christians, I suppose, would say that the question of life beyond death is marginal or irrelevant . . . and yet many seem to act as though they believed that the only salvation worth considering must be attainable in this world before death, if not by ourselves, at least by some future generation. The very exercise of asking ourselves whether we subscribe to this view can prove medicinal. Once we have explicitly reaffirmed the Christian understanding of salvation, we see the ambiguity of our previous behavior. We are alerted to the apparent implications of our silences and omissions, our enthusiasms and boredoms, our approvals and disapprovals. We often find evidence of tacit heresy in our own lives and in the lives of Christians whose professed beliefs are unexceptionally orthodox.[1]

When the eternal perspective of God's Word is obscured, Christian morality, spirituality, and mission very quickly become more vulnerable to the pressures of contemporary culture. John Paul II has also been drawing our attention to this essential eternal perspective, and in our approach to repentance we would do well to meditate on his words:

> Christianity is a programme full of life. Confronted with the daily experience of death, in which our humanity shares, it repeats tirelessly: "I believe in eternal life." In this dimension of life is found the final fulfillment of man in God himself: "We know that . . . we shall be like him, for we shall see him as he is" (1 Jn 3:2).[2]

It is clear that Jesus does not eliminate normal concern and pursuit of daily bread and of everything that can make human life more advanced, highly civilized, more satisfying. But life passes inevitably. Jesus points out that the real meaning of our earthly existence lies in eternity, and that the whole of human history with its dramas and its joys must be seen in the perspective of eternity.[3]

Jesus, speaking of the kingdom of heaven, wishes to teach us that human existence has value only in the perspective of truth, of grace, and of the future glory. Everything must be accepted and lived with love and for love in the eschatological reality revealed by him: "Sell your possessions, and give alms; provide yourselves with purses that do not grow old, with a treasure in the heavens that does not fail" (Lk 12:33).[4]

Since morally wrong behavior often ensues when our basic grasp of Christian truth becomes uncertain and our clear, eternal perspective clouded, we must ask ourselves:

Have I done things that are morally wrong, no matter what the rationalizations, no matter who told me it was all right?

Have I led others to believe and to do wrong things by my example and my active encouragement, or by my silence and passivity?

Our "Teaching." Besides reviewing the way we have lived our own lives, we also need to examine the faithfulness of our teaching. We teach in many ways—informally and formally, directly and through the delegation of others.

Have I faithfully and fully taught the gospel of our Lord and Savior Jesus Christ, as understood by the official teachers of the Catholic Church? Or have I taught the opinions of men as the Word of God?

Have I "affirmed" people in their pride, sense of self-sufficiency, and "autonomy," rather than leading them to submit themselves to God and His Word?

Have I presented a mixture of God's Word and the "current thinking of the academic community" which has left people confused and uncertain?

Has my own teaching, or the teaching of those I have delegated (in my children's school, in seminaries or religious education programs) led people to forsake sin and live lives of purity and holiness, zeal and dedication? Or has my teaching subtly communicated a cynicism concerning the possibility of knowing God's Word with any certainty, and therefore the possibility of living enthusiastically and heroically?

Here it may be useful to meditate on the reflections of a small group of European bishops who have begun to acknowledge the way in which some of the "wisdom of this world" has perhaps obscured some of their teaching:

Many of our decisions, of our beliefs, are linked to an anthropology influenced by contemporary philosophical currents, for which the phenomenon of "secularization" has left an irreversible mark on modern man. Don't such convictions now have to be relativized by this renewal of the transcendent which reminds us that all anthropology which forgets the spiritual dimension of man is a truncated anthropology? . . . And don't we have to reconsider some of our approaches so that our speaking about God doesn't exhaust itself simply in an abstract and rational modality which unfortunately sometimes marks our declarations and our publications?"[5]

Our Spheres of Responsibility

We must also examine how we have conducted ourselves in our spheres of responsibility, which are broader than our personal lives and example, or even of our teaching.

Most of us have a definite sphere of responsibility for the lives of others, beyond our personal lives and example. Parents, for example, are responsible to a certain extent for the lives of their children. Older children are to some extent responsible for the lives of younger children. Parish priests have a significant responsibility for the moral and spiritual lives of their parishioners. Leaders of religious orders have considerable responsibility for the personal lives and service of those in the order. Bishops are responsible for the overall moral and spiritual health and soundness of teaching in their dioceses, and with other bishops they share responsibility for their own regions, their countries, and the world.

Virtually all of the massive infidelity, false teaching, and moral and spiritual corruption in the years since the Council has taken place in situations for which others have pastoral responsibility. In many of these situations, those with the responsibility have done little to stop evil from being done, or have only weakly bemoaned the situation, as Eli did with his sons. They have failed to exercise their responsibility and use their authority effectively.

As we repent, we need to look closely at how we have discharged our God-given responsibility in the spheres where we have it.

As Regards People. Have I allowed people for whom I have been responsible to be exposed to false teaching?

Have I allowed those for whom I have been responsible to accept false teaching and to promulgate it?

Have I been passive in the face of unrepented immorality in the lives of these people?

Have I been sufficiently in touch with the lives of those for whom I am responsible to know what they are thinking and doing, and so to be able to effectively "pastor" them?

As Regards Institutions and Programs. Many of us have responsibility for institutions, programs, or communities. These include families, schools, CCD programs, adult education programs, seminary curricula, and diocesan institutions. We need to ask ourselves some questions regarding our stewardship or guardianship over these things too.

Have I allowed my family (seminary, diocese, etc.) to become lukewarm, lax in the faith?

Have I tolerated ambiguous teaching and moral counsel in my institution?

Have I overlooked unfaithful, disloyal belief and practice?

Have I taught clearly or arranged to have taught clearly:

—God's plan of salvation
—the Church's teaching on sexual morality
—the important differences between Christianity and the non-Christian religions.
—the authority of the Scriptures, tradition, and the authentic teaching authority of the Church?

In particular, those responsible for institutions need to ask questions like these:

Have I taken the path of "least resistance" and added people to my faculty who are ambiguous in their Christian life and teaching, because no one else was available?

Is the continued existence of my institution more important than its continued faithfulness to God?

Accountability before God

All of us need to answer to God for our care of what he has entrusted to us, be it people, institutions, our families, our students, other people, or our own lives and example. As we have seen, scripture teaches clearly that each Christian needs to give an accounting before God for how he has lived his life. Scripture also says that a special accounting will be asked of those who have been given pastoral responsibility.

John Paul II manifests this awareness of accountability before the Lord in the extraordinary efforts he is making to call his own diocese of Rome to conversion and holiness of life. In an address to the students and staff of the Pontifical Irish College, he spoke of this awareness of his accountability before the Lord:

> Because you are living in Rome, in a diocese for which I personally must give a particular accounting to the Lord, you will understand how ardently I desire that Christ should be formed in you (cf. Gal 4:19).[6]

We have already considered how the Lord held Eli responsible for failing to effectively discipline his sons (1 Sm 2:12-36). We have also seen how the Spirit admonished early Christian communities for tolerating infidelity in their midst (Rv 3:12-23). Now let us look specifically at God's expectations concerning those who hold pastoral responsibility, particularly as this pertains to the prophetic and pastoral role which those in authority among God's people share to some degree.

To not adequately exercise the teaching and warning function that God has given us is to run the risk of being held responsible for whatever may flow from such passivity.

> You, son of man, I have appointed watchman for the house of Israel; when you hear me say anything, you shall warn them for me. If I tell the wicked man that he shall surely die, and you do not speak out to dissuade the wicked man from his way, he (the wicked man) shall die for his guilt, but I will hold you responsible for his death. But if you warn the wicked man, trying to turn him from his way, and he refuses to turn from his way, he shall die for his guilt, but you shall save yourself. (Ez 3:17-19)

Today, those of us who are parents, teachers, priests, bishops, religious education directors, seminary rectors, theology department chairmen, college presidents—all of us share in this "guardian" and "watchman" role. The consequence of not exercising this role effectively is to be held responsible for the evil that is done under our responsibility.

Jesus' heartfelt remark that it is better to be thrown into the sea with millstones around one's neck than to allow simple believers to be corrupted in their faith indicates how he feels about leading—or allowing others to lead—the "little ones" astray.

While primary responsibility in these areas falls to those who have been given authority in various areas of life—namely, parents and Church leaders at all levels—there is a sense in which every Christian, simply by virtue of being a Christian, has a responsibility to challenge false teaching and immorality, even when we are not directly responsible. We have a concern for one another's welfare simply by virtue of our baptism; we are all brothers and sisters in Christ. It is often fitting for ordinary Christians to speak directly to those involved in corruptions of the faith, and to bring the matter to the attention of the appropriate authority—parents, pastors, bishops, or religious superiors. If the immediate authority does not make a satisfactory response, it is often appropriate to go to the next higher authority. At a certain point, matters like these then have to be left to the judgment of the appropriate authority, who in turn will have to answer to God for the situation. When exercising this basic level of responsibility simply by virtue of being a "concerned Christian," it is important to act with respect and with openness to the possibility that the situation is not being perceived correctly or that there is more to it than meets the eye. At the same time, when a real corruption of truth or life is at stake, working diligently and persistently to bring it to the attention of the people involved and to the proper authorities is a valuable service to the whole Church and to the Lord.

As we come before the Lord and reflect on His Word to us, as we measure our life and the discharge of our responsibilities against His Word, our next step is to actually turn to God in repentance. Let us now look at some of the elements involved in authentic repentance.

Receiving Forgiveness. Forgiveness must be specifically sought, not simply presumed. If we repent and acknowledge our sin to God and to those we have wronged, we can be sure that God and those who obey His Word will forgive us. All the same, this forgiveness is to be sought and received as a gift, not presumptuously.

Sorrow for Sin. As we acknowledge our sin and infidelity and turn to God to confess it and ask his forgiveness, it is appropriate for us to manifest sorrow. This is an important part of both individual and corporate repentance. In times past, when God's Word has been "rediscovered" and God's people have measured their life against it anew, their repentance has often included an appropriate manifestation of sorrow for sin and infidelity.

The foundation for authentic sorrow is a recognition of who it is that we have sinned against, and of the consequences that have come into the world and peoples' lives through our infidelity. Sorrow for sin does not necessarily have to be rooted in an emotional response. We simply need to recognize that wrong has been done and that it is fitting to express sorrow for that wrong. In other words, we do not have to wait for certain emotions to well up before we can express sorrow for sin. We can simply choose to express it in various ways. For most of us, feelings of sorrow will usually be a component of such expression; God's people have often given way to "mourning and weeping" as they returned to him. For example, when Ezra gathered together all the people and read to them the Word of God, they broke out into weeping, because they saw how far short they had fallen in their lives as individuals and as a people (Neh 8). On another occasion, when Ezra learned of the unfaithfulness of the people—including the leaders, who had married wives and adopted practices from the nations around them—he began to weep and mourn, praying and fasting for the people:

> While Ezra prayed and acknowedged their guilt, weeping and prostrate before the house of God, a very large assembly of Israelites gathered about him, men, women, and children; and the people wept profusely. (Ezr 10:1)

In the days of Ezra and Nehemiah, acknowledgement of sin and an expression of sorrow were essential elements of the process of restoring God's people to a close and faithful relationship with himself. Today, as John Paul II works for the restoration of the Church in faith, morality, and mission, the same thing holds true: we have to acknowledge sin and express appropriate sorrow for our sin, individually and as a people.

Bearing the Fruits of Repentance. When the crowds were coming to John the Baptist in an apparent show of repentance, he exhorted them to give some evidence of their change of heart in concrete actions and changes in their lives (cf. Mt 3:8).

This is the required expression of any true repentance: unrighteous behavior must yield to righteous behavior. Also, specific acts or reparation are often necessary if the damage occasioned by our action or lack of action is to be repaired.

Repairing the Damage. "They would repair, as though it were nought, the injury to my people" (Jer 6:14).

Repentance must be in depth. It must take responsibility for the wrong done and must seek to repair the damage and set things right. Just as repentance for thievery is inauthentic unless it includes restoring the stolen property, just as repentance for slander is inauthentic without effort to restore the injured party's reputation, so too must repentance toward God express itself in reparation and restitution in all its dimensions.

Where we have sowed doubt or have allowed doubt to be sown, we must sow certainty. Where we have produced ambiguity or have allowed ambiguity to flourish, we must restore clarity. Where we have permitted cynicism about the things of God to grow up, we must replace it with sincerity and purity of heart. To the extent that we have allowed

God's Word and ways to be distorted, neglected, or denied in our spheres of responsibility, we must see that God's Word is restored. Whether in our families, parishes, dioceses, schools, seminaries, publishing houses, religious orders—wherever our pastoral passivity or lack of courage or discipline has allowed God's Word and people to be corrupted—there must we take action so that restoration and repentance can take place. If we have recommended unsound books to our people, then we must de-recommend them. If in our institutions we have tolerated teachers who do not faithfully present God's Word as understood by the Church, we must take measures to lead them to repentance, and if unrepentant, to remove them. If we have permitted situations that undermine the Christian community life of our family, our parish, our diocese, we must work to change them.

A "Firm Purpose of Amendment." Another prerequisite for authentic repentance is what has traditionally been called a "firm purpose of amendment." This means making the resolutions and taking the steps that will ensure that the infidelity or abdication of responsibility will not recur. We must combat our weaknesses, change our circumstances, and do whatever else may be necessary so that we can faithfully fulfill our responsibility as "watchmen" and "shepherds" for ourselves and God's people.

Many of us in positions of pastoral responsibility in the Church today quite simply have not made the decisions or established the circumstances that will equip us to carry out our duties in faithfulness to God. I believe that it is virtually impossible to be a responsible Christian unless we are making room in our daily lives for prayer and sound spiritual reading, for study of Christian truth, and for contact with others who also want to live a fervent Christian life and serve God faithfully. Making time for the Lord, for studying His Word, and for regular contact in a support group of other earnest Christians shows the kind of "firm purpose of amendment" that genuine repentance calls for.

These activities need to be complemented by a decision to remove from our lives those contacts and situations that lead us to become lukewarm and unfaithful in the service of God. All of us need to discern where the work of the world, the flesh, and the devil have led us to sin and infidelity. Then we must take measures to renounce the specific works of the devil, crucify the flesh, and become crucified to the world, so as to live fully for God. The atmosphere of worldliness, sensuality, and cynicism that often pervades many, even in leadership positions in the Church today, needs to be renounced. An atmosphere of godliness, purity, and love for God must reign in its place.

C.S. Lewis put his finger on the kind of "separation" from the world that is required if a Christian is to be faithful to God and truly able to serve the world as God intends.

> Every attentive reader of the Psalms will have noticed that they speak to us severely not merely about doing evil ourselves but about something else. In 26:4 the good man is not only free from "vanity" (falsehood) but has not even "dwelled with," been on intimate terms with, those who are "vain." He has "hated" them (5). . . . In 50:18, God blames a man not for being a thief but for "consenting to" a thief. . . . Not because we are "too good" for them. In a sense because we are not good enough. We are not good enough to cope with all the temptations, nor clever enough to cope with all the problems, which an evening spent in such society produces. The temptation is to condone, to connive at; by our words, looks and laughter, to "consent." . . . "Lead us not into temptation" often means, among other things, "Deny me those gratifying invitations, those highly interesting contacts, that participation in the brillant movements of our age, which I so often, at such risk, desire."[7]

Oftentimes, the lack of real Christian community in the Church today, the absence of real Christian support, and the personal isolation of many of those in leadership positions foster a vulnerability to temptation and infidelity that must be faced and changed. Seeking appropriate Christian support is therefore essential for anyone who wants to live as a faithful servant of Christ today, and may be an essential fruit, for many of us, of authentic repentance.

CHAPTER FOURTEEN

A Time for Action

SINCE REPENTANCE involves a change of mind as well as a change of heart, it will inevitably affect our plans and goals, our life and action. I would like to sketch some of the elements of a sound foundation for action that is pleasing to God. Obviously an adequate discussion of this subject would fill a book. Consequently, I intend the following remarks to serve not as a comprehensive treatment, but as a starting point or reference point for reflection and action.

Based on the Truth

A main thrust of this book has been that the truth of the gospel must be clearly grasped, lived, and proclaimed so that healthy Christian life may exist and grow. Therefore, a firm and clear grasp of Christian truth must be the basis of our relationship with God and with those we are trying to serve. One of the great weaknesses of both the pre- and post-Vatican II Church has been a widespread tendency to presume that Catholics already understand and are trying to live the fundamentals of the faith. Many millions do not. As a result, many houses have been built on sand, with no sure foundation of Christian truth.

The basic truths of sin and forgiveness, the sacrifice of Christ on the cross, the resurrection, the gift of the Holy Spirit, the Church, evangelism, the Second Coming, and the judgment should never be presupposed. They must be solidly built into and constantly renewed in our own lives and the lives of those for whom we have responsibility.

In the Power of the Holy Spirit

There has been a tendency in the Catholic Church for the Christian truths to be intellectually held and perhaps accurately expressed, but not adequately incarnated in life or action. Often this has been due to what Spanish Bishop, Juan Hervas, one of the founders of the Cursillo Movement, calls the "minimalist corruption of the gospel." By this, Bishop Hervas means the tendency in practice to ask less of Catholics than what the gospel asks, and to offer less than what the gospel offers. This has resulted in the widespread practice of a "lukewarm" Catholicism. Scripture makes it clear that God does not look kindly on a lukewarm Christianity. (See Rv 3:16.)

An adequate Christianity must ask of people all that the gospel asks: total commitment. It must offer all that the gospel offers: most especially, for our purposes here, the gift of the Holy Spirit, which brings Christian truth to life, generates Christian experience, and motivates and guides Christian action. Christian truth is meant to bring life, to cause the release of the power of the Holy Spirit in the lives of Christians. Unless this happens, Christianity is subnormal.

Led by the Spirit

"All who are led by the Spirit of God are sons of God" (Rom 8:14).

While the firm and clear foundations of Christian truth and the empowering of the Holy Spirit are essential to any adequate vision of Christianity, the *guiding* action of the Holy Spirit is uniquely important. Only the Spirit of God knows the depths of God, the real situation of the world, and the truly wise course for the family, the parish, the diocese, the religious order, the universal Church. Seeking God directly for his guidance and developing a sensitivity to the leading of the Holy Spirit is crucial for adequate Christian life and action today.

One of the great sins we need to acknowledge and confess is our neglect of actively seeking God's guidance for the situations we face as a people. One of our great problems as a Church is that we have too many "natural" men and women—be they liberals or conservatives, pragmatists or intellectuals, educated or uneducated—and not enough men and women who are led by the Spirit in their life and work. This failure to submit our plans to God's Word and to the leading of his Spirit is one of the main causes for the emptiness and lack of fruit of so much "renewal." Dr. Coggan, the former Archbishop of Canterbury, adverted to this in a sermon: "Some of us have almost given up believing that God still speaks to the Church. May God forgive us."[1]

Realistic Attitudes Toward "The World"

One of the most notable sources of confusion in the life and mission of the Church in recent years has been an unclear, sometimes confused, and often naive attitude toward the world. This stems from an erroneous reaction to the fundamental pastoral thrust of the Second Vatican Council—the important and worthwhile attempt to overcome an excessively negative attitude towards the world, in order to regain a hearing for the Church in an increasingly secularized society. Handled with skill and understanding, as, for example, in the ministry of John Paul II and others, this "opening to the world" has had a good effect. Elsewhere, however, it has resulted in disastrous confusion, frequent infidelity, and an abundance of negative results.

A naive "love of the world" often overlooks the reality of the fallen world's hostility to God, the work of the evil one, and the lusts of the flesh. It can result in the acceptance and encouragement of profoundly anti-Christian values, attitudes, practices, and beliefs in the lives of many Christians. Future action for the Church must take into account the whole word of God concerning the "world." It must take into account the profound practical implications of scripture texts like the following:

> Have no love for the world, nor the things that the world affords. If anyone loves the world, the Father's love has no place in him, for nothing that the world affords comes from the Father. Carnal allurements, enticements for the eye, the life of empty show—all these are from the world. And the world with its seductions is passing away but the man who does God's will endures forever. (1 Jn 2:15-17)

The Desire to Be Accepted by the World

A naive and uncritical love for the world often goes with a deep desire to please the world, to be well thought of, to be accepted by it. Christians, of course, want the world to recognize the good things the Lord has done in them, and so to reveal Christ to the world. However, this very desire has sometimes led them to so want to please the world and be accepted by it that they have consciously or unconsciously grown silent about the things which would offend it. Most profoundly offensive, of course, is the word and work of God centered in the cross and resurrection of Jesus Christ. In practice, this approach has sometimes led to an emphasis on what Christians and non-Christians have in common that chokes off the "offensive" proclamation of the gospel, with its absolute claims on the life of every human being and its summons to be joined to Jesus Christ or to suffer the consequences of judgment.

This desire to be accepted by the world has profoundly affected the attitudes of many in the Church. In some Church leaders, the desire to lecture at a prestigious secular university, to attend a U.N. conference, or to be invited to a scientific conference, has been accompanied by a silence about the central message of the Christian gospel.

In forming our pastoral approach to the family and the Church, we need to take into account the profound truth of the "offensiveness" of the gospel to the "natural" man.

> Since in God's wisdom the world did not come to know him through "wisdom," it pleased God to save those who believe through the absurdity of the preaching of the gospel. . . . As for myself, brothers, when I came to you I did not come proclaiming God's testimony with any particular eloquence or "wisdom." No, I determined that while I was with you I would speak of nothing but Jesus Christ and him crucified. . . . My message and my preaching had none of the persuasive force of "wise" argumentation, but the convincing power of the Spirit. As a consequence, your faith rests not on the wisdom of men but on the power of God. (1 Cor 1:21; 2:1-2, 3)

Fixation on a Passing Historical Moment

One of the goals of the Second Vatican Council was to help the Church develop a fresh approach to modern realities that would make its mission of evangelization more effective. The pastoral strategy of the Church had in some ways become fixated in stances taken at the time of the Reformation, the French Revolution, and the "age of revolution" in Europe. The realities engendered by these historical events needed to be taken into account in the Church's pastoral strategy, but ensuing events demanded consideration too. The Council was an attempt to do this.

Today, however, fifteen years after the Council, we face the danger of fixating on another particular historical moment—the moment during which the Council formed its pastoral strategy. Signs of stagnation are apparent. For example, the German-French theological preoccupation on dialogue with the theoretical European "modern man" can lead to overemphasis on a pastoral strategy that is not really applicable to vast areas of the Church outside of Europe. James Hitchcock perceptively points to the danger in continuing to operate with notions of political philosophy that were once useful in shaping the Church's relations to secular governments, but that are now quickly becoming inapplicable because of the shrinking base of viable world democracies. This stagnation will prevent us from taking stock of today's rapidly shifting historical circumstances. Just as the Church itself is always in need of renewal, so also is its pastoral strategy.

In his second encyclical, John Paul II pointed out that Vatican II only alluded to dangers in modern culture and society that have grown much clearer and more menacing in the last fifteen years:

> In the span of the 15 years since the end of the Second Vatican Council, has this picture of tensions and threats that mark our epoch become less disquieting? It seems not. On the contrary, the tensions and threats that in the Council document seem only to be outlined and not to manifest in depth all the dangers hidden within them have revealed themselves more clearly in the space of these years; they have in a different way confirmed that danger, and do not permit us to cherish the illusions of the past.[2]

Another danger is the Church's propensity for disastrous "time lags"—its habit of responding to yesterday's problems today when today's problems are of quite a different sort. Michael Harper, the Anglican author, made this perceptive comment about the Anglican Church in England and political and social movements:

> The Church has an unfortunate knack of saying and doing the right things at the wrong time. . . . In the last century when social conditions cried out for reform and when socialism as a political force was almost non-existent, the Church largely supported the status quo, and appeared on the side of the exploiters rather than the exploited. But now many of our Church leaders are vociferously on the other side. Whereas before the Church was the Tory party at prayer, now it seems to be the Socialist party, most of whom do not say their prayers. When the Word of God needs to be directed at the harmful effects of socialism and the so-called welfare state and the need for a more truly Christian approach to community life, the Church seems to be repeating the message which the 19th century needed to hear![3]

Today many Christian directives for the right ordering of society are not at all what the Spirit of God would lead his people to do. The most "relevant" action taken by God's people in the days just before the flood of judgment broke on the ancient world was the painstaking construction of the ark by Noah—an action that met with the hostility and ridicule of his fellow citizens. Are we not again in a time in God's plan when judgment approaches and one of the greatest services the Church can render the human race is to raise once again, loud and clear, the cry of the apostles: "Save yourselves from this generation which has gone astray" (Acts 2:40b)?

Intercession

All of us are expected to take responsibility for a certain sphere; if we go beyond this area we become what the scriptures refer to as a "busybody." Nevertheless, in addition to our sphere of responsibility, we all share a common responsibility for the Church as a whole. This duty is most appropriately fulfilled through intercessory prayer.

As we repent for our individual sins and turn back to God, we also need to beseech God on behalf of the whole Church, asking him to have mercy on us, to forgive us our sins, and to restore us to strength and wholeness as a Church through a new outpouring of his Spirit.

Paul VI viewed intercession for the coming of the Holy Spirit as a key to solving the present Church crisis:

> Men committed to the Church are greatly influenced by the climate of the world; so much so that a danger bordering on dizzying confusion and bewilderment can shake the Church's very foundations and lead men to embrace most bizarre ways of thinking, as though the Church should disavow herself and take up the very latest and untried way of life. . . . Now it seems to us that to check the oppressive and complex danger coming from many sides a good and obvious remedy is for the Church to deepen her awareness of what she really is according to the mind of Christ, as preserved in Sacred Scripture and in tradition, and interpreted and developed by the authentic tradition of the Church. The Church is, as we know, enlightened and guided by the Holy Spirit, who is still ready, if we implore him and listen to him, to fulfill without fail the promise of Christ: "The Holy Spirit whom the Father will send on my account, will in his turn make everything plain, and recall to your minds everything I have said to you."[4]

Paul VI thought that the hopes of John XXIII for the Second Vatican Council could really be fulfilled only through the experience of a new Pentecost. We have seen signs of this new Pentecost in a number of spiritual renewal movements following the Council, most notably and literally in the charismatic renewal. Yet, if the Church is to be truly equipped to carry out its mission in the world, it seems that a greater and deeper outpouring of the Spirit is needed—and not just among a few or on the periphery. As Paul VI said:

One must also recognize a prophetic intuition on the part of our predecessor John XXIII, who envisaged a kind of new Pentecost as a fruit of the Council. We too have wished to place ourself in the same perspective and in the same attitude of expectation. Not that Pentecost has ever ceased to be an actuality during the whole history of the Church, but so great are the needs and the perils of the present age, so vast the horizon of mankind drawn toward world co-existence and powerless to achieve it, that there is no salvation for it except in a new outpouring of the gift of God. Let him then come, the Creating Spirit, to renew the face of the earth![5]

Praying for the outpouring of the Spirit is one necessary focus of intercessory prayer. Another is praying against the work of the evil one.

Our battle is not simply against "flesh and blood" but against "powers and principalities." Unless we take this seriously, we will be neglecting the only weapons that are effective in this spiritual combat. John Paul II has pointed out that any analysis of reality that does not take into account the "prince of this world" is inadequate and is doomed to frustration and failure.

Does man have within himself the strength to face with his own forces the snares of evil, selfishness and—let us say so clearly—the disintegrating snares of the "prince of this world," who is always active to give man, first, a false sense of his autonomy, and then to bring him, through failure, to the abyss of despair? . . . Entrust yourselves to the grace of the Lord who cries within us and for us: courage!

Victory over the world will be Christ's. Do you want to take his side and face with him this battle of love, animated by invincible hope and courageous fortitude?

You will not be alone; the Pope is with you. He loves you and blesses you.[6]

Intercessory prayer, focused on specific situations to overturn and block the work of the evil one, is one way of contributing to the spiritual combat in which we all are caught up.

Appropriate Action

Another important response to the circumstances in which we find ourselves is appropriate action in response to the widespread undermining of God's Word.

In recent years, too many of us at every level in the Church have allowed God's Word to be undermined in our midst by our passivity or perhaps fearfulness. As we turn back to God as a people, many of us will be required to speak out or take action in our particular spheres of responsibility.

The basic principle of our action must be that we will not stand by as God and His Word are dishonored in our midst, and his people, our brothers and sisters, misled. In order to be effective and fruitful, our action must at the same time be humble, wise, righteous, and courageous.

Our action must be humble in that we are not speaking out or taking action from a position of "self-righteousness" or a "holier than thou" stance, but out of love and obedience—love for God and his people, and obedience to His Word and the promptings of his Spirit. We do not speak out and act because we enjoy confrontation, but because we *must* speak out and act in order to be faithful to God and His Word and to our covenant relationship with our brothers and sisters in Christ.

Our action must also be humble in the sense that we may not be right in our interpretation of a particular situation. We may, indeed, see only one side of a situation and not have an adequate grasp of all the relevant factors. We need to have the humility to be ready to discover this.

We must also act out of love. Our concern for the truth is precisely that—a concern for the truth and not a desire to prove someone wrong. This attitude of humility will generally mean that we will present our concerns to the appropriate people in such a manner as this: "My experience of your teaching is . . ."; "The students I talk to seem to be taking some ideas from your teaching that perhaps you don't intend, namely . . ."; "People have told me that they are interpreting your advice and counsel this way. . . . Are you aware of this?"

We should not presume that others are guilty of bad motives or conscious intention to undermine God's Word. In some situations, those who are doing the damage may not be aware of the results of their actions. On the other hand, as we have seen, some people involved in undermining the truth seem to be very aware of what they are doing and are consciously intent on this course.

Our action must also be wise. We must seek God for guidance to answer many questions. When should we speak and act and when should we remain silent? What has he given us responsibility for and what is the responsibility of others? When should we act alone and when should we consult others? When do we know enough about a situation and when is more study needed? These can be difficult questions. God gives his Holy Spirit to guide us if we seek him.

A good part of wisdom is acting within our immediate sphere of responsibility. It is there we have the greatest authority and clearest responsibility. On the other hand, all of us have some measure of responsibility to express our concern when fundamental issues are at stake, even though we may have little authority and can only express our concern to those who have responsibility.

Another part of wisdom is to act and speak according to the gifts and abilities God has given us. Not all of us are equally well equipped to deal with every situation. Sometimes our best contribution may be to pray for God to equip someone to deal with a situation that we are not able to.

Wisdom also means acting in a way appropriate to the situation. Often we should deliberately encourage what is good. For example, a word of encouragement after a sound homily, or an expression of support for a pastor trying to establish a sound religious education program, may be much more useful in a particular situation than denouncing unsound teaching and practice. It may be appropriate to write a letter to the diocesan newspaper about a public issue. On the other hand, when a private matter comes to our attention, private discussion with those directly involved will usually be in order. Sometimes we should withdraw our financial support from activities which do not clearly support the truth and authority of God's Word. In such cases, we should look for worthy God-centered activities more deserving of our financial support.

Wisdom means making sure that all of our resources—time, talent, and money—are working for the Lord and His Word and not against it, and encouraging others to do the same.

Our action must also be righteous. Normally we should approach those directly involved in activity which appears to be undermining God's Word before discussing the matter with a wider group of people or higher authority. The procedure for handling such difficulties is described in Matthew 18. Righteousness also means taking reasonable precautions against being rash in our judgments or loose in our talk. We should never unfairly damage someone's reputation. Nevertheless, it is entirely fitting for publicly taught and published material which undermines God's Word to be identified for what it is. Also, since the bishop is fully responsible for the soundness of all the teaching, preaching, and pastoral counsel in his diocese, it may be entirely appropriate to inform him of our concern at an early stage.

Our action must also be courageous. It must be said again that the dominant background of the crisis of truth is the silence and passivity of too many of us in the face of a massive undermining of God's Word. We need courage to act, to overcome our natural inclinations to "not rock the boat," or to "let George do it." We need to have the courage to run the risk of being wrong, to cheerfully acknowledge our mistake if we are wrong. We need to have the courage to run the risk of encountering the opposition and perhaps persecution and defamation that we almost certainly will encounter if we speak out and take appropriate action. But we still need to act. Only by courageous action will the cloud of darkness now choking the lives of many be dispelled and replaced with the life-giving light of Christ and His Word. As one Catholic observer of the contemporary scene has remarked:

> Genuine religious believers—as distinct from those for whom church membership is mainly a matter of habit—will be forced more and more to define precisely what the important differences are between themselves and non-believers. They may well have to accustom themselves to living in ways which the world around them will find strange and bizarre and which will require almost heroic decisions. The day may be coming once again when, as Christ foretold, those who persecute his followers will think they are doing something virtuous.[7]

Or, in the words of John Paul II:

> It is less possible than ever today to stop at a Christian faith that is superficial or of a sociological type; times, as you well know, have changed. . . . It is necessary to arrive at the clear and certain conviction of the truth of one's Christian faith, namely, in the first place, the historicity and divinity of Christ and the mission of the Church willed and founded by him.
>
> When one is really convinced that Jesus is the Word Incarnate and is still present in the Church, then one accepts his "word" completely, because it is a divine word which does not deceive, which does not contradict itself, and which gives us the true and only meaning of life and eternity. He alone, in fact, has "words of eternal life." He alone is the way, the truth and the life!. . . Jesus is not an idea, a sentiment, a memory! Jesus is a "person," always alive and present with us! . . . To seek, love and bear witness to Jesus! This is your commitment; these are the instructions I leave you![8]

John Paul II has also pointed out how a fervent Christian life may lead to persecution in today's world. It is the eternal perspective we receive from a knowledge of the basic truths of the gospel that gives us courage in times of difficulty:

> The Christian must live in the perspective of eternity. Sometimes his truly Christian life may give rise even to persecution, open or underhand: "Let us see if his words are true: let us test him with insult and torture, that we may find out how gentle he is, and make trial of

his forbearance." The certainty of the eternal happiness that awaits us makes the Christian strong against temptations and patient in tribulations. "If they persecuted me," the Divine Master said, "they will persecute you." (Jn 15:20)[9]

The day after he was elected pope, in his very first audience, John Paul II reminded the cardinals of the price they may be asked to pay for their faithfulness to Christ and the Church. These are words that can apply to all of us.

The faithful have really understood, revered Brothers, that the purple you wear is the sign of that faithfulness "unto the shedding of your blood," which you promised the Pope with a solemn oath. Yours is a garment of blood, which recalls and presents the blood that the Apostles, the Bishops, the Cardinals have shed for Christ in the course of the centuries. . . . May this unshakeable faithfulness to the Bride of Jesus be always the badge of honor and the preeminent boast of the College of Cardinals.[10]

And of all of his people, redeemed by his blood.

CHAPTER FIFTEEN

Unity, Division, and the Sword of the Spirit

IN RECENT YEARS, we have come to see that many of the historic divisions among the Christian Churches have been caused by worldly pressures, especially the political and economic kind, and the work of Satan. The divisions have not been primarily "led by the Spirit." Popes, patriarchs, and denominational leaders have acknowledged that all parties to the existing divisions among the Christian Churches share in the responsibility for them. We have become aware of the impact of the role played by communication problems, misunderstandings, and pride, and we are rightly determined not to provoke further divisions or to unnecessarily perpetuate those that already exist.

However, this praiseworthy goal has led some Church leaders to seek unity "at any price"—even at the price of infidelity to central Christian truths. This tendency has been emerging within the wider ecumenical movement, as well as within particular Churches, including the Catholic Church.

The World Council of Churches, the central body of the wider ecumenical movement, has been characterized by a tendency among its members to minimize differences regarding Christian truth that exist among themselves in the interests of being able to collaborate in the social and political field. The emphasis on a "plurality of expressions of the Christian faith" has sometimes concealed mutually exclusive and contradictory understandings of Christian truth. Sometimes a vision of the Church is projected as a collection of diversely believing people—including those who hold orthodox and unorthodox understandings of basic truth—who are united in adherence to particular political and economic values.

The lack of a secure foundation of truth in some of the Churches with which the Catholic Church has devoted most of its ecumenical efforts, has led some Catholic analysts to suggest a refocusing of the ecumenical effort. Avery Dulles, a prominent Catholic theologian engaged in the ecumenical effort, has warned against what he calls "secret infidelity"—the profound accomodations to contemporary secular culture which now characterize many of the Churches involved in official ecumenical dialogues:

> The official ecumenical movement, as represented by the World Council of Churches and by many regional and local councils, has largely forsaken the task of confronting the new paganism. Theological ecumenism, as represented by the bilateral consultations, has concentrated on special doctrinal questions that have arisen out of the divisions of the eleventh and sixteenth centuries. Neither of these two main currents of ecumenism shows any sign of addressing itself to the massive problem posed for all the churches by the rampant immanentism, humanism, secularism, psychologism, sociologism of our age—a convergent movement that leaves no room for the transcendent except as a kind of psychological "peak experience."[1]

James Hitchcock, another prominent Catholic thinker, suggests that the erosion of orthodox faith in many major Protestant Churches may call for a change in Catholic ecumenical strategy. The Catholic Church, he says, should probably be paying more attention to the evangelical and pentecostal segment of world Christianity. Exploring what Catholics and Evangelical Protestants have in common about basic doctrine might result in a more fruitful collaboration to withstand the undermining of basic truth now going on in the major Christian Churches and in society at large.

> The real ecumenical task, which presents both the greatest difficulties and possibly the greatest rewards, is to begin explorations with the Protestant groups broadly called evangelical. The greatest difficulties are found here, because these groups take their own beliefs very seriously and will not compromise easily. However, the greatest rewards are also to be found here. . . .

Short of actual doctrinal agreements, this new kind of ecumenical dialogue can be especially fruitful in terms of a reinvigorated Christian influence over American culture—the insistence that Christian beliefs and Christian moral principles be treated with respect and given proper weight in the formulation of public policy.[2]

Harry Blamires, an Anglican commentator, sees a new alignment in Christianity today that cuts through all the old divisions. Almost all the major Churches, he contends, are divided between those who hold to the biblical faith as understood in its basics through the centuries, and those who want to "accommodate" and "reinterpret" Christianity in order to place it at the service of contemporary causes and ideologies. He points out that a new ecumenical situation may be developing, one that would make it possible for Christians from many different Churches to support and encourage one another in the struggle for the core of Christian truth.

> We Christians today, of every confessional background alike, are surrounded by active secularizers of thought and life even within our own Christian bodies. A realignment is called for to gather together across denominational barriers those who have fully worked into their intellectual systems the implications of a faith whose powerhouse lies beyond the reach of time and change. It must gather these people together in phalanxlike resistance to every movement towards uprooting the faith from its eternal grounding and robbing it of its supernatural essence. Whatever good works we Christians may involve ourselves in—and the more the better: there is no question about that—we enter upon them carried on a flood tide of inspiration and zeal which submerges the familiar milestones of secular measurement; for the spring and source of it is a wounded side.[3]

Since the Second Vatican Council, the Catholic Church has emphasized unity and has officially committed itself to seeking unity with the divided Christian Churches. At the same time, it has made it clear that this desired unity, willed by Christ, must be based on a common adherence to his truth. This insistence that unity be based on truth has been met with hostility on the part of many Christians who would like to blur the distinction between the Church and the world and to use Christianity as a vague proponent of unity in a syncretistic mix of world religions in the service of political ideologies. In earlier sections of this book we saw how deeply this effort runs and how explicitly it is being pursued.[4]

It is important to see clearly that truth not only unites, it divides. Truth unites those who adhere to it and divides its followers from those who reject it. There are unnecessary divisions in Christianity that we should do everything to avoid—divisions based on misunderstanding and bad communication, works of the flesh, influences of the world, and the strategy of the evil one. Yet some divisions are necessary if we are not to yield to infidelity. We who share some responsibility for the future of Christianity and most particularly for the Catholic Church must be aware of this.

In every generation, a faithful presentation of Jesus shows him to be a "sign of contradiction" (Lk 2:3), a stumbling stone (1 Cor 1:23; 1 Pt 2:11), the occasion for the "fall and rise of many" (Lk 2:34). Jesus came both to unite and to divide the human race. God's will is for all to be saved, but some perhaps many, may reject God's will; these men and women will be forever divided from God and from those who obey God.

Maintaining the scriptural standards of faith and morality in the Church today, in every field of its work and life, is a solemn responsibility, not easily fulfilled yet severely judged. The salvation of the world depends on its being faithfully carried out. The pain of disunity is less than the pain of infidelity.

As I have tried to make clear in this book, there is a severe crisis of truth in the Catholic Church today, a crisis that affects its very foundations in the core of the gospel message of salvation and redemption. The time has come for the "sword of the Spirit, the Word of God," to do its work. "Sharper than any two-edged sword," the Word of Truth must be proclaimed and responded to. As that happens, there will be division; in our own hearts, the sword of the spirit will divide true from false, the unclean from the clean; the same will happen in our families, our parishes, our seminaries, our dioceses, our ecumenical relationships.

There is a need for us to be "made clean" (Jn 15:3) once again, "consecrated in truth" (Jn 17:17) through the powerful ministry of the word of God, proclaimed in its purity and power. Then will we be restored to that relationship with God and with one another which will truly and authentically reveal to the world that Jesus has come from the Father, that he contains within himself the words of life, that he is indeed the very door to heaven.

As Jesus is proclaimed and the Word of Truth is announced in the power of the Holy Spirit, those who respond will experience new and profound unity and peace. Those who persist in disobedience, however, will suffer division, hostility, and war. The hostility directed against God's followers will grow deeper and fiercer. Yet, at the same time, the light, power, and glory of his body will grow brighter and more powerful. What has wrongly been kept separate will be joined together. What has wrongly been united will be separated. We will see the truth of Irenaeus' description of humanity as two distinct races with eternally diverging destinies. Every man and woman will choose for one of these two opposing forces. Those who have rallied to the banner of Christ will be more certain about who they are and what they are working for; so perhaps will those who have rallied to the banner of Satan.

Scripture uses the image of two women to describe the two groupings of people that will exist at the Lord's coming. One is a harlot, the "whore of Babylon"—rebellious, unsubmissive, proud, and lustful, perpetrator of all foul things, seducer of the ungodly, persecutor of Christ and his Body, "drunk with the blood of the saints" (Rv 17, 18). The other, a bride, stands "pure and radiant," ready to meet her bridegroom who is Christ the Lord (Rv 21). She is an image of the Church, purified and made holy, fulfilling the promise and prayer of Mary who herself is the image and foreshadowing of our destiny, the one whose offspring, promised long ago in Genesis, was to crush the head of Satan. And he has. And he will.

In the years ahead, all of our personal decisions will contribute to the outcome of what is unfolding in the Church and the world. Developments of great consequence rest on our fidelity, on our courage, on our obedience to Christ our Lord, to His Word and his Church.

In an address to a group of people responsible for the training of seminarians, John Paul II indicated what he thinks awaits us in the years ahead. While his words were specifically addressed to rectors of seminaries, I believe they can be applied to us all; I have indicated this in my parenthetical additions. These words succinctly sum up the message of this book:

> In a word, the first priority for seminaries [the Church] today is the teaching of God's Word in all its purity and integrity, with all its exigencies and in all its power. The word of God—and the word of God alone—is the basis for all ministry, for all pastoral activity, for all priestly [Christian] action. . . .
>
> In the years ahead all of us must work for the purification of the Church, in accordance with the Gospel, and following the directives of the Second Vatican Council. In so doing, we hope to offer to the Savior His Church—holy and worthy of his love: a Church in which numerous young men [multitudes] are imbued with the mystery of Christ, and, basing their lives on his word, given themselves in generous preparation for his ministry.[5]

May it be so!

Notes

I have abbreviated two publications which are cited frequently in these notes. *L'Osservatore Romano*, the Vatican newspaper, is abbreviated *LOR*. The *National Catholic Reporter*, an American periodical, is abbreviated *NCR*.

Chapter One
A Crisis of Truth

1. *Ecclesiam Suam*, 26.
2. "Le futur pape sera affronté au problème de la pastoral," *La Libre Belgique* (October 12, 1978).
3. Quoted in *Our Sunday Visitor* (May 27, 1979).
4. *LOR* (April 23, 1979), address to Institutes of Catholic Education, April 3, 1979.
5. *Time* (European ed.) (December 24, 1979), p. 44.
6. For example, George Gallup's research indicates that 45% of U.S. Catholics do not attend church in a given week, and 20% are not members of a parish (*Catholic Trends*, May 13, 1978, p. 4). In Britain, only 57% of the public believes in heaven, 22% in the devil or hell (PRRC Emerging Trends, vol. 1, no. 10, December 1979, p. 1). In France, 40% believe that there is no life after death (*Origins*, November 22, 1973).
7. Paul VI, June 29, 1972, at a mass commemorating his ninth anniversary as successor to St. Peter.
8. *LOR* (December 3, 1979), p. 11, address to the religious communities of St. Pius V parish, October 28, 1979.

Chapter Two
Undermining God's Word

1. R. Scroggs, "Tradition, Freedom and the Abyss," *New Theology, No. 8*, ed. Martin E. Marty and Dean G. Peerman (New York: Macmillan, 1971), pp. 85, 100. See also the article by Schubert Ogden, theology professor at Southern Methodist University, "How My Mind Has Changed," in *The Christian Century* (December 17, 1980), p. 1234. Ogden declares that "what historians and exegetes now take for granted about the composition of the New Testament" now means that "none of the writings of scripture as such can be held to satisfy the early church's own criteria of canonicity."
2. Hans Küng, "Preface to A.B. Hasler's book, *Wie der Past unfehlbar wurde*," quoted in *The Küng Dialogue* (enc. 55) (Washington D.C.: United States Catholic Conference, 1980), p. 161.
3. Rosemary Reuther, quoted in *Consensus in Theology?* ed. Leonard Swidler (Philadelphia: Westminster Press, 1980), p. 65.
4. David Tracy, *Blessed Rage for Order* (New York: Seabury Press, 1975), pp. 6-7.
5. From a letter from Sr. Joan Gormley, S.N.D., leading official in the Maryland Province of Sisters of Notre Dame De Namur, quoted in "Fellowship of Catholic Scholars Newsletter" (June 1980), p. 18.
6. R. Barr, Editorial, *Today's Parish* (January 1980), p. 5ff.
7. St. Augustine, *On Christian Doctrine*, II, VII, 9 (38-9).

8. In one eighteen-month period, *U.S. Catholic* published articles attacking the Church's teaching on sexual morality, and questioning the reality of hell and the teaching authority of the pope, often in an extremely disrespectful flippant tone. It regularly advocates the ordination of women and has given five American archbishops and bishops the "*U.S. Catholic* Award" for furthering the cause of women in the Church. Cf. January 1980, p. 1; April 1980, pp. 2, 37-40; July 1980, p. 46; August 1980, pp. 26-31; November 1980, pp. 20-26; January 1981, pp. 2, 3; February 1981, pp. 31-32; March 1981, pp. 31-38; May 1981, pp. 7-9.

9. Elizabeth Farians, *Andover-Newton Quarterly* (March 1972), p. 199. Abundant examples of this type of theologizing and exegesis among Catholic scholars are contained in the recently published volume in the Concilium series: *Women in a Men's Church*, ed. Virgil Elizondo and Norbert E. Greinacher (New York: Seabury Press, 1980).

10. R.C. Devor, "When We're Blindsided by the Gospel," *Encounter* (Autumn 1975), p. 381.

11. Ralph Martin, *Husbands, Wives, Parents, Children* (Ann Arbor, Mich.: Servant Books, 1978).

12. Unfortunately, Mrs. Curran's remarks about the American Bishops Family Life Plan proved to be rather accurate. The Plan, designed to lead the American Catholic Church into a renewal of family life in the decade of the 1980s, is very nebulous and focuses mainly on a process of listening to people, giving the impression that perhaps God and the Church do not have much to say about family life. The scriptural foundations of family life and the whole matter of what God's Word says about it is not dealt with. The only teaching foundations offered in such a critical area are a very partial selection of quotes from recent Church documents which omit the challenges and "hard" parts of God's Word even as presented in contempory documents. (See *Parish Family Ministry Resources*, published by the United States Catholic Conference Commission on Marriage and Family Life, specifically, "The Plan of Pastoral Action for Family Ministry: A Vision and Strategy.")

The following is an excerpt from an unpublished paper, "Salvation for the Christian Family: New Programs or New Culture, A Critique of 'Plan of Pastoral Action for Family Ministry,'" written by Fr. John Dreher:

The subtitle of the Plan is "a vision and strategy." A reading of the description of the Plan indicates that it is more a strategy for action than a vision.

The Plan is primarily a step by step process for *HOW* to go about establishing programs to minister to families. Its practicability and action orientation make it appealing to Americans. . . . *WHAT* to administer—somewhat surprisingly—is not specified in the plan. . . . The most prominent feature of the Plan is a process for "listening" to the people. It is appealing to our modern democratic mind to determine how we will be served. Whether it is entirely open to Christian families to define who they are is a central issue I will raise in this critique. . . .

I feel the problem facing Christian families today is more one of dealing with its situation in modern culture, than the lack of programmatic service by the Church. I feel the problem is more deeply rooted than the Plan envisions and that the "salvation of the family" is more a matter of conversion than ministry, more a matter of the very culture and model of the family than of ministering to it in its current operating model. The issue is whether a Plan for Family Life today should not put primary emphasis upon examining in light of revelation the basic nature and fundamental relations of the family and not simply service. If vision is primary, then the first concern must be to listen to our Creator and the One who is Father of every family. This is not to negate listening to the people but to make sure that we have the mind of Christ to give us understanding of what the people say.

13. Dolores Curran, *St. Anthony Messenger* (January 1979), p. 48.

14. "Readers Forum," *The Catholic Messenger* (Davenport, Iowa) (September 13, 1979), p. 8.

15. St. Hippolytus of Rome, "Fragment" in Eusebius, *History of the Church*, 5, ch. 28.

16. Dogmatic Constitution on Divine Revelation, III, 11, *The Documents of Vatican II*, ed. Walter M. Abbott, S.J. (New York: America Press, 1966), pp. 118-19.

17. *LOR* (December 3, 1979), p. 8, address to the International Theological Commission, October 26, 1979.

18. *LOR* (April 17, 1979), p. 12, Declaration concerning the book "Quand je dis Dieu," by Fr. Pohier, issued by the Congregation for the Doctrine of the Faith.

19. *LOR* (April 17, 1979), p. 12.

20. *LOR* (July 13, 1981), pp. 4-5, Letter from the Sacred Congregation for the Doctrine of the Faith to Fr. E. Schillebeeckx.

21. Harvey D. Egan, S.J., "Reviews: Jesus: An Experiment in Christology," *NCR* (July 27, 1979), p. 14.

22. Joseph Sobran, "Finding a Faith in Modern Times," (*Los Angeles Times* Syndicate) *Winston-Salem Journal* (Winston-Salem, North Carolina) (October 6, 1979), p. 4.

23. For a description of this personal struggle and process, see *Hungry for God* (New York: Doubleday & Co., 1974).

24. Cardinal William Baum, "The Distinctiveness of Christian Morality," an address given at the Symposium on Principles of Catholic Moral Life (June 1, 1979), pp. 3, 4. The document that Cardinal Baum quotes here is the Congregation of the Doctrine of the Faith's *Mysterium Ecclesiae* (June 24, 1973).

25. Dogmatic Constitution on Divine Revelation, I, 6, *The Documents of Vatican II*, ed. Walter M. Abbott, S.J. (New York: America Press, 1966), p. 114.

26. *Catechesi Tradendae*, VIII, 60, *LOR* (November 12, 1979), p. 9.

27. *Catechesi Tradendae*, VIII, 60.

28. William G. Doty, *Contemporary New Testament Interpretation* (Englewood Cliffs: Prentice Hall, 1972), p. 19.

29. James Dunn, "Demythologizing—The Problem of Myth in New Testament," *New Testament Interpretations*, ed. Howard Marshall (Grand Rapids, Mich.: Wm. B. Eerdmans Publishing Co., 1978), p. 300.

30. See G. Maier, *The End of the Historical Critical Method* (St. Louis: Concordia Publishing House, 1977); W. Wink, *The Bible in Human Transformation: Toward a New Paradigm for Biblical Study* (Philadelphia: Fortress Press, 1977); Peter Stuhlmacher, *Historical Criticism and Theological Interpretation of Scripture* (Philadelphia: Fortress Press, 1977); George T. Montague, S.M., "Hermeneutics and the Teaching of Scripture," *The Catholic Biblical Quarterly* (January 1979), pp. 1-17; and S. Clark's essay, "Modern Approaches to Scriptural Authority," *Christianity Confronts Modernity*, ed. Peter Williamson and Kevin Perrotta (Ann Arbor, Mich.: Servant Books, 1981), pp. 163-86.

31. R.E. Brown, S.S., "The Myth of the Gospels Without Myth," *St. Anthony's Messenger* (May 1971), pp. 47-48.

32. Sr. Ann Patrick Ware, quoted in *Evangelical Newsletter* (April 4, 1980), p. 1, from her address before an interfaith gathering of feminists in New York City.

33. Mary Daly, *Beyond God the Father* (Boston: Beacon Press, 1973).

34. "I knew that Ba'al was a real god, the revelation of the mystery of life, the expression of the depths of being which had broken through into the lives of the people and gave them a key to the mystery of death and rebirth. . . . As for the defects of Ba'al, were they more spectacular than the defects of the biblical God or Messiah, or perhaps less so? . . . I could not give allegiance to any "jealous god" on the level of historical particularity. . . . I could not tell her (a nun) that my devotion to Mary was somewhat less than my devotion to some more powerful females that I knew: Isis, Athena, Artemis." (Rosemary Ruether, quoted in *Journeys: The Impact of Personal Experience on Religious Thought* [New York: Paulist Press, 1976].)

35. D.E. Miller, "The Truth of the Christian Fiction: Belief in the Modern Age," *The Christian Century* (January 31, 1979), pp. 97-100. See also Robert M. Price, "The Personal Savior—Reclaiming the Language of Piety," *The Reformed Journal* (August 1981), pp. 10-14.

36. *LOR* (February 4, 1980), p. 12, homily during mass at Capranica College, January 21, 1980.

37. Cardinal William Baum, "Doctrine and the Ecumenical Movement," an address given to the National Workshop on Christian Unity, published in *Origins* (May 10, 1979), p. 750.

38. Fr. William Most has done a great deal of research regarding the question of

whether the Catholic Church has ever changed, in the sense of repudiated, something it had previously taught in the area of faith and morals. He states: "Yes, there are claims of many errors made by the Church. I have personally checked every one—including many reported on in this column—and have found only one in 2000 years which holds any water at all: the Galileo case. But that was not from the Pope himself, just from a Vatican agency. And, basically, it was not a matter of doctrine, but of natural science anyway." (*National Catholic Register* [June 15, 1980], p. 5.) Fr. Most deals with many related questions in his column in the *National Catholic Register*, and in his book *The Consciousness of Christ* (Front Royal, Virginia: Christendom Publications, 1980).

39. *LOR* (March 2, 1981), p. 5, from the mass on February 19, 1981.

40. Archbishop Joseph Bernardin, "On The Teaching of Religion in the Archdiocese," Address to Religious Educators (Cinncinati, Ohio).

Chapter Three
Knowing God's Word

1. W.J. Burghardt, S.J., "This World Desperately Needs Theologians," *The Catholic Mind* (March 1981), p. 36.

2. St. Augustine, *Reply to Faustus*, 115; *On Christian Doctrine*, II, VII, 9(38).

3. St. Justin Martyr, *Dialogue with Trypho*, par. 65.

4. Cardinal John Newman, *Parochial and Plain Sermons*, vol. 1, serm. XIV.

5. *LOR* (February 16, 1981), p. 4, homily to priests of St. Paul's College, January 24, 1981.

6. *LOR* (February 4, 1980), p. 12, homily during mass at the Capranica College, January 21, 1980.

7. *LOR* (February 5, 1979), p. 10, homily to clergy and religious of Santo Domingo, January 26, 1979.

8. *LOR* (November 19, 1979), p. 12, address to Pontifical Universities and Roman Ecclesiastical Colleges, October 15, 1979.

9. *LOR* (February 4, 1980), p. 12, homily during mass at the Capranica College, January 21, 1980.

10. *Ibid.*, p. 11. Universities and Roman Ecclesiastical Colleges, October 15, 1979.

11. *Ibid.*, p. 12.

12. Dogmatic Constitution on the Church, XXV, 2, *The Documents of Vatican II*, ed. Walter M. Abbott, S.J. (New York: America Press, 1966), p. 47f.

13. Dogmatic Constitution on Divine Revelation, X, 2, *The Documents of Vatican II*, p. 117f.

14. Cardinal Hoffner's declaration (December 18, 1979) on Fr. Hans Kung, *Origins* (January 3, 1980), p. 465.

15. *LOR* (November 19, 1979), p. 12, address to Pontifical Universities and Roman Ecclesiastical Colleges, October 15, 1979.

16. Cardinal William Baum, "The Distinctiveness of Christian Morality," opening address at the Symposium on Principles of Catholic Moral Life (June 17, 1979), p. 1.

17. *Catechesi Tradendae*, I, 6, *LOR* (November, 12, 1979), p. 2.

Chapter Four
Silencing the Gospel

1. Ralph Martin, *Unless the Lord Build the House* (Notre Dame, Ind.: Ave Maria Press, 1971).

2. *The Catholic Herald* (London, England) (September 14, 1979).

3. *The Catholic Herald* (October 12, 1979), p. 4.

4. "Un Rendez-vous des Enfants à la Cathedrale," *Dimanche a Uccle* (Belgium) (September 23, 1979), p. 3.

5. M. Sandoval, "Friends Not Enemies," *Maryknoll* (May 1980), p. 3.

6. D. Berceli, M.M., "Christianity Through Islam," *Maryknoll* (May 1980), p. 45.

7. J. Eposito, "What is Islam," *Maryknoll* (May 1980), p. 13.

8. *Columban Mission* (December 1980). See especially Fr. Frank Hoare's article, "Prasad" (pp. 4-5), and Edward Rice's "Lord of the Harvest Moon" (pp. 6-9).

9. See also *Maryknoll* (November 1981), especially pp. 9, 34, 51-54, for signs of this type of influence. The works of Raimundo Pannikar are especially influential in this regard. See his *The Unknown Christ of Hinduism* (Maryknoll, N.Y.: Orbis, 1981).

10. E. Kieser, "Evangelization Through Electronics," *America* (May 6, 1978), p. 359.

11. Melissa Jones, "The Rite of Changing Women," *NCR* (November 9, 1979), p. 19.

12. "An Interview with Fr. Bruce Vawter," *U.S. Catholic* (August 1980), p. 31.

13. Thomas E. Power, *Invitation to a Great Experiment: Exploring the Possibility That God May Be Known* (New York: Doubleday & Co., 1979), p. 4.

14. *Sign* (March 1979).

15. "Classics of Western Spirituality," published by Paulist Press.

16. "Focus On Resources," *The New Review of Books and Religion* (May 1979), pp. 22-26.

17. The Spring 1980 Schedule of Dialogue House, New York City.

18. For information, see, for example, "Silva Mind Control—Is It Really Demonic?" in *National Communications Office Newsletter* (June 1980), and "The Consciousness Movement I: The Selling of the Swami," by Jim Manney, *New Covenant* (March 1977), p. 4.

19. "Buddhists Exchange Ideas," *The Catholic Herald* (London, England) (October 12, 1979), p. 3.

20. Declaration on the Relationship of the Church to Non-Christian Religions, par. 2, *The Documents of Vatican II*, ed. Walter M. Abbot, S.J., New York, America Press, 1966), p. 662.

21. *Ibid.*

22. *Ibid.*

23. *Evangelii Nuntiandi*, 53 (Washington, D.C.: United States Catholic Conference Publications Office, 1976), p. 36f.

24. *LOR* (May 7, 1979), p. 4, remarks to the members of the Plenary Assembly of the Secretariat for Non-Christians, April 27, 1979.

25. *Ibid.*

26. *LOR* (March 9, 1981), p. 9, remarks at a meeting with representatives of non-Christian Religions, February 24, 1981.

27. Karl Rahner, "Christianity and the Non-Christian Religions," Theological Investigations, vol. 5 (Baltimore: Helicon Press, 1966). See related essays in vols. 6, 9, 12, and 14, and in *God's Word Among Men* (ed. G. Gispert) (Sauch, Delhi, Vidyajyoti, 1973).

28. It must be said that some voices among prominent contemporary Roman Catholic theologians have attempted to point out the dangers of the "anonymous Christianity" approach. One is Walter Kasper in *Jesus The Christ* (New York: Paulist Press, 1976), p. 189: "These [views of Christ] are all splendid and ingenious projects of a Christocentric total view of reality. Nevertheless, their intrinsic danger must not be overlooked, which consists in transforming the uniqueness of Jesus Christ into something universal and ending with a Christianity which is found anonymously everywhere in mankind, paying for its universality by the loss of its concreteness and uniqueness of meaning."

29. Denis Murphy, "A Church in the Minority," *America* (August 25, 1979), p. 75.

30. *Ibid.*

31. *Ibid.*

32. Peter Gowing, quoted by Theresa McClellan, "Missionary Strives to Maintain Christian-Moslem Relationships," *The Grand Rapids Press* (Grand Rapids, Michigan) (January 31, 1981), p. 4A.

33. Dr. Deane Ferm, " "The Road Ahead in Theology' Revisited," *The Christian Century* (May 9, 1979), p. 527.

34. Other examples of this effort to deny the uniqueness of the identity and claims of Jesus can be found in John Hick's *The Center of Christianity* (San Francisco: Harper & Row Publishers, 1968, 1978). See especially pp. 70-79. See also the collection of articles edited by John Hick entitled *The Myth of God Incarnate* (Philadelphia: Westminster Press, 1978).

35. See, for example, *Maryknoll* (September 1981), p. 28.

36. Murphy, p. 75, quoting a bishop from Thailand.

37. Murphy, p. 75, quoting a bishop from Bangladesh.

38. *LOR* (December 3, 1979), p. 10, address to religious communities of St. Pius V's parish, October 28, 1979.

39. *LOR* (November 26, 1979), pp. 3, 4, from the mass for World Mission Sunday, October 20, 1979.

Chapter Five
Is Jesus the Only Way?

1. *LOR* (December 3, 1979), p. 16, address to members of the Italian Union of Secondary Teachers, November 3, 1979.

2. Declaration of the Relationship of the Church to Non-Christian Religions, 2, *The Documents of Vatican II*, ed. Walter M. Abbot, S.J. (New York: America Press, 1966), p. 662.

3. Decree on the Missionary Activity of the Church, 7, *The Documents of Vatican II*, p. 593.

4. See, for example, 1 Cor 15:24-28; Eph 1:9-10; Col 1:15-20.

5. *LOR* (June 18, 1979), p. 10, address to eleven bishops of India, May 31, 1979.

6. *LOR* (May 14, 1979), p. 9, address to bishops from India, May 5, 1979.

7. *LOR* (November 26, 1979), p. 3, from the mass for World Mission Sunday, October 20, 1979.

8. Dogmatic Constitution on the Church, 16, *The Documents of Vatican II*, p. 35.

9. *Evangelii Nuntiandi*, 80, (Washington, D.C.: United States Catholic Conference Publications Office, 1976), p. 63. Office, 1976), p. 63.

Chapter Six
Christianity and Social Concern

1. For a brief account of some of the main line of the Church's social teaching see my "Perspective" in *New Covenant*, April, 1982.

2. While today the greater danger seems to be an identification of Christianity with leftist ideology, in the past and perhaps again in the future the danger of identifying with rightest ideologies has been and may again be the predominant danger. See in this regard Dale Vree's article, "Politicized Theology," in *Christianity Confronts Modernity*, ed. Kevin Perrotta and Peter Williamson (Ann Arbor, Mich.: Servant Books, 1981), pp. 57-78.

3. Msgr. Helder Camara, quoted by Nicolette Franck, "Mgr. Camara crèe à Genévè la "Symphonie des Deux Mondes,"' *La Libre Belgique* (March 8/9, 1980), p. 28.

4. For a current account of Chinese efforts to bend the Church today in China to the State's purposes, see "China and the Church Today" (September-December 1979), distributed in North America by Partnership in Mission, 1564 Edge Hill Rd, Abington, PA 19001.

5. Bishop Francis Stafford, "Synod Reflections IV," *The Catholic Review* (Baltimore, Md.) (October 31, 1980).

6. *Le Monde* (Paris, France) (May 23, 1979), p. 15.

7. Quoted by Rev. Msgr. J.T. Ellis, "American Catholics in 1979," *The Pilot* (Boston, Mass.) (September 21, 1979), p. 9.

8. It is clear that one of John Paul II's main concerns is to properly locate the building of a more human world in the context of fundamental Christian truths about God and man. His first three encyclicals have made a significant contribution to establishing a context and enunciating principles which can guide Christians in judging the relative suitability of various political programs and systems. Of course, even when the principles have been well enunciated, agreed on, and used in coming to political judgments, sincere and well-informed Christians may still find themselves judging differently about the relative suitability of various political and economic approaches, which are more relative and open to debate than the principles themselves. Nevertheless, what John Paul II appears to be doing in providing criteria to judge the suitability of political alternatives is of great significance. British religious writer Clifford Longley recently said it well:

> We are, I believe, witnessing the rebirth of a new Catholic Humanism with Pope John Paul's brilliant synthesis of Catholic theology and human rights philosophy, and the result is a genuinely Christian criterion for measuring the success or failure of this or that political system.
> It specifies ends, while leaving the means to the economists and politicians who are the experts. It might or might not, for example, be better to strike early or late; strikers

might or might not be greedy and selfish; hospital workers might be callous, or they might be desperately poor. (*The Catholic Herald* [London, England] [February 23, 1979]).

See also the contributions of the Latin American bishops in this regard in the Medellin and Puebla documents.

9. Raul Macin, cited by William Conard, "Liberation Theology to Leftist Politics," *Christianity Today* (June 8, 1979), p. 61.

10. Gonzalo Baez-Camargo, cited by W. Conard, p. 61.

11. Moises Hassan, quoted by Charles Roomey, "Revolution Gives Credit to Catholics," *NCR* (December 7, 1979), p. 6.

12. *NCR* (April 4, 1980), p. 22.

13. See, for example, the "Conscientization Kit" published by the World Council of Churches in 1975.

14. Gustavo Gutiérrez, *A Theology of Liberation* (Maryknoll, N.Y.: Orbis Books, 1973), p. 9.

15. Translated from "Diario La Prensa" (San Pedro Sula) (July 19, 1980).

16. See *Maryknoll,* (September 1981), pp. 15-21.

17. L.J. Cardinal Suenens and Dom Helder Camara, *Charismatic Renewal and Social Action* (Ann Arbor, Mich.: Servant Books, 1979).

18. Information contained in this paragraph comes from actual Communist documents that have come into the hands of top Church leadership in this particular country. For obvious reasons they cannot yet be published.

19. *Catechesi Tradendae,* VII, 52, *LOR* (November 12, 1979), p. 8. See also in this connection the letter from Jesuit Superior General, Pedro Arrupe, to Jesuit Superiors in Latin America, *Origins* (April 16, 1981), pp. 690-93.

Chapter Seven
Secular Humanist Influence on the Church

1. Although Marxist ideology is not the predominant influence in the United States, it is worth noting that some leadership elements involved in work with Spanish-speaking Catholics in the U.S. are working to move things in this direction. A participant in the "Theology in the Americas" Conference held in the summer of 1980 in Detroit documented for me that one Hispanic priest publicly declared "progressive" political forces should use language that the Church feels comfortable with and once the Church is won over to assisting the revolution, then it too can be destroyed, and there will no longer be a need for theologians. A selective account of this conference appeared in the August 15, 1979, issue of *NCR.*

Also worth noting is a proposal by a group of American Jesuits that appeared in the *National Jesuit News* (February 1972, pp. 6-7). It speaks of the need for "the construction of a revolutionary social strategy for the Society of Jesus which is explicitly neo-Marxist and Maoist. . . . To effect this role authentically, the Society of Jesus must purge itself of its bourgeois consciousness and identify with the proletariat, acknowledging that only the proletariat, as the living negation of advanced monopoly capitalism and as the subject of history, can achieve correct and objective social knowledge—the proletariat simultaneously knows and constitutes society. It is at this point that we are very close to understanding the mystery of Jesus' own proletarian background."

2. A concise but penetrating analysis of "secular humanism" appeared in the July 1979 issue of *Columbia* magazine, in an article entitled "The Secular Sickness," by Dr. James Hitchcock.

3. "Humanist Manifesto II," *The Humanist* (September/October 1973), p. 4.

4. James Hitchcock, *Catholicism and Modernity* (New York: Seabury Press, 1979), p. 86.

5. *Catechesi Tradendae,* VII, 52, *LOR* (November 12, 1979), p. 8.

6. *NCR* (January 25, 1980), p. 3f.

7. *Ibid.*

8. Quoted by Mary Bader Papa, "ERA: Catholics Debate Its Effects . . ." *NCR* (December 28, 1979), p. 16.

9. See, for example, "Is There an ERA-Abortion Connection?" by Jim Lackey, *The Pilot* (October 24, 1980), p. 1; "Prolife News," by Sally Greene, *National Catholic Register* (October 12, 1980).

10. Quoted by M. Papa, p. 16.

11. *Notre Dame Magazine* (October 1979).

12. *Notre Dame Magazine* (February 1980), p. 5.

13. Eugene Kennedy, "Friendship: The Mysterious Bond," *Notre Dame Magazine* (October 1979), p. 10ff.

14. Patricia O'Brien, "Women Friends," *Ibid.*, p. 13.

15. Kevin Lamb, "Journeys of an Ex-Viking," *Ibid.*, p. 41.

16. Rev. Theodore Hesburgh, C.S.C., "A Priest in the Land of the Dragon," *Ibid.*, p. 25.

17. "Les Jesuites mettent en cause la 'societé de consommation,' " *La Libre Belgique* (September 18, 1979).

18. Fr. John McNeill, S.J., author of *The Church and the Homosexual* (Mission, Kans.: Sheed, Andrews, and McMeel, 1976), has been in the forefront of the leadership of Dignity. Fr. Bill Callahan, S.J. of the Quixote Center in Washington, D.C., has been in the forefront of the women's ordination effort (see footnote 16, Chapter Eleven). Chapter Eight.

19. "Project 1: The Jesuit Apostolate of Education in the U.S.: Some Options," published by the staff of the Jesuit Conference of North America, pp. 123-26.

20. Parents troubled by the condition of many Catholic universities and colleges often ask me if I know of reliable institutions where their children can go. There seems to be something of a Catholic revival going on in the forming of new Catholic colleges solidly rooted in the faith, but as of yet I have no personal experience with them. One Catholic university that I can wholeheartedly recommend is the University of Steubenville, located in Steubenville, Ohio, and run by a group of Franciscans.

21. *La Libre Belgique*, "Dossier Special" (September 15, 1979), p. 3.

22. *Redemptor Hominis*, 10, *LOR* (March 19, 1979), p. 6.

23. *LOR* (April 9, 1979), p. 10, homily to the Vatican Polyglot Printing House, March 30, 1979.

24. Fr. John Egan, quoted in *Catholic Trends* (April 28, 1979), pp. 2-3.

25. Fr. Richard McBrien, "Essays in Theology," *The Catholic Transcript* (Hartford, Connecticut) (July 21, 1978). Fr. McBrien is here just articulating a position held by some and is not claiming it as his own.

26. Ellwood Kieser, C.S.P., "Evangelization Through Electronics," *America* (May 6, 1978), p. 359.

27. Fr. Richard McBrien, *The Catholic Transcript* (July 21, 1978). Again, McBrien is not personally identifying with this formulation.

28. Walter Kasper, *Jesus The Christ* (New York: Paulist Press, 1976), p. 96.

29. Avery Dulles, S.J., "Unmasking Secret Infidelities: Hartford and the Future of Ecumenism," *Against The World For the World*, ed. Peter L. Berger and Richard J. Neuhaus (New York: Seabury Press, 1976), p. 55.

Chapter Eight
The Undermining of Sexual Morality

1. Anthony Kosnik, William Carroll, Agnes Cunningham, Ronald Modras, and James Schutte, *Human Sexuality: New Directions in American Catholic Thought* (New York: Paulist Press, 1977).

2. *Ibid.*, pp. 92-94.

3. *Ibid.*, pp. 151f.

4. *Ibid.*, pp. 231-32.

5. *Ibid.*, p. 232.

6. *Ibid.*, pp. 148-49.

7. Ronald Modras, "The Devil, Demons and Dogmatism," *Commonweal* (February 4, 1977), pp. 71-75.

8. For example, Fr. Richard McBrien, chairman of the theological department at Notre Dame, has published a two-volume work called *Catholicism* (Minneapolis, Minn.: Winston Press, 1980) which is being heralded by some as a new synthesis for our time. In it he states the teaching of the Church in regard to moral questions, but also states the opinions of various theologians including those of the authors of *Human Sexuality*. This method gives the impression that we should reflect on all the opinions and decide for ourselves what we find most meaningful. McBrien condescendingly acknowledges the "right" of the Church to teach in preference to the contradictory opinions of certain theologians. See, for example, his treatment of homosexuality (pp. 1027-32) and contraception (pp. 1016-1027). Such "polished" and subtle distortions of the rightful place of the teaching authority of the Church in the area of faith and morals can be even more damaging than blatant attacks. The bishops of Australia perceived the undermining effect of Fr. McBrien's *Catholicism* and issued a public declaration in regard to it:

> We, the Catholic bishops of Australia, feel obliged to issue a statement on (*Catholicism*). On one hand, the book has been praised as a masterly summary of Catholic teaching. On the other, it has been criticized for deviating from authentic Catholic teaching.
> In particular, it has been suggested that the book is an excellent medium for use in Catholic schools.
> We disagree. . . . *Catholicism* has some strong features, but it also has real weaknesses. For example, it puts side by side two things which cannot be equated:
> The Church's authentic teaching.
> The opinions of theologicans, some of them quite radical ones.
> The result can easily be confusion about what the Church really teaches. Therefore, this book needs to be read with discrimination and an alert critical sense. . . .
> We do not recommend *Catholicism* to primary or secondary school teachers, even as a reference or resource book. . . . We do not recommend it to the ordinary layman or laywoman as a book in which to look up some point of Catholic teaching. (*The Leader* (Australia) (September 7, 1980).)

See also, "Controversy over *Catholicism*," by Andrew Zwernerman, *Scholastic* (Notre Dame's student publication) (November 1980), pp. 11-13.

9. Joan Turner Beifuss, "Sex and the Divorced Catholic," *NCR* (May 25, 1979), p. 15.

10. Beifuss, p. 14.

11. See the Dogmatic Constitution on the Church, par. 25, *Documents of Vatican II*, ed. Walter M. Abbott, S.J. (New York: America Press, 1966), pp. 47ff.

12. Beifuss, p. 15.

13. "Letter from the Sacred Congregation for the Doctrine of the Faith to Archbishop Quinn," *LOR* (December 17, 1979), p. 9.

14. "Declaration on Certain Questions Concerning Sexual Ethics," Sacred Congregation for the Doctrine of the Faith (December 29, 1975).

15. Ralph McInerny, "Do Moral Theologians Corrupt Youth," *New Covenant* (November 1979), p. 4.

16. McInerny, pp. 5, 7.

17. Rev. Joseph Creedon, quoted by Richard C. Dujardin, *The Providence Sunday Journal* (March 22, 1981), p. A-24.

18. *Today's Parish* (January 1980).

19. R.H. Springer, S.J., "Holy God, Gays Want In!" *Today's Parish* (January 1980), pp. 10-13.

20. Springer, p. 13.

21. Theodore Jennings, "Homosexuality and Christian Faith: A Theological Reflection," *The Christian Century* (February 16, 1977), pp. 137-42.

22. See, for example, Letha Scanzoni and Virginia Ramey Mollenkott, *Is the Homosexual My Neighbor?* (San Francisco: Harper & Row Pub., 1978); *The Record* (Newsletter of Evangelicals Concerned, Inc., New York) (Fall 1980); J. Harold Ellens, "Homosexuality: The Biblical Claim," *The Bulletin*, a publication of the Christian Association for Psychological Studies, 4, no. 2 (1978), p. 5; Lewis B. Smedes, *Sex for Christians* (Grand Rapids, Mich.: Wm. B. Eerdmans Pub. Co., 1976).

23. Dignity and New Ways Ministry would fall into this category. For an understanding of the perspective of New Ways Ministry see the following articles written by co-director Robert Nugent, S.D.S.: "Homosexuality and the Hurting Family," *America* (February 28, 1981), pp. 154-57; "Gay Ministry," *Ministries* (December 1980), pp. 26-28. Joan Beifuss, in her article "Gays 1980: "Out of Both Closet and Confessional'" (*NCR*, November 21, 1980), euphemistically states, "Many Catholic gays, buoyed by groups such as Dignity and New Ways and by the climate of opening discussion, are making their own decisions of conscience about sin and sexuality and their own relationship to the church" (p. 10). She also quotes the head of Dignity, Frank Schueren, as saying, "I believe God gave me the ability of personal conscience. . . . I myself have been through psychiatric analysis and every other means I've had available, including clergy counseling. I've used all those things to form my conscience. And in my conscience, which the church says is my final guide, I do not believe that I'm doing anything wrong as long as it's part of a meaningful relationship." Beifuss then gives the following description of Schueren's life: "Schueren, 38, lived for 11 years with a male friend whose wife had died. During that time they raised his friend's son and daughter. "Both of them are heterosexual,' he notes dryly. Although Schueren and his friend have ceased living together, they still consider themselves "family'" (p. 2). For an understanding of Dignity's position, see *Homosexual Catholics: A New Primer for Discussion* (Washington, D.C.: Dignity, 1980), prepared by Robert Nugent, S.D.S., Jeannine Gramick, S.S.N.D., and Thomas Oddo, C.S.C.

24. Roger LeLievre, "Working to Regain Spiritual Ties," *Ann Arbor News* (Ann Arbor, Mich.) (June 24, 1979).

25. See, for example, the interview with Brian McNaught (a leader of Dignity), "Is Our Church Big Enough for Gay Catholics?" *U.S. Catholic* (June 1980), pp. 10-11; Henry Fehren, "A Christian Response to Homosexuals," *U.S. Catholic* (September 1972), p. 10; Edward Vacek, S.J., "A Christian Homosexuality?" *Commonweal* (December 5, 1980), p. 683; Gregory Baum, "Catholic Homosexuals," *Commonweal* (February 15, 1974), pp. 479-82; Jeannine Gramick (a leader of New Ways Ministries), "Set the Captives Free," *New Catholic World* (November-December, 1977), pp. 292-95; Robert H. Springer, "Holy God, Gays Want In!" *Today's Parish* (January 1980), p. 11; Robert Barr, "Urgent for the 80s," *Today's Parish* (January 1980), p. 6; Joan Turner Beifuss, "Gays 1980: "Out of Both Closet and Confessional,'" *NCR* (November 21, 1980), pp. 7-8; Richard Wagner, "Being Gay and Celibate—Another View," *NCR* (November 21, 1980), p. 16; Robert Griffin, C.S.C., "A True Confession," *Notre Dame* (February 1981), pp. 68f; Charles E. Curran, *Catholic Moral Theology in Dialogue* (Notre Dame, Ind.: Notre Dame University Press, 1976); Philip S. Keane, *Sexual Morality: A Catholic Perspective* (New York: Paulist Press, 1977); John J. McNeill, S.J., *The Church and the Homosexual* (Mission, Kans.: Sheed, Andrews & McMeel, 1976); Richard Woods, *Another Kind of Love: Homosexuality and Spirituality* (Garden City, N.Y.: Image-Doubleday, 1978).

26. Edward Vacek, S.J., "A Christian Homosexuality?" *Commonweal* (December 5, 1980), p. 683.

27. *National Catholic Register* (April 5, 1981), p. 1.

28. An example of this appeared in *Notre Dame*, the alumni magazine of the University of Notre Dame, where one of the Notre Dame chaplains told the story of how he didn't have the heart to tell a young man in a stable active homosexual relationship that what he was doing was wrong. (Robert Griffin, C.S.C., "A True Confession," *Notre Dame Magazine* (February 1981), p. 68f.

29. Rev. Richard A. McCormick, quoted by Gene Luptak, "Catholic Theologian Proposes Exceptions to Moral Teachings," *The Arizona Republic* (September 20, 1980), p. 1, Religious Section.

30. Fr. James Young, transcribed from a tape recording of his talk given at the "Parish Service Program," Trinity College, Washington, D.C.,on December 12, 1978.

31. Bishop John A. Marshall, quoted in *The Pilot* (Boston, Mass.) (October 17, 1980), p. 13.

32. Sr. Carol Ann Gotch, quoted in *NCR* (April 20, 1979), p. 19.

33. One such reliable source is *The Teaching of Christ*, ed. Ronald Lawler, O.F.M., Donald Wuerl, and Thomas Comerford Lawler (Huntington, Ind.: Our Sunday Visitor, 1976).

34. Harold Ivan Smith, "Sex and Singleness the Second Time Around," *Christianity Today* (May 25, 1979), p. 18.
35. *NCR* (December 14, 1979), p. 11.
36. McInerny, p. 6.
37. Letter from Conrad W. Baars, M.D., *National Catholic Register* (August 31, 1980), p. 4.
38. Robert Eldridge, "Sex Seminar Questioned," *National Catholic Register* (November 30, 1980), p. 1f. See also the report prepared by the U.S. Coalition for Life. For information write to the U.S. Coalition for Life, Box 315, Export, PA 15632.
39. David Armstrong, "Catholicism—The Quiet Revolution," *The Bulletin* (Australia) (December 18, 1979), p. 54.
40. *Ibid.*, pp. 55, 56.
41. *Ibid.*, p. 55.
42. *Ibid.*, p. 56.
43. *Ibid.*, p. 57.
44. *Ibid.*, p. 56.
45. *LOR* (November 30, 1978), p. 5, address to the bishops of Canada, November 17, 1978.
46. *LOR* (February 2, 1981), p. 10, address to the Sacred Roman Rota, January 24, 1981.
47. *LOR* (April 21, 1981), p. 4, homily during a mass for university students, March 26, 1981.
48. *LOR* (April 9, 1979), p. 2, Angelus Message of April 1, 1979.
49. Cardinal William Baum, "The Distinctiveness of Christian Morality," opening address at the Symposium on Principles of Catholic Moral Life (June 17, 1979), p. 16f.
50. "Declaration on Certain Questions Concerning Sexual Ethics," Sacred Congregation for the Doctrine of the Faith (December 29, 1975).
51. Quoted by Armstrong, p. 59.
52. Donald Coggan, quoted in *Catholic Trends* (January 5, 1980), p. 3.
53. Charlotte Bunch, interviewed by Gloria Steinem, "Two Feminists Tell How They Work," *MS* (July 1977), p. 92.
54. Sheila Collins, quoted by Mary Bader Papa, *NCR* (November 2, 1979), p. 2.
55. Mary McDermott Shideler, "An Amicable Divorce," *Christian Century* (May 5, 1971), p. 555.

Chapter Nine
Seeing and Not Seeing

1. E.E.Y. Hales, *The Catholic Church in the Modern World* (New York: Image Doubleday & Co., 1958), pp. 45-46.
2. A letter of St. Francis Xavier, quoted in *The Apostolate of Prayer and Service* (Rome, Italy) (October 1979), p. 277.
3. In an unpublished paper, "St. Paul's Letters to the Corinthians: A Word to a Community," Fr. Francis Martin points out how an apparent lack of "proportion" in a prophetic word can be understood:

How is it possible to call a community to repentance? What is intended by such a call? The basic presupposition in such a situation is that once described by Abraham Heschel as: "Few are guilty, all are responsible." Or, as Paul approvingly quotes Menander as saying: "Evil company corrupts good manners" (1 Cor 15:33). In sociological terms, we might say that general attitudes of complicity in wrong-doing have reached such a stage that the community is more and more responsible for the guilt of some of its members. These people are acting at variance with the will and word of God. They find it easier and easier to act in such a way, because the atmosphere in which they move is tolerant of such behavior. In such a situation, it is not rare for someone sent by God to hit upon certain key events in the life of the community— some of which may appear to be a bit trivial, or at least blown out of proportion. However, what a true prophet sees at this moment is what historians would call a "paradigmatic event": that is, an incident in which there is a certain coming together of component factors in a way which at once distills and illustrates the tone or tenor of a group. (p. 3)

Chapter Ten
Powers, Principalities, and Organizations

1. See, for example, "The Renaissance Magus and the Modern Messiah," by Stephen A. McKnight, *Religious Studies Review* (April 1979), p. 81.

2. E.E.Y. Hales, *The Catholic Church in the Modern World* (New York: Image-Doubleday & Co., 1958), pp. 43-44.

3. Two biographies of Marx are *Marx*, by Robert Payne (New York: Simon & Schuster, 1968), and *Karl Marx*, by Saul Padover (New York: McGraw-Hill Book Co., 1978).

4. Quoted by William Shirer, *The Rise and Fall of the Third Reich* (New York: Fawcett, 1978), pp. 153-54.

5. Although Kübler-Ross now admits to having contact with "spirit guides" as early as a few years after the publication of *On Death and Dying* (New York: Macmillan Publishing Co., Inc., 1969), and claims now never to have believed orthodox Christian doctrine on the reality of sin, the need for redemption, and the reality of judgment and eternal reward and punishment, the first published statements in this direction appeared in connection with her introduction to Raymond Moody's book, *Life After Life* (Covington, Georgia: Mockingbird Books, 1975), and in comments in the book *Death: the Final Stage of Growth* (Englewood Cliffs, New Jersey: Prentice-Hall, 1975), which she edited. In informal remarks in lectures she had been more open about her occult involvement. (See the review of her work up until 1977 in *Spiritual Counterfeits Project Journal* (April 1977), pp. 7-8.) An article in *Time* (European ed., November 12, 1979, p. 55) brought the whole situation to public notice from the point of view of some of her collaborators, and she subsequently was even more open in public lectures about her spiritualistic, reincarnational views (*Orlando Sentinel-Star* [February 19, 1981], p. B16), and spoke quite openly about her occult involvement for formal publication in her 1981 interview for *Playboy* (May 1981, pp. 69-106).

The Spiritual Counterfeits Project article gives a good analysis of the whole "thanatology" movement and its threats to Christian truth and life. See also *The Other Side of Death*, by Tal Brooke (Wheaton, Illinois: Tyndale House Pubs., 1979), for one Christian analysis of the death studies and movement.

6. *Time*, European ed. (November 12, 1979), p. 55.

7. Marcia Seligson, "Interview with Elisabeth Kübler-Ross," *Playboy* (May 1981), p. 94.

8. Quoted by Joan Saunders Wixen, "Explaining Death, After Death and the Living," *Ann Arbor News* (September 4, 1981), p. B8.

9. Fr. Ronald Modras, "The Devil, Demons and Dogmatism," *Commonweal* (February 4, 1977), p. 75.

10. Quoted in "To Manipulate a Housewife," Concerned Women for America, P.O. Box 82957, San Diego, CA 92138, from *Saturday Review of Education* (March 1973).

11. Quoted in "To Manipulate a Housewife," from *Tulsa Sunday World* (August 21, 1977).

12. Quoted in "To Manipulate a Housewife," from a brochure previously available from P.O. Box 7064, Powder Horn St., Minneapolis, MN 55407.

13. *Los Angeles Times* (April 10, 1978), pt. 1, pp. 3ff.

14. Rosemary Ruether, in Gregory Baum's *Journeys: The Impact of Personal Experience on Religious Thought* (New York: Paulist Press, 1976), pp. 41, 43, 45.

15. Mary Daly, *Beyond God the Father* (Boston: Beacon Press, 1973).

16. *National Catholic Register* quotes The Most Rev. Maurice Dingman of Des Moines, Iowa, as saying, "When you are speaking about the feminist movement in the Church you are speaking about the Spirit moving in the Church" (June 7, 1981), p. 3).

17. Robert J. Lifton, quoted in *Time* (European ed.) (June 25, 1979), p. 33.

18. Sr. Mary A. Walsh, "Planned Parenthood Seeks to Change "Teen' Morality," *The Pilot* (Boston, Mass.) (July 18, 1980), p. 14.

19. *Ibid.*
20. Gary Bergel, "The Monstrosity of Planned Parenthood," *Intercessors for America Newsletter* (May 1, 1981), p. 3.
21. Associated Press report, October 4, 1980.
22. A summary of the available material on the life and work of Margaret Sanger and Planned Parenthood, with the relevant references, is available from Intercessors for America (P.O. Box D, Elyria, OH 44036), in an article in their May 1, 1981, newsletter. Two particularly helpful sources are Lawrence Lader, "The Margaret Sanger Story and the Fight for Birth Control," (Westport, Conn.: Greenwood Press Publishers, 1975) and Sanger, *An Autobiography* (New York: Dover Publishers, 1971).
23. A detailed description and evaluation from a Christian viewpoint of many of these programs is available from "Christian Family Renewal" (P.O. Box 78, Clovis, CA 93613), which publishes a periodic report on recent developments in the area, including accounts of successful parental resistance to the imposition of Planned Parenthood-sponsored sex education programs on school systems. "Sex Education and Mental Health Report," vol. 10, no. 1 (Winter 1980), contains reports documenting the above paragraphs. For an account of the type of sex education program that is already in use in some California schools, see the book *Slaughter on Main Street*, by Jacqueline Kasun (Clovis, California: Valley Christian University Press, 1980).
A secular, professional organization, Council for Basic Education, also had the following to say about sex education programs: "Our encounters with sex education (and sex educationists) have led us to question its virtue (and theirs); . . . One book that came to hand, for example, was little more than a guide for having fun without getting caught. For another reason, public interest in sex education appears to center more on the incidence of teenage pregnancy and venereal disease than on the "deeper functions' of sexual behavior." (*Basic Education*, issued by the Council for Basic Education, April 1981, p. 5.)
24. "Sex Education and Mental Health Report," vol. 10, no. 1 (Winter 1980), p. 9.
25. *Ibid.*
26. Erica Carle, quoted in "Sex Education and Mental Health Report, p. 9.
27. Even secular journals of professional educators are expressing concern. Here is a quote from "Teaching the Young About Sex," by William J. Bennett (*American Educator* [Winter 1980], p. 20):

One rarely, if ever, sees the sex education advocates arguing for less sexual activity itself. More "responsible" activity, more "thoughtful" activity, more "well-planned-out in advance and with precautions taken" activity, yes, but rarely, if ever, the simple counsel that teenagers should have less intercourse. Caution and precaution are recommended, but not restraint. In the literature and in the arguments, the idea of abstaining more often than indulging rarely comes up.

The message to the young is clear, or in time, it becomes clear enough: the young learn that, in the eyes of these adults, sexual activities, namely masturbation and intercourse, are either all right or are matters about which these adults are agnostic or do not wish "to impose their values." The only clearly "bad things" are either to get the clap or to get pregnant.

Jacqueline Kasun's article, "Turning Children Into Sex Experts," *The Public Interest* (Spring 1979) provides information on this.
Results of a survey on sex education in the United States are also very interesting:

The Mathtech report describes in five volumes the real goals of sex education. "Sex education is very different from many other classes," the Mathtech report says. "The purpose of sex education is not simply to fill the gaps in the knowledge of adolescents. . . . The goals of sex education are much more ambitious; they involve . . . the changing of attitudes and behaviors." The Mathtech report describes with enthusiasm the success in "changing" students' attitudes. The goals of these changes are identified by Mathtech as "broadly humanistic."
The students who take sex courses become more "liberal or tolerant of the sexual behavior" of others. They develop "a greater acceptance of homosexuality and mas-

turbation." They become "more comfortable" with the idea of their future marriage partners having had sexual relations with someone else.

(Quoted by Father Robert Fox, "Changing Values," *National Catholic Register* [August 23, 1981], p. 5.)
   28. Jacqueline Kasun, "Turning Children Into Sex Experts," *The Public Interest* (Spring 1979), p. 7.
   29. Robert Eldridge, "Sex Seminar Questioned," *National Catholic Register* (November 30, 1980), pp. 1ff. See also the report prepared by the U.S. Coalition for Life. For information, write to the U.S. Coalition for Life, Box 315, Export, PA 15632.
   30. See *National Catholic Register*, (June 22, 1980, p. 1), and (October 26, 1981, p. 4).
   31. Dr. Armand Nicholi, "The Fractured Family: Following It Into the Future," *Christianity Today* (May 25, 1979), pp. 11, 12.
   32. *Ibid.*, p. 15.
   33. *Ibid.*, p. 15.
   34. *LOR* (December 3, 1979), p. 14, homily at Campo Verano, November 1, 1979.

Chapter Eleven
Pastoral Passivity

   1. "On Evangelization in the Modern World," par. 2, (Washington, D.C.: U.S. Catholic Conference Publications Office, 1976), p. 6.
   2. Of special note here is James Hitchcock's *Catholicism and Modernity* (New York: Seabury Press, 1979).
   3. It should be noted here that the traditional understanding of "development of doctrine," as articulated by patristic sources such as St. Vincent of Lerins and by modern thinkers such as Cardinal Newman, considers authentic development to be just that: a development of what is in some real sense already there, in a way which doesn't deny the truthfulness or reliability of what is already there. Paul VI's *Ecclesiam Suam* and "Credo of the People of God," as well as *Mysterium Ecclesiae*, issued by the Congregation for the Doctrine of the Faith, are all attempts to contribute clarity to this area.
   4. Edward J. Foye, "Reviews," *NCR* (November 23, 1979), p. 16.
   5. *LOR* (May 21, 1979), p. 10, Declaration of the Bishops of the European Community.
   6. *LOR* (November 2, 1978), p. 12, address of the pope, October 22, 1978.
   7. *Newsweek* (European ed.) (October 8, 1979), p. 16.
   8. St. Augustine, "Faith and Works," 1737a.
   9. See, for example, John Sheets, "The C.T.S.A. and the Ordination of Women," *Communio* (Winter 1978), p. 387:

How does the Catholic Theological Society of America expect professional respect when it leads a task force with people who have the same opinions on the subject, and who call in consultants who share these opinions? . . . Has the CTSA ceased to be a body of professional scholars interested in the serious investigation of the truth, or has it become a politicized advocacy group? Every serious body of scholars realizes that the truth is not served by simply turning up the volume, hoping to drown out other points of view.

   10. Fr. John Meier, quoted by Joan Beifuss in *NCR* (February 22, 1980), p. 20.
   11. Foye, p. 16.
   12. C.S. Lewis, *The Screwtape Letters* (New York: Macmillan Publishing Co., 1961), p. 56.
   13. Cardinal Hume, "Address to Friends of Newman," in *Briefing* (November 2, 1979), p. 5.
   14. Billy Graham, "The Seven Churches of Asia," *Christianity Today* (November 17, 1978), p. 20.
   15. Catharina Halkes, quoted in *NCR* (January 18, 1980), p. 15.
   16. Fr. Bill Callahan, S.J., quoted in *NCR* (January 18, 1980), p. 3.
   17. Dr. Randolph Nugent, quoted in *NCR* (January 11, 1980).
   18. Quoted by DeCourcey H. Rayner in *Christianity Today* (April 6, 1979), p. 50.

Chapter Twelve
Signs of the Times: Pointing Toward Judgment

1. Msgr. John Tracy Ellis, "American Catholics in 1979: Certain Signs of the Times," an address given on September 12, 1979, Park Plaza Hotel, Boston, Massachusetts; the text is published by *The Boston Pilot*.

2. Billy Graham, "The Seven Churches of Asia," *Christianity Today* (November 17, 1978), p. 22.

3. Dr. James Packer, quoted by Michael Harper, *Beauty or Ashes?* (Hounslow, England: Hounslow Printing Co., 1979), p. 2.

4. Michael Harper, *Beauty or Ashes*, p. 14.

5. *LOR* (October 26, 1978), p. 4, from John Paul II's "Urbi et Orbi" message, October 17, 1978.

6. From Karol Cardinal Wojtyla's farewell speech after a visit to the U.S. in 1976, reprinted in *The Wall Street Journal* (November 9, 1978).

7. Concerted efforts to trace the history of this prophetic word have not raised any question regarding its authenticity, although it has not yet been successfully traced. Since much of St. Nilus' work has not yet been translated from the Russian, and since even dedicated Orthodox scholars consulted are not familiar with all his work and influence, this is understandable. The repeated publication of this prophecy in respected Orthodox journals such as *The Orthodox Word* (July-August 1968) and *The Orthodox Christian Witness*, attests to its at least preliminary trustworthiness. In any event, since much of the prophecy is merely a gathering together of various scriptural themes, apart from its reference to the twentieth century, this in itself serves a useful purpose.

8. For an overall account of the Marian apparitions of the nineteenth and twentieth centuries, see *The Immaculate Heart of Mary*, Joseph A. Pelletier, A.A. (Worchester, Mass.: Assumption Pub., 1976).

9. Prophecy delivered by Fr. Michael Scanlan, T.O.R., at the National Advisory Meeting of the Catholic Charismatic Renewal, January 13, 1980. For those interested in fuller acquaintance with the prophetic word emerging in this renewal movement, see the May 1980 issue of *New Covenant*.

10. *LOR* (January 7, 1980), p. 11, from a letter of Archbishop Fulton Sheen to Pope John Paul II, dated November 26, 1979.

Chapter Thirteen
A Time for Repentance

1. Avery Dulles, S.J., "Unmasking Secret Infidelities: Hartford and the Future of Ecumenism," *Against the World For the World*, ed. Peter Berger and Richard Neuhaus (New York: Seabury Press, 1976), pp. 59-60.

2. *LOR* (December 3, 1979), p. 14, homily, November 1, 1979.

3. *LOR* (August 20, 1979), p. 3, mass for an Italian Solidarity Center.

4. *LOR* (August 27, 1979), p. 3, mass for religious sisters.

5. An evaluation by the episcopal sub-group studying the charismatic renewal presented to the Secretariat Général de l'Episcopat de France, Circulaire 1979-4 (February 15, 1979), p. 2.

6. *LOR* (February 4, 1980), p. 5, address to the Pontifical Irish College, January 13, 1980.

7. C.S. Lewis, *Reflections on the Psalms* (New York: Harcourt, Brace & World, 1958), pp. 66, 72, 74.

Chapter Fourteen
A Time for Action

1. Dr. Coggan, quoted by Michael Harper, *Beauty or Ashes? The Ashe Lecture 1979* (Hounslow, England: Hounslow Printing Co., 1979), p. 6.

2. *Dives in Misericordia*, VI, 10.

3. Michael Harper, *Beauty or Ashes*, p. 9.

4. Paul VI, *Ecclesiam Suam*, par. 26.

5. Paul VI, *Gaudete in Domino*, ch. VII.

6. *LOR* (November 23, 1978), p. 1ff, address, November 15, 1978.

7. James Hitchcock, "The Secular Sickness," *Columbia* (July 1979), p. 11.

8. *LOR* (November 16, 1978), p. 1ff, from the general audience of November 8, 1978.

9. *LOR* (April 9, 1979), p. 10, homily to personnel of the Vatican Polyglot Printing House, March 30, 1979.

10. *LOR* (October 26, 1978), p. 1, address to the Cardinals, October 18, 1978.

Chapter Fifteen
Unity, Division, and the Sword of the Spirit

1. Avery Dulles, S.J., "Unmasking Secret Infidelities," *Against the World For the World*, ed. Peter L. Berger and Richard J. Neuhaus (New York: Seabury Press, 1976), p. 59.

2. James Hitchcock, *Catholicism and Modernity* (New York: Seabury Press, 1979), p. 231.

3. Harry Blamires, "The Uprooting of Christianity," *Pastoral Renewal* (October 1979), p. 32.

4. See the previous discussions on this topic in Chapter Four.

5. *LOR* (March 12, 1979), p. 10, address to the rectors of English, Scottish, and Maltese seminaries, March 3, 1979.

Index